Katsina

Katsina

Commodified and Appropriated Images of Hopi Supernaturals

Zena Pearlstone

With contributions by

BARBARA A. BABCOCK

MARSHA C. BOL

LEIGH J. KUWANWISIWMA

ALPH SECAKUKU

VICTORIA SPENCER

PETER M. WHITELEY

BARTON WRIGHT

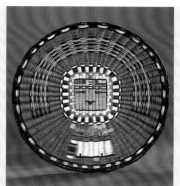

UCLA Fowler Museum of Cultural History   Los Angeles

Funding for this publication
has been provided by

The Rockefeller Foundation

The Ahmanson Foundation

The Times-Mirror Foundation

**Manus, the support group of the UCLA
Fowler Museum of Cultural History**

James H. Kindel Jr.

The American Folk Art Society

The Fowler Museum is part of
UCLA's School of the Arts and Architecture

Lynne Kostman, *Managing Editor*
Daniel R. Brauer, *Designer and Production Coordinator*
Don Cole, *Principal Photographer*

UCLA Fowler Museum of Cultural History
Box 951549
Los Angeles, California 90095-1549

Requests for permission to reproduce material from
this volume should be sent to the UCLA Fowler Museum
Publications Department at the above address.

Printed and bound in Hong Kong by
South Sea International Press, Ltd.

Library of Congress Cataloging-in-Publication Data

Katsina / [edited by] Zena Pearlstone with contributions by
    Barbara A. Babcock, Marsha C. Bol…[et al.].
          p. cm.
          Includes bibliographical references.
          ISBN 0-930741-82-X (hard)—ISBN 0-930741-83-8 (soft)
          1. Kachinas. 2. Indian art—Southwest, New.
      I. Pearlstone, Zena. II. Babcock, Barbara A., 1943–
      III. Bol, Marsha.
E99.H7 C62 2001
745.592'21'0899745—dc21   00-057765

To Hopi friends,
past and present,
who have enriched my life.

We need exhibitions that question the boundaries of art and the art world, an influx of truly indigestible "outside" artifacts.

James Clifford,
The Predicament of Culture

Contents

Foreword   8

Preface: Five Hundred Years of Tourism
Barbara A. Babcock   9

Acknowledgments   13

Notes on Orthography   15

CHAPTER 1
Introduction: From the Sacred
to the Cash Register—Problems
Encountered in Protecting
the Hopi Cultural Patrimony
Leigh J. Kuwanwisiwma   16

CHAPTER 2
Hopi Histories
Peter M. Whiteley   22

ARTIST PROFILE I   *Neil David Sr.*   34

ARTIST PROFILE II   *Diane Branam*   36

CHAPTER 3
The Contemporary Katsina
Zena Pearlstone   38

ARTIST PROFILE III   *Esther Jackson*   128

ARTIST PROFILE IV   *David Freeland*   129

ARTIST PROFILE V   *Ramson Lomatewama*   130

CHAPTER 4
Early Euro-American
Ethnographers and the Hopi *Tihu*
Marsha C. Bol   132

ARTIST PROFILE VI   *Michael Horse*   142

ARTIST PROFILE VII   *John Farnsworth*   144

CHAPTER 5
The Drift from Tradition
Barton Wright   146

ARTIST PROFILE VIII   *Gerry Quotskuyva*   158

ARTIST PROFILE IX   *Christopher Pardell*   160

CHAPTER 6
Authentic Hopi Katsina Dolls
Alph Secakuku   162

ARTIST PROFILE X   *Clark Tenakhongva*   166

ARTIST PROFILE XI   *Poteet Victory*   168

CHAPTER 7
Intellectual and Cultural
Property Rights and Appropriation
of Hopi Culture
Victoria Spencer   170

ARTIST PROFILE XII   *Verma Nequatewa*   178

ARTIST PROFILE XIII   *Jean Healey*   179

CONFERENCE STATEMENT
Wallace Youvella Sr.   180

Appendix: The Gourd Rattles
of Edmund Nequatewa   182

Endnotes   187

References Cited   193

Foreword

The appropriation and commodification of expressive culture have been prominent themes in many of the Fowler Museum's most important publications on Africa, Asia, and Latin America—and rightly so. Few if any admired artistic traditions from these regions have escaped exploitation in the Western marketplace—from the ivory carvings in *Elephant: The Animal and Its Ivory in African Culture* to the wonderfully popular *molas* in *The Art of Being Kuna* to the intricate pictorial embroideries of *Threads of Light: Chinese Embroideries from Suzhou and the Photography of Robert Glenn Ketchum*. Clearly in each of these instances, there would be entirely different stories to tell without the presence of the commodity. The words *appropriation* and *commodify* have become commonplace in contemporary discourse concerned with much of the world's art, so much so that each merited its own essay in Robert S. Nelson and Richard Shiff's *Critical Terms for Art History* (1996). These catchwords in turn beg questions of "authenticity" and "tradition" that run throughout the discussions of Hopi Katsinam that form the subject of the present volume.

Unlike many of the Fowler Museum's previous studies, however, this publication deals with objects that are firmly rooted in the realm of the sacred. The hybrid compromises that may be seen as permissible with certain secular traditions become considerably more problematic when they entail religious beliefs. Also unlike our previous studies where the modes and means of production have largely remained within the originating culture, Hopi Katsinam have been imitated and exploited by their immediate neighbors as well as by manufacturers halfway around the world. Imitation and production compromises aside, what believer—regardless of religion—could help but being offended at seeing revered figures featured as comic book characters, whiskey bottles, or corn chip logos. These are just a few of the problems addressed in this provocative anthology.

I would like to thank Zena Pearlstone for her remarkable efforts in researching and preparing this insightful volume. Working closely with Hopi scholars and artists, she has organized an ambitious examination of some of the most important considerations in contemporary Hopi life, including issues of religious privacy, intellectual copyright, and artistic freedom. Zena brings her characteristic thoughtfulness and thoroughness to a set of problems that extend to the artistic and religious practices of many cultures throughout the world. Her patience with funding delays, scheduling changes, and the Museum's competing priorities has been greatly appreciated.

It is always a pleasure to thank the publications staff of the Fowler Museum for their efforts Director of Publications Danny Brauer designed this book with his customary thoughtfulness and care. Lynne Kostman edited the text with the same consummate skill that has characterized all her remarkable work at the Museum. The substantial photographic workload was superbly handled by Museum photographer Don Cole.

Fran Krystock, Anna Sanchez, and Teva Kukan of the Museum's Collections staff and Sarah Kennington and Farida Sunada of the Registration Department expended extra effort and care in moving objects in and out of the Museum for photography. I would especially like to thank John Selmer and Barbara Goldeen as well as Tom and Nancy Juda for making their spectacular collections available to this project.

Generous funding has been provided by the Rockefeller Foundation, and I would like to thank Tomás Ybarra-Frausto in particular for his support and stewardship of this and other Fowler projects at the Foundation. Additional funding has also been graciously supplied by the American Folk Art Society and by James H. Kindel Jr.

Our most enthusiastic appreciation goes to Leigh J. Kuwanwisiwma, director of the Hopi Cultural Preservation Office, and to all the other Hopi who have shared their time and thoughts with Dr. Pearlstone and the Fowler Museum.

Doran H. Ross, *Director*
UCLA Fowler Museum of Cultural History
JUNE 2001

Preface: Five Hundred Years of Tourism

BARBARA A. BABCOCK

> Economics and tradition meet in the field
> of Indian art.
>
> Oliver LaFarge,
> *As Long as the Grass Shall Grow*

In 1992, in recognition of the five hundredth anniversary of the Columbian encounter between Europeans and Indians, the National Museum of American History of the Smithsonian Institution opened an exhibition entitled *American Encounters*, which presented the history of relations among Hispanics, Euro-Americans, and Native Americans in New Mexico from 1539 to the present. Among its curators, however, the exhibition's unofficial, working title was *500 Years of Tourism*. While that humorous yet sobering title was not on display at the exhibition, it was published as a bumper sticker for sale in 1992 at such popular tourist sites as Taos Pueblo. The truth of this message is that for nearly five hundred years now, the Southwest has been a site/sight of much significance and a destination of desire for countless numbers of Euro-American "pilgrims/tourists," be they Spanish conquistadores, Catholic priests, anthropologists, Mormon missionaries, health seekers, Santa Fe Railway passengers, artists, New Agers, nuclear physicists, or postwar families traveling by automobile on Route 66— each group and each generation reinventing "the mythology of place" (Riley 1994, 229).

Spaniards thought the fabled Seven Cities of Cíbola were located in the Southwest and came in the sixteenth century in search of gold. Beginning in 1821, many Americans migrated to the Southwest via the Santa Fe Trail by horse, wagon, and foot. When armed Native American resistance ended and the railroad reached the Southwest in the 1880s, the region became more accessible and more desirable for settlers, for miners, for missionaries, for merchants, for circuses and carnivals, and for tourists. Starting in 1882, tourists were transported by what T. C. McLuhan has referred to as the "dream tracks" of the Atchison, Topeka, and Santa Fe, and later, its "Indian Detours" to "the romantic corner of the United States," "a last refuge of magic, mountains and quaint ancestors" (Santa Fe advertisements, quoted in McLuhan 1985). "The Great Southwest" that the Santa Fe Railway created

in collaboration with the Fred Harvey Company was, in Marta Weigle's words, a "desert-turned-Disney-World" (1989, 135), "a regional world's fair staged for railroad tourists in northern New Mexico and Arizona" (1992, 118). With the automobile and the completion of Route 66 came yet more and other tourists, drawn like those before them to "the magnetic Southwest"—to sites of perhaps too much significance like the Grand Canyon or Monument Valley, Chimayo or Carlsbad Caverns, Sedona or Taos, Trinity or Roswell, living and abandoned Pueblo villages, dude ranches, and sanitariums.

If there are many such desired destinations in the Southwest, there are also, as James Byrkit describes, many Southwests and many debates as to its boundaries—boundaries that may extend in all four directions but always enclose Arizona and New Mexico at the least (1992). As geographer D. W. Meinig observed, "The Southwest is a distinctive place to the American mind but a somewhat blurred place on American maps, which is to say that everyone knows that there is a Southwest but that there is little agreement as to just where it is" (1971, 3). Or, as another geographer, Yi Fu Tuan politely suggests, "The American Southwest reminds us how little the popular images of a place depend on scrupulous historical knowledge" (quoted in Byrkit 1992, 385). More recently, Michael Riley has described the Southwest as "a composition of continually contested, positioned, and linked visions of place," and suggested that "inasmuch as the Southwest exists as a socially shared image, we must grapple with the question of why and how there is such a region in the minds of its residents and visitors" (1994, 222, 239).

For over a century now, this "exceedingly picturesque" landscape inhabited by "colorful" natives has been endlessly commodified and consumed. As D. H. Lawrence remarked in 1924 after returning to Taos from the Hopi Snake Dance, "The Southwest is the great playground of the White American... and the Indian, ...he's a wonderful live toy to play with" (quoted in Rushing 1995, 29). More recently and more soberly, Michael Riley has remarked that "the Southwest relies on a linked construction of ethnicity and place as a means of providing for and driving its ability to enchant" (1994, 224). This is especially true of the Land of Enchantment, the state of New Mexico, which even in the 1990s advertises itself with an image of Taos Pueblo and a Pueblo woman in the foreground baking in a *horno*, or traditional earthen oven:

> the bread of her ancestors from a centuries-old recipe. Every morning, Crucita Romero rises before the sun to bake the day's bread.... Quiet dramas like this are played out every day in the nineteen pueblos of New Mexico, each one a glimpse of less complicated times.... Native American pueblos. They're just a few of the many wonders of New Mexico. [New Mexico Department of Tourism advertisement in *Endless Vacation* (March–April 1993)]

Such linked and fabricated construction of place and ethnicity—epitomized by the Grand Canyon and its Mary Colter "insisted-on-authenticity" Hopi House, inhabited by Indian men who danced and Indian women who made pottery—was a staple of the touristic discourse and experience produced by the Fred Harvey Company and the Santa Fe Railway in the early decades of this century (Weigle 1996). Now as then, anthropologist Peter Whiteley has observed that "in addition to their intrinsic attraction as performers of exotic rituals and producers of acquirable tribal art, Hopis are on a major American tourist circuit because of their proximity to the Grand Canyon and Monument Valley" (1993, 135).

While proximity of the Hopi Mesas to the Grand Canyon and Monument Valley facilitated that seductive linked construction of place and ethnicity in Southwest tourism, there was also the attraction of "authenticity." For the past century, the Hopi have been presented in words and images as "Pueblo life, pure and undefiled" (Dorsey 1903, 100). And Hopi culture has been identified as the most ancient, for the Hopi village of Orayvi is the oldest continuously inhabited town in North America. These "ancient ways of life" were inscribed as well in countless well-preserved ruins throughout the Southwest. Here, situated in a stark, spacious, and spectacular landscape, was a truly American antiquity and national identity "indigenous to the soil" that attracted archaeologists as well as tourists. Artists, anthropologists, and tourists have all trafficked in this cultural primitivism and exploited a landscape as "picturesque" as its inhabitants and their dwellings. The limitless space and the "quality and abundance of light" have especially attracted and enabled

countless painters and photographers (Zwinger 1987, 146). For many, the Southwest was/is, in the words of Gretel Ehrlich, "a geography of possibility" (1985, 9).

In the 1880s, this "fantasized periphery" was invented for Americans and incorporated into the national imagination primarily through the efforts of four individuals: landscape painter Thomas Moran, photographer William Henry Jackson, journalist Charles Lummis, and anthropologist Frank Hamilton Cushing. Their words and images were the first Southwest that many Americans, not to mention the United States Congress, experienced and were persuaded to invest in; they were instrumental in turning a colonial frontier into a United States national region and in transforming hostile savages into peaceful, domestic, artistic, and picturesque natives. Not surprisingly, the work of these individuals was the basis of the discourse that the Santa Fe Railway and the Fred Harvey Company elaborated and sold in books and brochures, on calendars and postcards.

"'Picturesque,'" Charles Lummis wrote in 1893, "is a tame word for it. It is a picture, a romance, a dream, all in one. It is our one corner that is the sun's very own" (1893, 2–3). Wisely, William Simpson, general advertising agent for the Santa Fe Railway, as well as J. F. Huckel, director of the Fred Harvey Indian Department, and Herman Schweizer, manager of the Indian Department, employed Moran, Jackson, and Lummis, in addition to anthropologist George Dorsey and several Taos painters, to provide texts and artwork for such company publications as *American Indians: First Families of the Southwest* (1920) and advertisements like the Santa Fe's famous annual calendar (D'Emilio and Campbell 1991; McLuhan 1985). These verbal and visual images were endlessly manipulated and reproduced on everything from postcards to menus to advertisements and souvenir playing cards. Because of his work for Detroit Publishing Company and the Santa Fe/Harvey enterprise, photographer William Henry Jackson has come to be known as "the father of the picture postcard." The discourse Santa Fe/Harvey produced, the corporation's marketing practices, and the assumption that a region and a people could be presented as object and exhibition still inform representations of the Southwest, its indigenous inhabitants, and tribal objects and performances (Babcock 1990a; Weigle and Babcock 1996).

Such aestheticization of the Other in general and the "romantic inflation" of the Pueblo in particular (Frost 1980)—"art not ethnology"—are not only crucial to ethnic tourism but are, as David Spurr (1993) points out, key tropes of colonial discourse, for these seemingly positive transformations of natives and their handicrafts into art are in fact symbolic domination (Mullin 1995). As Nicholas Thomas has also remarked, "the frequent tendency to set other places up as picturesque exhibits, as things to be seen rather than locations in which action occurs, effects a displacement into the domain of the aesthetic and the ornamental" (1994, 53). This process, with its displacement, denial, and differential awareness, is termed "artistic mystification" by Sylvia Rodriguez in her essay on the Taos art colony (1989, 90, 93). And in *Cannibal Culture,* Deborah Root describes art used "to explain and naturalize the display of authority" as an "alibi of appreciation" (1996, 18). In discussing the manipulation of and "promiscuous traffic" in Hopi representations, Peter Whiteley similarly remarks, "They involve a subtler process of cultural hegemony, a politics of representations wherein a dominant group appropriates and refigures a subaltern's cultural symbols to its own purposes" (1993, 132).

Lummis, Dorsey, innumerable painters and photographers, and the Fred Harvey Indian Department created an artistic world inhabited by "adjectival natives." "It was an accident," Lummis wrote

that the Santa Fe route, when it followed the line of least resistance across "the Great American Desert"… skimmed the cream of the artist's interest of the Southwest. There is no railroad in the world… which penetrates such a wonderland of the pictorial in geography and in humanity. [Quoted in McLuhan 1985, 19]

The "wonderland of the pictorial" that Lummis and company created for the Santa Fe, however, was no accident at all (Padget 1995). Their natives were overwhelmingly Pueblo, even though they were obviously not the only natives in the Southwest. They were, however, the only "semi-civilized" natives, being sedentary, domestic, and producers of beautiful objects, as well as being themselves beautiful-to-look-at. In short, these "semi-savages" were (and still are) regarded as aesthetic, colorful, "picturesque," Oriental, and romantic (Babcock 1990b, 1993; Dilworth 1996a). In contrast to the Navajo and Apache, the Pueblo were settled in villages, which the Spaniards called *pueblos,* and were regarded as "America's first penthouse dwellers." And, Pueblo

life, material culture, and ritual performances were/are informed by an elaborate and compelling cosmology that Lummis et al. hyperbolized.

As a consequence, the Pueblos were declared non-Indians by the New Mexico Supreme Court in 1869 and again in 1877. This decision was revoked, not only because it would deprive the Pueblo of their lands but because then and now our primitivist desire needed a significant Other, an alternative to industrial capitalism, a meaningful spirituality or "place of grace," whether in the 1890s or 1990s. As Peter Whiteley remarks in discussing "New Age" interest in Hopi spiritual beliefs, "The Hopi are held up as icons of spiritual wisdom, exemplars in a quest toward new meaning in the malaise of modern life" (1993, 130).

Indeed, for over a century, the aestheticism and spirituality of Pueblo Native Americans have fueled the conversion of culture to commodity and "ritual to retail" (Ed Ladd, quoted in Green 1995). As early as 1897, Aby Warburg remarked of his own desire,

what drew me, as an art historian, to visit the groups of Pueblo Indians in New Mexico and Arizona was that the conjunction of pagan religious representations and artistic activity is nowhere more recognizable than among the Pueblo Indians and that in their culture one can find rich material for the study of the question of the development of symbolic art. [1995, 96]

Not surprisingly, Hopi Katsina dances and carved wooden Katsina dolls especially became objects of the Euro-American gaze, fetishes of difference. Among all the Pueblos, figurative forms were made (1) as wooden katsina dolls, (2) as stone, wood, or clay fetishes, or (3) as ceramic figurines and effigy vessels, all of which originally had some religious efficacy and were connected with an ideology of reproduction.

Such shapings of ethnicity have been condemned and destroyed as "pagan idols"; devalued by some as "primitive *monos*" or "curiosities" or "grotesques"; yet promoted and used as logos by such nineteenth-century traders as Jake Gold in Santa Fe. This commercial practice led a later generation of scholars and collectors to dismiss most figurative forms as "tourist trash." Such dismissals were, however, ambivalent and problematic. A "curiosity" is, as Nicholas Thomas suggests in speaking of material culture and colonialism in the Pacific, an "unstable" object "not authorized by any methodological or theoretical discourse, and grounded in passion rather than reason" (1991, 127). These savage "idols" were also ambivalently valued because they

> provided an extremely powerful mechanism through which the fact of conversion could be materially expressed and displayed.... any ritual object.... could stand in the first place for the foolishness of indigenous beliefs and secondly for the islanders' willingness to abandon them. [N. Thomas 1991, 156–57]

Not surprisingly, the discourse of primitivism is focused on native bodies and on such anthropomorphic Pueblo forms as Katsinam or war gods or effigy vessels, which connote difference and embody an alien spirituality.

The first recorded date of the Euro-American collection of a Hopi *tihu*, or "doll," is 1857. The exhibition and commodification of Hopi Katsinam did not begin until almost fifty years later when the Indian Department of the Fred Harvey Company began to market and display these figures. These were first publicly exhibited by the company in 1904 at the Louisiana Purchase Exposition in Saint Louis and subsequently became a popular collectors' item. Presumably because of the sacredness of these figures and their making, Katsina carvers were noticeably *not* among the Indian artists that Santa Fe/Harvey put on display at its various venues and in its publications—noticeable because the Indian artisan and the spectacle of Indian craftsmanship was such a "central icon of Fred Harvey's Southwest" (Dilworth 1996a, 96).

Beginning in 1930, another Southwest institution, the Museum of Northern Arizona, changed this practice with its annual Hopi Craftsman Exhibits. The "Hopi Show" with its displays, awards, and demonstrations popularized Katsinam and encouraged their manufacture. The presence of such "subject-producers-of-objects" demonstrations, which have become a staple in the Indian art world, not only constructed the Indian as artist but attested to handcrafted authenticity, as well as endless reproducibility—a rare combination in a world of assembly lines and mechanical reproduction (Todorov in Babcock 1990b; Babcock 1993, 1996).

Whether a Katsina doll, a Storyteller doll, or an *olla* maiden, these metonyms of Pueblo culture, which we are endlessly reproducing on a global scale, are themselves representations of reproduction, both cultural and biological (Babcock 1993, 1996). And, of course, there is now coyote as well, and we all know about his promiscuity. These figures have all become *logos* for the Southwest, which are now international signifiers as well. Such "logoization" is, as Benedict Anderson asserts, made possible by precisely such "infinite quotidian reproducibility" (1991, 182–83). Stephen Greenblatt also contends that

> the assimilation of the Other is linked to... the reproduction and circulation of mimetic capital, and with capitalism, the proliferation and circulation of representations (and devices for the generation and transmission of representations) achieved a spectacular and virtually inescapable global magnitude.... The images that matter, that merit the term capital, are those that achieve reproductive power. [1991, 6]

Similarly, Homi Bhabha argues that the power of colonial discourse depends on fixity, on repeatability, and thus on the manipulation of such stereotypes, which he goes on to analyze in terms of fetishism (1994, 66–84). And, in addition to their reproducibility and ambivalence, "stereotypes must circulate endlessly, relentlessly throughout society" in order to be effective (Owens 1992, 195). In this sense, too, Hopi Katsinam have become powerful and important, for they are everywhere in the modern world of mechanical reproduction—not only in the Southwest in highway signage and Navajo replicas but in Marvel Comics and in countless souvenir images, from plastic key chains to expensive reproductions sold in Southwest "curio" shops. ●

Acknowledgments

The seeds of this project were sewn in 1985 when Doran H. Ross, then the deputy director of the Museum of Cultural History at UCLA, asked me to organize a small exhibition of the Museum's holdings of Katsina gourd rattles. The rattles in question were created by Edmund Nequatewa and his sons from Songoopavi, Second Mesa, Hopi. While the exhibition never took place due to the complexities of the Museum's move to its present quarters and its transformation into the UCLA Fowler Museum of Cultural History, the research started me on the journey that led to the present volume.

I visited the Nequatewas during the summer of 1985 with their dealers, Richard and Margo Mehagian. Although Edmund, who was ill and had been hospitalized, was unable to reminisce about the history of Katsina rattles, I was able to spend some time with his family—in particular his wife, Annabelle, and his son Merrill. On that visit and several that followed, Merrill was particularly giving, escorting me to meet other artists, providing me with information, and teaching and introducing me to aspects of Hopi art that I would otherwise have missed—he was a special friend. His death in a car accident in January of 1996 has robbed this project of a sensitive and intelligent voice. He was proud and excited at the prospect of seeing his family's work featured. His mother, Annabelle, continues to welcome me warmly into her home every time I visit Hopi.

In the years following that initial encounter, the project grew to encompass the multitude of Katsina representations that appear on these pages. Ideas for the volume in its present form were first discussed at Hopi in 1994. Leigh J. Kuwanwisiwma, the director of the Hopi Cultural Preservation Office, arranged this meeting, which proved to be invaluable for the project. Throughout the years of research, Leigh has offered me direction and made available all the resources of his office and his staff. This book is incalculably richer for his contributions, and I am most grateful to him for his help and involvement. In addition to Leigh and myself, this initial meeting was attended by Susan Secakuku, at that time Leigh's assistant, and Gloria A. Lomahaftewa, then assistant to the director of the Heard Museum for Native American Relations. Issues of Hopi commodification and non-Pueblo appropriation were discussed, and Leigh and Susan came to the conclusion that a publication relating to these issues would "be supportive of Hopi viewpoints."

On February 11, 1995, a planning meeting was held at the Fowler Museum of Cultural History; attending were Barbara A. Babcock, Regents Professor and Director, Comparative Cultural and Literary Studies, University of Arizona; J. J. Brody, Professor Emeritus, Department of Art and Art History, University of New Mexico; Leigh J. Kuwanwisiwma; Emily Meyer, then a research assistant at the Fowler Museum of Cultural History; Betsy Quick, Director of Education, Fowler Museum of Cultural History; Doran H. Ross; Susan Secakuku; and myself. I presented slide images illustrating instances of appropriation of the Katsina image. These were viewed and evaluated to determine their suitability for inclusion in the book. Also discussed were commercial carving by Hopis, the question of public domain, cultural and intellectual property rights, and future considerations.

Leigh reiterated his belief that a publication would be beneficial in educating the public about Hopi feelings concerning commodification and appropriation. The reactions of the Hopi to colonial appropriation have changed as they have negotiated their own way through the postmodern world. Members of the Hopi Cultural Preservation Office underscore their postcolonial status as they actively seek some degree of control over their cultural property and a venue for presenting their point of view. It is my sincere hope that through this publication their expectations will be realized.

I have come out of the Katsina and imitation Katsina immersion program in which I have been a student over the past fifteen years, a wiser if somewhat overwhelmed researcher. The Katsina "phenomenon," the only word that can capture the explosion of representations over the past decades, now encompasses much of the world. This volume should make it clear that the situation is far from simple. There are no easy answers and, sometimes, no easy questions. Not all Hopis agree on what the present and future course of Katsina representations should be, and as a result, there is no "quick fix." I have tried to acknowledge all points of view—Hopi and non-Hopi. Some are represented only summarily. I did not meet a Navajo carver or painter of Katsina forms who would agree to be interviewed. I talked with only one Rio Grande Katsina artist—from Isleta Pueblo.

This publication has drawn on the talents of many. It is not a project that I could ever have managed alone. Above all I am indebted to the people at Hopi. Many living in the villages contributed to my education over the years. To the following I owe particular thanks: Neil David Sr., Janice Day, Philbert Honanie, Esther Jackson, Michael Kabotie, Marlinda Kooyaquaptewa, Milland Lomakema Sr., Ramson Lomatewama, Ferrill Nequatewa, Verma Nequatewa, Michael Pavatea, Susan Secakuku, Marlene Sekaquaptewa, Clark Tenakhongva, and Judy and Phillip Tuwaletstiwa.

My lifelines at Hopi throughout this project have been, and continue to be, Alph Secakuku and Joseph Day. Alph has been an advisor, teacher, and friend. I cannot imagine a better one and am constantly appreciative of my good fortune. I thank him for his wisdom, his expertise, and his willingness to explain things one more time. I also thank him for his careful attention to the figure captions for this book. Joe has always been available to interpret for another *pahana*, on many occasions informing me about things that I did not realize I needed to know. I thank Alph and Joe for their humor and camaraderie.

I am extremely fortunate in the chapter authors who agreed to participate in this volume. They have provided historical and cultural information and unique perspectives that collectively allow the reader a more comprehensive analysis of Katsinam and Katsina art. I am indebted to all of them for their understanding of deadlines and probably unreasonable requests. The artists who were interviewed and whose thoughts and words appear in the profiles were always gracious and often made time for me when it was inconvenient for them. The following have provided additional assistance in bringing this publication to completion: Andy P. Abeita, Barbara A. Babcock, Robert Breunig, Elisabeth Cameron, Dexter Cirillo, Joy L. Gritton, Michael Horse, Tom and Nancy Juda, Carol Herselle Krinsky, James Ostler, Victoria Spencer, and Barry Walsh. I thank Richard and Margo Mehagian for first introducing me to Hopi and for their assistance over the years. John Selmer and Barbara Goldeen have been pillars of support and extraordinarily good friends. This publication would be much poorer without their intellectual and physical contributions.

Janet Catherine Berlo, Cecelia F. Klein, Peter M. Whiteley, Victoria Spencer, and Barton Wright read my contribution to this volume and offered constructive advice. Many of their suggestions have been incorporated in the essay. Special thanks go to Margaret Ann Hardin for being my sounding board and a voice of reason throughout this project. Margaret also helped me to find needed objects and images at the Natural History Museum of Los Angeles County, as did Tony Marinella at the Museum of Northern Arizona, Marian E. Rodee at the Maxwell Museum of Anthropology, Tatiana Lomahaftewa Slock at the Institute of American Indian Arts Museum, and Louise I. Stiver at the Museum of New Mexico.

The exceptional staff of the Fowler Museum of Cultural History has turned a concept into a reality. Again and again, each has done the impossible. Doran H. Ross has steered the project to completion, providing insights and suggestions at every stage. I am grateful to him for arranging time for me to complete my essay. Danny Brauer has performed his special magic for this publication. Don Cole produced eye-catching photographs of a great range of objects. Lynne Brodhead worked to secure financial support. I am grateful as well to Polly Nooter Roberts for support and encouragement and to Betsy Escandor for many favors along the way. Finally, I thank Lynne Kostman. Not only has she been the wisest and most conscientious of editors, but she took on tasks surely well beyond her job description. She has ignored no detail, abandoned no potential photograph. I shudder to think of how I would have managed without her. To all, including those not mentioned by name, my thanks for your consummate professionalism. This project was supported by the National Endowment for the Humanities through a 1997 Summer Stipend that facilitated my research.

Zena Pearlstone

Notes on Orthography

All Hopi words in this volume follow the orthography of the *Hopi Dictionary: A Hopi-English Dictionary of the Third Mesa Dialect,* compiled by the Hopi Dictionary Project Bureau of Applied Research in Anthropology, University of Arizona (Tucson: University of Arizona Press, 1998). Hopi words appearing in quotations are cited as they were published.

The term *Katsina* (plural, *Katsinam*) has many variant spellings. Most common are: Kachina, Katchina, and Katcina. Katsina is the closest phonetic equivalent to the Hopi pronunciation. The term cannot be translated. It is not a Hopi word and is probably borrowed from outside the Pueblo area (Adams 1991, 4; Secakuku 1995, viii). The names of the Hopi villages are also spelled in various ways. In the following table, compiled by Peter Whiteley, the new orthography used in this text is listed along with some orthographic variants.

Hopi Dictionary Spelling	Spelling Variants
First Mesa	
Walpi	Gualpi
Sitsomovi	Sichomovi
Tewa	Hano, Hanoki
Second Mesa	
Songoopavi	Chumopavy, Shongopavi, Shumopavi, Shungopavi, Shungopavy
Supawlavi	Shipaulovi
Musangnuvi	Mashongnavi, Mishongnovi
Third Mesa	
Orayvi	Oraibi
Kiqötsmovi	Kiakochomovi, Kykotsmovi, New Oraibi
Paaqavi	Bacavi, Bacobi, Bakavi
Hotvela	Hotavila, Hotevilla
Munqapi	Moencopi, Moenkopi

Introduction: From the Sacred to the Cash Register—Problems Encountered in Protecting the Hopi Patrimony

LEIGH J. KUWANWISIWMA
DIRECTOR, HOPI CULTURAL PRESERVATION OFFICE

The Seeds of Change

Much has changed in the Hopi world since its first encounter with European culture in 1540. Exposure to this completely different value system proved a decisive influence, one that would contribute to the shaping of Hopi thought. It was the Spanish who introduced the Hopi to the concept of value as determined by the price assigned to tangible items. Spain's motivation for financing explorations across the ocean into the "New World" was, it should be remembered, to fill an almost insatiable appetite for wealth; hence, the quest for the fabled "cities of gold." The Christian mandate to "conquer the world" also played a significant role in the way in which the Spanish, and later the Mexican and American governments, treated the Hopis. The Hopi traditional value system, which was based entirely on a religious philosophy, was manipulated to serve the ends of Christianity.

The consequences of this sudden introduction to foreign peoples and their beliefs linger into the twenty-first century and continue to influence the way in which Hopis determine value within their own culture. Debate rages today within the Hopi villages as to what is appropriate to sell. One needs only to look at the written record to understand the process by which Hopis gradually began to place monetary values on their religious objects.

Setting the Stage

Between 1869 and 1872 the famous geographer John Wesley Powell first explored the Colorado River system and visited the Hopi Mesas. Fascinated by the thriving Hopi culture, he was especially impressed with its material manifestations, among them Katsina dolls, or *tithu* (singular, *tihu*) as the Hopis call these carvings. Highly significant within the context of the Katsina religious traditions, these were much more than mere "dolls" to Hopis. They were a part of a girl's rite of passage as she matured. Quite simply, these *tithu* were religious objects. Many collectors and Hopis have, however, unfortunately placed more weight on the seemingly secular role that these "dolls" play in a young girl's development. This mentality and essential lack of understanding of the *tithu* have made it easy for Hopi carvers to place a price on these "dolls."

When Powell offered several Hopi families a quarter for a Katsina doll, the Hopis engaged in the first episode of the sale of religious items. To be fair, one must understand that at this time, a quarter bought a twenty-five-pound sack of flour, a highly valued commodity to a culture that was just beginning to feel the dominance of a cash economy. Powell left word that he would be back the following year to purchase more Katsina dolls. True to his promise, he returned and bought more material goods, including *tithu*, ceramics, and miscellaneous artifacts. Thus the stage was set.

Tithu as an "Art Form"

There is no equivalent in the Hopi lexicon for the term *art*. Hopi imagery—as observed in paintings and other tangible forms of expression—always carries a symbolic meaning within the context of Hopi culture. Thus, the way a Hopi Katsina doll is painted is purposeful. Each color, color combination, and area of paint application is a standard way of expressing a Hopi message. The Hopi Katsina dances have been described as "beautiful," "colorful," and "entertaining." Today, tour companies, travel agencies, airlines, economic coalitions, and a consortium of cities and states have invested huge marketing budgets to attract visitors to the Southwest. As one leafs through the pages of advertisements, it is not surprising to see that the Hopi Reservation is promoted as a central reason for visiting Arizona.

The reality is that today's image of the Hopi people is a product of history—from Powell to America West Airlines to the Hopi Cultural Center Motel and Restaurant. Within the context of an immense marketing network, Hopis and their culture have been relegated to "art." On one hand, the tourism industry promotes and profits; on the other, the individual Hopi carver is motivated by economics to subtly compromise a religious image. An intricately carved Hopi Katsina doll by a well-established Hopi carver will today bring more than five thousand dollars. In between, there are Hopi politicians, cultural preservationists, religious leaders, and entrepreneurs, all objecting to certain aspects of the situation; it seems impossible, however, to arrive at a middle ground.

Hopi views concerning the commercialization of the Katsina doll seem increasingly to differ. This is especially true today when Hopis, in general, are publicly voicing their objections to the proliferation of imitation (non-Pueblo made) "Katsina" dolls and demanding that the tribal government do something about this situation. This pressure from its own constituency presents an interesting situation. Does the Tribal Council take the initiative to "protect" the Hopi artists from unfair practices (on the part of non-Hopis who use the Hopi term *Katsina* to market imitation wares)? Or is it the council's responsibility to protect the intellectual property of its religious community? To what degree is the tribal government willing to take the issue internally? These are interesting questions reflecting a very complex state of affairs.

The Hopi Cultural Preservation Office and the Issues

The Hopi Cultural Preservation Office deals with issues of intellectual and cultural property rights and religious privacy, in other words, with how Hopis should deal with the appropriation of cultural information without permission. When the office was established in 1989, we couldn't imagine that these issues would become so complex. In dealing with matters of cultural preservation, I have had to learn a great deal about domains of which I previously had very little knowledge—intellectual property law, copyright, patents, and trademarks. I think I know what the issues are, and I think I know generally what the goals of our office are in terms of protection, but legally the situation is very, very complicated.

Hopi society is intricate. We have twelve villages, each of which is under its own jurisdiction and authority. We have about thirty-four living clans, about forty extinct clans whose interests still have to be represented, and about fourteen to fifteen religious societies. It works, but having to deal with all of these entities and to get a consensus of support for something that the Cultural Preservation Office wants to accomplish is difficult. There is overall general opposition to what is happening with religious objects, and Hopis voice these objections over and over again. But because our society has always functioned at the village level, it is difficult to reach any general consensus, much less agreement, on the kind of position we should take.

Being a Hopi, growing up Hopi, one does care for the culture. I catch myself having my personal and cultural bias come into play because I'm a Hopi. I don't carve for commercial reasons and never did, and I probably never will. That is basically because of my upbringing, my teaching. You only carve at appropriate times; you do not carve publicly. That is the oath I took and that is what I personally intend to uphold. As a Hopi who highly respects these religious teachings, I do not feel good about the present situation because religious teachings are no longer kept private. As an individual Hopi, I can tell myself and my family that it is basically wrong. In our tradition you never say someone carved a doll. We always say the Katsina gives it. That is again based upon religious and cultural teachings that I sincerely respect. In some cases contemporary carvings of Katsinam (plural of *Katsina*) do directly violate the religious viewpoints of other Hopis. The Katsina society, the Katsina clan, probably feel infringed upon. They are the people who are vested with certain ceremonial obligations, with maintaining the integrity of all that pertains to Katsinam. I have debated these issues with them on occasion, but, like me, they don't know how to deal with the situation because peoples' livelihoods are at stake. The sale of arts and crafts ranks right behind the Hopi tribal government and the federal agencies as a major contributor to the Hopi cash economy. Furthermore, for a long time carving has been a common, and probably a socially acceptable, practice.

I always bring my religious viewpoint to the table, but I also know that there is a special interest group out there—the Hopi carvers—and that I, as director of the Hopi Cultural Preservation Office, must also represent them. When it comes to Katsina doll carving, I have to assume a contemporary perspective if I want to protect the interest of those Hopis who are in fact carrying on a tradition. I'm the one who has to try to bring the ends of the spectrum together.

Some of today's Hopi artisans are renowned, and as artists they are properly recognized within their respective artistic communities. They do, I submit, in many cases successfully convey Hopi aesthetics. Their carving may be nontraditional, but it still manages to capture some essence of Hopi culture. There are also issues of artistic integrity that must be confronted. Today you have specific styles of carving, and an individual Hopi carver may feel that his or her style is being infringed upon. One carver began to carve Katsina dolls with removable tops, or "masks," and we protested that. The carver reacted that it was none of the tribe's business, but his work is culturally offensive because it infringes on what we are taught to protect and uphold, that is, the integrity of our initiations.

It is an internal problem. There is the question of what the Katsina means to us as Hopis versus what it means to individual Hopis who choose to commodify. Lines have already been drawn, probably by default, probably on the basis of the history of carving. Because we are a modern society, I don't feel that the tribe is in the business of regulating private rights. On the other hand, we are in the business of protecting cultural property rights. It is a direct question, a Hopi question, and frankly it is one that we just don't have any good answers for at this point. We don't even have any productive ways to talk about it. I know that the other Pueblos have voiced their objections to Hopis, and we are quite aware of that. There are some Zuni carvers who sell their work and some other miscellaneous

Pueblo carvers but nothing as extensive as what goes on at Hopi.

Even though there are no good answers, I do think that a general representation of tribal interest begins where non-Hopis exploit what is intrinsically proven to be Hopi. I think I can safely draw the line there and represent the interests of those Hopis who are making a living and making their artistic reputations. I feel I have a right to protect that aspect of Hopi against those people who intrude and choose to exploit our intrinsic cultural value. Whether or not the Cultural Preservation Office can succeed in this endeavor is another question. At the same time the Hopi Cultural Preservation Office must address the interests of the more religious elements of the community.

Non-Hopi Infringement

There are a lot of people making money by using the Hopi name. They advertise Hopi blue corn seeds, Hopi sweet corn seeds, Hopi this, Hopi that (fig. 1.1). I've got a Hopi blue cornmeal that is manufactured in Phoenix. There are Hopi blue cornflakes marketed in Southern California. There are Hopi-Navajo tours. The same situation exists for Katsinam.

I once asked an intellectual property attorney if anything could be done about the use of the terms

1.1   1.2

Navajo-Kachina and *Kachina doll*. Specifically, I wanted to know what were the Hopis chances of getting a trademark for the Hopi word *Katsina* (*Kachina*). The attorney was pretty familiar with the issue and turned to the *k*'s in *Webster's Dictionary*. *Kachina* is an entry. It is already in the public domain. The word *Hopi* is in the public domain as well. I think I understand that when the White man says "public domain," it means that by not protecting something, you basically allow others to have what was once yours. You allow others to have and to claim an interest by not protecting it. The attorney also told me that it would be difficult to deal with the Katsina doll issue because the Hopi themselves are selling these carvings. So unless the artist specifically acquires a trademark for a particular style of carving or a design on a carving, there is no way of protecting Hopi art.

As a consequence, there are many people mimicking Hopi dolls all over the world (see Pearlstone, this volume). Perhaps the greatest proliferation of imitation dolls right now is occurring on the Navajo Reservation where they are made by individual Navajos and by Navajos working in doll factories (fig. 1.2). These are advertised as "Navajo-Kachina" dolls, and I tell people there's nothing Navajo about Katsinam. The Navajos never believed in Katsinam. They are appropriating our tribal term without our permission.

Some of the artists who are imitating *tithu* make their objects look pretty authentic. They use either watercolor or acrylic paint and mix it with different kinds of sand so it kind of looks like natural pigment. Then they sandblast the carvings so they look old. They have perfected the techniques. The Cultural Preservation Office tries to keep tabs on the auctions where these objects are shown. Auction catalogs will say—and this is really clever advertising—"turn-of-the-century kachina doll" or "authentically Puebloan

turn-of-the-century doll." What does that really mean? But people are naive about these issues and will pay a lot of money for these items (fig. 1.3).

Sometimes situations are very complex. A few years ago, a Navajo college student called me and said she had bought some Katsina dolls at a Phoenix swap meet and wanted to return them to Hopi because in her opinion they were significant (fig. 1.4). She was respectful of Hopi culture. She did not know what they were but thought that they were meaningful to Hopis because they were advertised as Hopi Katsina dolls. She called the dorm at her college in Colorado, and the students contributed money—I think almost four hundred dollars—and they mailed it to her in Phoenix. She bought the dolls to get them off the market. She brought them home to Window Rock and called me. She told me what she had done and said she wanted to return them to the Hopis because she didn't feel good

1.1 A bag of "Hopi Blue Popcorn" produced by Bag O' Beans, Reno, Nevada, features a Katsina-like figure. Private collection.

1.2 An imitation, modern "Katsina" doll of Navajo manufacture. Collection of the Hopi Cultural Preservation Office.

1.3 An imitation, modern "Katsina" doll of unknown origin. Collection of the Hopi Cultural Preservation Office.

1.3

about them out there. She brought them in, and I saw that they were imitation dolls.

We have also seen a significant influx of commercially made—I hate to use the word *mask* because we don't call them that—Katsina "masks," which are proliferating in the tourist market. It's another example of cultural exploitation that is difficult to deal with as a Hopi Tribe. In a case such as this Hopis would like the Katsina clan or the Katsina society to make a decision. Yet because their responsibilities are of such religious significance, they cannot support something that's going to be politicized even though they object to it. They would object to these cases being debated in court. Making things more public is not the Hopi way. That is not what religious leaders want to do.

The Smokis were a group of Anglos both male and female in Prescott, Arizona, who got together around 1929 and thought it would be a great idea to represent tribal cultures. They did a lot of research, came to Hopi, and witnessed a lot of the dances, and began to mimic a lot of the ceremonials. They would go through the whole process of initiations and related events and mimic different Hopi societies. Hopis generally knew of these things and protested. In 1991 we finally publicly protested these ceremonials and were successful basically in forcing the group to go bankrupt. They lost a lot of money because we picketed and publicly protested.

The Smokis were followed by a primarily female group who called themselves the Kachina Dolls. These are "wanna-bes"; they wear fringed leather, braids—New Ager types. In 1987 there was something called the "harmonic convergence." It was a worldwide phenomenon, a spiritual kind of thing. Because Hopi is so popular, this group had apparently organized something at the Pueblo that we didn't even know about. A farmer going up from Old Orayvi on foot to his own area stumbled upon a bunch of New Agers who were apparently involved in the "convergence." He had no idea what was going on. Hopis protested, and the tribal police escorted those people off the Pueblo. But then they erected what they called a shrine. After the Home Dance I checked the so-called shrine just out of curiosity. They had gone beyond mimicking offerings and had placed objects on the shrine resembling prayer sticks; they also left sacred fresh spruce. Another time, we discovered a Lutheran minister who was conducting workshops in Native American rituals. He was actually teaching people, who paid $175 for a workshop, how to make "Katsina masks,

1.4 An imitation "Katsina" doll purchased at a Phoenix swap meet by a Navajo college student. Collection of the Hopi Cultural Preservation Office.

altars, prayer sticks, songs." When confronted, his reaction was "to give the Hopis a good fight" (see Spencer, this volume).

In 1992 Marvel Comics published an issue demeaning Katsinam (see Pearlstone, this volume). By the time we got in touch with the publisher's New York office, there was not much they could do because they had sold their rights to their distributorship nationwide. They did initiate a recall, but by then the comic book had already been out for two to three weeks. There is always a catch-22. When we protested publicly, that particular issue became a collector's item. So, ironically, it tripled in price.

About all we can do is to protest these issues publicly. They are certainly important, but to invest considerable resources in a protest, you at least want to be assured of a good chance to win, and basically the odds are against us. Freedom of speech is an important principle in American government—academic freedom as well. It is a real problem at Hopi. We are overwhelmed at the number of cases where others are imitating Hopi life and art. We don't have the time or means to deal with activities in foreign countries. We are aware that if we protest and succeed in shutting down a local publisher, he can then go to Germany or some other European country and publish the same thing there.

Hopis have never intruded on the rights of other people. Our religion is private. We don't convert, we don't proselytize. I'm not interested in Navajo products. I have no desire to mimic them. But commercialism is rampant, and we ourselves are at fault in some ways. There are so many people to reach. There are 3,500 universities and colleges in the United States alone, all of which are, of course, dealing with different kinds of research. There are many visitors, domestic and foreign, to Hopi. It is my sincere hope that this volume will present some of these issues objectively and help to make the public aware that there is a significant problem, particularly in the cases of non-Hopi carvers who take advantage of something that is culturally proven to be Hopi. ●

Hopi Histories

PETER M. WHITELEY

History and Time

Hopi culture reaches deep into the remote past like the roots of the reed that Hopis ascended to enter this, the Fourth World. The Hopi chart their arrival via Sipaapuni, the emergence point, in the Grand Canyon, near the confluence of the Little Colorado and Colorado Rivers. Prior to emergence onto the earth's surface, Hopi life passed through three earlier phases—time/spaces of gradually coming-into-being.

Linguists argue about "time" in the Hopi language.[1] Benjamin Lee Whorf claimed that strictly speaking, there are no tenses in Hopi and thus no way to conceive historical events as distinctly "past." Challenging this, Ekkehart Malotki points out numerous ways of referring to time in Hopi. Malotki is correct technically, but Whorf's view hits upon the essential philosophy of Hopi historical consciousness. Whorf shows the Hopi perspective on "being and time" as a continuous emergence-into-presence (not dissimilar from Heidegger's philosophy of existence). The seeds of all that is or will be have always existed: the temporal process is simply one of manifestation—of the endlessly manifesting working itself into the actually manifested. How it does this does not entail a wholly mystical sense of causation: rather it depends on the intentional thoughts and actions of conscious agents—especially human beings conceiving plans and carrying them out. Hopi historical consciousness thus includes both the cosmically ordained and the pragmatically determined. Hopi historical ideas, like others, are shaped by narrative frameworks that specify what is valuable and important. Hopi narratives emphasize repetitions, especially by fours: important events occur four times, each successively attaining definition toward completeness. The tetradic quality reappears in numerous contexts, for example, cosmology, geography, song forms, and architecture; it is also common among the Pueblos of New Mexico. The following four histories make no claim to speak for Hopi thought directly; I hope, however, that they will reflect some of the Hopi historical imagination,

as well as Western conventions of knowledge about the past.

History 1

Emergence into the present world was both ultimately predestined, and proximately thought and consciously acted into being. In the Third World below, the *momngwit* (leaders), saw the signs: life had become corrupt—*koyaanisqatsi* (chaotic life). People neglected their duties and were constantly gambling, cheating, and practicing witchcraft. So the leaders sat and smoked and deliberated: they formed a plan of *naavotsiwni*, or life purification and renaissance. They decided to escape chaos by reaching up through the sky and beginning again. The sound of footsteps had been heard above, on top of the sky-roof. The *momngwit* molded *pavawkyaya* (a swallow) out of clay, breathed life into it, and sent it up to seek a passage into the new world. It proved too weak, so they tried again, with *tòotsa* (a hummingbird); and again, with *kiisa* (a hawk). Finally, on the fourth try, *motsni* (a shrike) passed through the gap and found the guardian of the Fourth World, Maasaw, sitting at his cornfield. "The leaders sent me to ask your permission to come and live here," said the shrike. "Well, the permission is not mine to give," responded Maasaw. "I am just taking care of this earth for the Creator. Life up here is hard. If they are willing to live this hard life, they can come: it is up to them."

The *momngwit* now had to decide how to ascend into this new life. First, they magically grew *salavi* (a Douglas fir). But it did not reach far enough. They tried again and again. On the fourth occasion, *paaqavi* (a reed) was strong enough and tall enough to push right through the opening. They climbed up inside the reed, planning to leave the corrupting *popwaqt* (witches) down below, so that their new world would remain pure and without death. But one *powaqmana* (witch girl) managed to come up with the rest before the *kikmongwi* (principal leader) had pulled up the reed. Escape from mortality was thwarted; the *kikmongwi's* own son was the first to die. To divine the cause, he made a cornmeal ball and threw it up in the air; it landed on the witch girl's head. He made a move to kill her, but she said, "Come back to the *sipaapuni* and look down. Your son is playing happily down there." So he allowed her to live, and the world below—uniting the axis of temporal process with that of vertical space—became both the repository of past life and the spiritual destination for mortal humanity. At its end, life returns to the point of beginning, emergence.

Maasaw gave the leaders four things: maize seeds, a jug of water, a planting stick, and a philosophy of life prescribing modesty, caution, cooperation, environmental care, and enduring determination. He instructed the people to split up and migrate to the four corners of the earth, gradually returning to a central place when ordained signs appeared. As they migrated, each group became a separate clan and built several villages along the way. When the signs—such as constellation movements—appeared, they left one village and moved on to build another. As they left a village, marks were left, reminders of their presence and guarantors of their ancestral interest: the ruins, Hopis say, are the footprints of their migrations.

2.1 A. C. Vroman, *Walpi Village from the Northeast, 1895.* Seaver Center for Western History Research, Los Angeles County Museum of Natural History, V-509.

Eventually the migrants neared their destiny, Tuuwanasavi, the earth's center. The first to arrive was the *kikmongwi's* group, now known as Honngyam (Bear clan). They reached a point below Second Mesa and built a village, Old Songoopavi. Gradually, other clans arrived and sought the Bear clan's permission to move in—the Patkingyam (Water clan), Pipngyam (Tobacco clan), and Taawangyam (Sun clan), all coming from Homol'ovi (near present-day Winslow), Nuvakwewtaqa, Sakwavayki, and other old villages in the south. The Tsu'ngyam (Snake clan), Alngyam (Horn clan), Lenngyam (Flute clan), and others came from several villages around Tokoonavi (Navajo Mountain). The Kookopngyam (Fire clan) and Kòokyangwngyam (Spider clan) came via Kawestima (the Tsegi Canyon area—"Navajo National Monument," including the villages of Keet Seel and Betatakin). The Honanngyam (Badger clan) and Poliingyam (Butterfly clan) came from the northeast—Salapa (Mesa Verde) and ruins along Chinle Wash and Laguna Creek. The Aawatngyam (Bow clan), Paaqapngyam (Reed clan), and Tepngyam (Greasewood clan) came from villages in the west beyond present-day Munqapi. And numerous clans came from the east—from Canyon de Chelly and Chaco, from the Rio Grande and Acoma. Not all came to Old Songoopavi. Other villages were being built—some by in-migrating clans, others through fission in the existing villages. At Songoopavi, the *kikmongwi*, Yaho'ya, and his brother Matsito had a dispute. Matsito went off to found Orayvi on Third Mesa, which in time became the largest village, granting entry to many incoming clans.

As a clan arrived, the leaders had to prove its worth by showing the *kikmongwi* a useful ceremony or some other capability that would enhance the life of the community. From Tokoonavi the Snake clan brought the Snake ceremony; from Kawestima, where it had also stayed prior to migrating to the Hopi Mesas, the Flute clan brought the Flute ceremony; from Kiisiwu the Badger clan brought many Katsinam, or supernatural helpers who performed the Patsavu ceremony during Powamuya (the purifying moon), which occurs around February, as their contribution. In time, the gradually consolidating form of Hopi society became an integrated structure of clans with their ceremonies arranged at different junctures of a liturgical cycle—each giving an elemental part to the vitality of the whole. The contemporary Hopi villages continue to organize much of their lives in this way with matrilineal clans and religious societies performing hereditary duties—economic, religious, political, and aesthetic.

Hopi Society and the Katsinam

The twelve modern Hopi villages all lie high in the Colorado Plateau country of northern Arizona, stretched out on a generally southeast-northwest axis roughly sixty miles as the crow flies (figs. 2.1, 2.2). The villages cluster in groups around the tips of three fingerlike promontories, known as the Hopi Mesas, which form the southwesternmost extensions of Black Mesa, an upthrust plate of the Colorado Plateau. From east to west the mesa-top villages are arranged as follows:

First Mesa: Walpi, Sitsomovi, Tewa
Second Mesa: Songoopavi, Supawlavi,
    Musangnuvi
Third Mesa: Orayvi, Kiqötsmovi, Paaqavi,
    Hotvela

Forty-five highway miles to the west of Third Mesa lie the two villages of Upper and Lower Munqapi, which trace their principal heritage to their mother village, Orayvi.

Hopi is a "Puebloan" culture identifiably descended from the "Anasazi" and other prehistoric Southwest town-dwelling Indians. According to the archaeological record, the Hopi Mesas have been continuously occupied for at least fifteen hundred years, and Orayvi on Third Mesa is the oldest continuously inhabited town in North America. Significant aspects of culture and religious practice are shared with other Pueblo peoples, including the Zuni and the Rio Grande Pueblos. The so-called "Katsina cult" is in evidence archaeologically among all the Pueblo peoples and is reported on throughout the historic records from the Spanish and Mexican periods (1540–1848) and from the Anglo-American period (1848–present).[2]

A calendar of elaborate ritual performances can be divided into the Katsina season—roughly from December to July—and a season of ceremonies by other religious sodalities—from August to December. The latter include the Snake, Flute, Wuwtsim (Manhood) and Maraw (Womanhood) societies, Lakon and Owaqöl (women's "Basket Dance" societies), and the Soyalangw society festival in midwinter. A great deal of traditional Hopi religion remains intact. Katsina performances are key religious rituals in all the villages, and all Hopis are initiated into either the Katsina or the

Powamuy order, which are chiefly responsible for Katsina ceremonies.

Katsina rituals occur both inside the kivas at night—especially from January to March and in the *kiisonvis* (plazas) during the day, especially from March to July. Of the major Katsina ceremonies, perhaps the most important are Powamuy (the Bean Dance), in February and Nimaniw (the homegoing, or Home Dance) in July, when the Katsinam depart for their spiritual homes in the high, moist places around Hopitutskwa (Hopi country). Some Katsinam only appear at specific ceremonies; others may appear throughout the Katsina season. Some come in groups, others singly or in pairs; some dance and sing, others may mime or speak or engage in many

permutations of action, gesture, and communication—directed to the world of nature and to the community of living human beings. There are several "classes" of Katsinam—Mongkatsinam (Chiefly Katsinam), Wawarskatsinam (Runner Katsinam), Kipokkatsinam (Warrior/Guard Katsinam), and so on. They appear in different contexts and serve different purposes.

Katsinam embody a fundamental principle in Hopi religion. In use, *Katsina* is a triune concept, referring to spirits of the dead, to clouds, and to the personated spirits who appear in ceremonies. While in English the term *Katsina* is often used to refer to dolls; in Hopi the term is *tihu* (doll) or *Katsintihu* (Katsina doll). The Hopi term *Katsina*

2.2. A. C. Vroman, *View Looking over Mishongnovi, Shipaulovi in the Distance, 1901.* Courtesy of the Southwest Museum, Los Angeles, 268.G, photo no. N.41687.

is only used to refer to the spirit beings. As Barton Wright puts it:

> To Hopis, it is essential to preserve harmony with the world around them, not only with man and other animals but with objects in nature, such as rocks, clouds, sky, etc., which the Hopis believe to be possessed of life. *Since the Kachinas embody these spirits they are the spiritual guardians of the Hopi people and their way of life. And since they can insure human, animal, and plant fertility, they insure life itself.* [B. Wright 1973, 2; emphasis added]

In ritual, the personators take on Katsina spiritual form, becoming the Katsinam themselves:

> When Kachinas are personated by the men of the villages, they assume visual form and appear in the streets and plazas of the town. It is here that the Kachina is his most magnificent, for the Hopis feel that when they impersonate a Kachina, they *become* the supernatural. As supernaturals they may cure disease, grow corn, bring clouds and rain, watch over ceremonies and reinforce discipline and order in the Hopi world. [B. Wright 1973, 2; emphasis in original]

History II

Archaeologically, the Southwest bears some of the oldest traces of human presence in the Americas, especially with the Clovis culture, dated to circa 10,000 B.C.E. The marks of "Paleo-Indians," the succeeding "Archaic" and "Basketmaker" periods, and the great agriculture-based traditions—Anasazi, Mogollon, Hohokam, and Hakataya (as archaeologists call them; Hopis prefer Hisatsinom, or "ancestors")—are all present within or close to Hopi country. The core of Hopi country stretches from Tokoonavi and Kawestima in the north to the Mogollon Rim in the south, from the Canyon de Chelly in the east to Öngtupqa (the Grand Canyon) in the west.

Evidence of emergence from belowground pit houses to aboveground masonry room-blocks, and from small house-blocks to Anasazi towns around 1100 C.E., is clear and abundant around the Hopi Mesas. Some Basketmaker sites dating to 500 C.E. are close to contemporary villages, and the pattern of occupation is clearly continuous. Walk in any direction from a modern Hopi village, and within a mile or two you will run into prehistoric potsherds or building rubble—some of the "footsteps" of which Hopis speak.

With the great Southwest drought from 1275 to 1300 C.E., Puebloan settlements contracted. Towns both large and small were replaced by clusters at reliable water sources. In the period 1300–1450 Hisatsinom villages in the areas Hopis call Tokoonavi, Kawestima, Homol'ovi, and Nuvakwewtaqa ceased to be occupied: centripetal migrations into the Hopi Mesas with their abundant spring flows swelled the population, and larger villages appeared. In the fifteenth century, there were numerous small villages on the three Hopi Mesas and on Antelope Mesa to the east.

History III

In 1540, Pedro de Tovar and Fray Juan Padilla, emissaries of conquistador Francisco Vásquez de Coronado—who was encamped at Zuni—arrived at Hopi. At that time, there were probably five major Hopi towns: Awat'ovi on Antelope Mesa, Walpi at First Mesa, Musangnuvi and Songoopavi at Second Mesa, and Orayvi on Third Mesa. The First and Second Mesa towns were below the mesa tops, and only Orayvi remains today where it was then. Tovar attacked Awat'ovi and the *qaletaqmongwi* (war chief) sued for peace: numerous gifts were presented—cotton textiles, hides, corn and cornmeal, piñon nuts, and turquoise. A second Coronado party later explored the area from Hopi to the Grand Canyon, while Coronado himself burned and battled his way among the Eastern Pueblos, attacking all who put up resistance.

Spanish colonization of the Provincia de Nuevo Mexico under Don Juan de Oñate began in 1598. Oñate established a brutal regime, levying forced labor and tribute—cotton mantas, turkey-feather cloaks, turquoise, food, and so forth—from the Pueblos; its direct impact at Hopi was, however, initially minimal. The first Franciscan mission was built in 1629 at Awat'ovi. Father Porras apparently made some converts after he restored a blind boy to sight, but his presence also caused dissent: he died, probably poisoned, in 1633. The mores of the Inquisition still held sway, and brutal repression of "idolatry" is illustrated in an account of 1655, when Orayvi emissaries went to Santa Fe in protest:

> They stated that an Orayvi Indian named Juan Cuña had been discovered in some act of idolatry. In the presence of the entire pueblo, Father Guerra gave him such a severe

beating that he was bathed in blood. Then inside the church, the Friar administered a second beating, following which he took burning turpentine and larded the Indian's body from head to feet. Soon after receiving this brutal punishment the Indian died. [Scholes 1937, 144–45]

His offense is not recorded, though it may have been no more than making prayer feathers or even carving a Katsina doll.

Other missions were established at "San Francisco de Orayvi" (whence the "San Francisco Peaks" by modern Flagstaff) and "San Bartolome de Xongopabi" with small chapels at Walpi and Musangnuvi. Hopis refer to the Spanish missionaries as *tota'tsim* (tyrants) and cite abuses such as that reported above to account for a deep antipathy to missionary Christianity that persists into the present. Hopi religious activities were taken underground during this period: Katsina ceremonies were performed at a remote mesa, Kaktsintuyqa (Many Katsinam point), south of Orayvi.

In 1680, all the Pueblos, from Pecos in the east to Orayvi in the west conspired to end the Spanish colonial regime. Led by Popé, a Tewa from San Juan Pueblo, messengers ran with coded, knotted strings to the other towns, and acting simultaneously, the Pueblos put missionaries, soldiers, and colonists to death with the remnant fleeing south to El Paso. At Hopi five priests were killed. Orayvi tradition states that the resident priest was killed by Tseeveyo, a Warrior Katsina who carries a sword. After the revolt, there was a good deal of movement. Some Pueblo people went to live with the Navajo at Dinetah (old "Navajo country") along the upper reaches of the San Juan River. The Zunis consolidated their six villages into one. And numerous Eastern Pueblos sought refuge with the Hopi. Tiwas from Sandia Pueblo founded Payupki on Second Mesa, Tewas built Hanoki on First Mesa, and other towns were founded too: Hopi country became the "refuge of the irreconcilables," and the Spanish never reestablished a presence there.

New clans were probably adopted into Hopi society at this point, along with their ceremonial contributions. The widely known Hemiskatsina, who performs at the Home Dance, originally came from Jemez Pueblo; Angaktsina, the Long-Hair Katsina, was likely introduced from the Rio Grande Pueblos; and it may be at this point that the Piikyasngyam (Side Corn clan) came with its *wu'ya* ("ancient")

the Ahooli Katsina, and the Tsa'kwaynangyam (Tsa'kwayna clan) came with their Katsinam of the same name.

Despite concerted efforts by Hopi leaders to prevent missionary reestablishment, in 1700 converts at Awat'ovi began to rebuild a church with disastrous consequences. In a conspiracy with Awat'ovi's Tobacco clan leader, Taapolo, warriors from the other Hopi villages, probably including Rio Grande refugees, attacked Awat'ovi at night during Wuwtsim initiations when all the men were in the kivas. They pulled up the kiva ladders and threw ristras of burning chile peppers down the hatchways, suffocating all inside. Women and children and some men were taken to a point below First Mesa, Mastsomo (Skeleton mound), where some were killed and others taken and distributed among the villages. Awat'ovi crumbled into a ruin, never to be reinhabited.

The Spanish launched a series of punitive campaigns between 1701 and 1716, but all were repulsed. In 1716, for example, Governor Phélix Martínez tried to parley at First Mesa:

Coming halfway down the cliff with a gun in his hand, one of the caciques, after abusing the reverend father custodian, the governor, and the religious [priests] with insulting words, fired, while his people let fly an infinitude of arrows; the result was a war against them, with the laying waste of cornfields and some deaths. [Quoted in Brew 1949, 25]

After the revolt, all the existing Hopi villages, except Orayvi (and Awat'ovi), moved their sites: Walpi, Songoopavi, and Musangnuvi all relocated to more defensible positions on the mesa tops. During this period also, Supawlavi was founded as a colony of Songoopavi by the Bear and the Sun Forehead clans on a rocky knoll a stone's throw from the new Musangnuvi. First Mesa got two villages, when Walpi allowed Tewas from the Galisteo Basin to build Tewa village, or Hanoki, a quarter-mile up the peninsularlike finger from Walpi's new site. The other addition, Sitsomovi, a Walpi colony, was also built in the eighteenth century between Walpi and Hanoki, and later received additional migrants from Zuni.

Other influences now appear in the Hopi world. "Apaches de Navajo," today's Navajo Nation, and the largest group of Native American people, were in the mid-eighteenth century a small group of

Apacheans living in north-central New Mexico. They began to depend on livestock acquired initially in trade and from raiding Pueblos and Hispanic towns. Navajo success with livestock heralded an exodus from Dinetah (old "Navajo country") to the south around Mount Taylor and then west to the Lukachukai and Chuska Mountains and the Canyon de Chelly. Navajo relations with Hopis seem always to have been ambivalent. Trading and intermarriage were combined with Navajo raids on Hopi villages for livestock and slaves to be sold to the Spanish. In 1780, Hopi leaders complained to visiting governor Don Juan Bautista de Anza about "continuous war" made on them by Navajos and Utes. Having learned of a terrible drought and smallpox epidemic, de Anza had come to invite Hopis to settle on the Rio Grande (continuing the policy of *reducción*, or consolidation of indigenous peoples, for purposes of control). While two-hundred families agreed to go, the leaders of Walpi and Orayvi adamantly refused. A contemporary account records that, despite "hunger, pestilence, and war… the chief priests of the nation were inexorable in their purpose of remaining heathen, preserving their customs, and remaining in their desolated pueblos" (A. Thomas 1941, 109). Hopi sovereignty was strong, as visiting priest Francisco Garces had found out four years earlier. Though introduced by Havasupai guides, the Orayvis would not house him or allow him to proselytize. He slept two nights in an Orayvi street, but the next day, July 4th, they drove him out: "And on the very day that representatives of a new American nation were proclaiming their independence in Philadelphia, July 4, 1776, the old nation of Oraibi was reaffirming theirs" (Brew 1949, 36).

After de Anza's visit, continuous Spanish-Navajo conflict resulted in Hopi isolation from the colonial regime. No visits of record are mentioned until 1823, following Mexico's independence from Spain. In that year, New Mexico's governor José Antonio Vizcarra led an expedition against the Navajos; they chased Navajo parties to the Hopi Mesas and there gathered intelligence about their movements.

Ripples from another nation's expansion were felt in the 1820s. Trappers from Saint Louis reached the area, and in 1827 Bill Williams stayed at Hopi for a while; the following year, George Yount lived for some months in Walpi and kept a journal of his experiences. But in 1834, a trapping party led by Williams shot somewhere between fifteen and twenty Hopis gardening below present-day Hotvela—an inauspicious beginning for Hopi-Anglo relations.

History IV

With the Treaty of Guadalupe Hidalgo in 1848, Hopis were soon keenly aware of the American takeover. Long before any government representative came to them, the Hopi sent prominent emissaries to Santa Fe in 1850:

> Their object, as announced, was to ascertain the purposes and views of the government of the United States toward them. They complained bitterly of the depredations of the Navajos. The deputation consisted of the cacique of all the pueblos, and a chief of the largest pueblo, accompanied by two who were not officials. [Donaldson 1893, 25]

Further, in 1852, the Hopi had a communiqué of peace and amity—a "unique diplomatic pacquet," including prayer feathers, honey, tobacco, and a pipe—delivered by Tesuque Pueblo representatives to President Millard Fillmore in Washington. This is particularly noteworthy given the widespread tendency to assume imperial powers always took the historical initiative, while indigenous peoples were merely passive recipients of an exogenous history enacted upon them. The 1850s witnessed increasing antagonisms between the United States and the Navajo, occasionally flaring into open warfare. Fort Defiance was established in 1851 as a beachhead into Navajo territory, pushing some Navajos to settle farther west in Hopi country, an encroachment that continues to be felt in the ongoing land disputes. In 1863, in the middle of the Civil War, Navajo pressures against Anglo settlers and Hispanic and Pueblo villages led to the infamous Navajo roundup and "long walk" to incarceration at Fort Sumner in eastern New Mexico. Typical of their ambiguous relationship, Hopis hid some Navajo individuals and their livestock from the army; but Hopis also aided in the roundup and then undertook punitive expeditions—particularly on Black Mesa—against Navajos who had evaded the army.

In the late 1850s yet another colonizing force made its presence felt: Mormons from the new "Kingdom of Deseret," or Utah Territory, reached Hopi and sent several missionaries annually from 1858 to 1873. Then they built colonies along the Little Colorado River. With the aid of Orayvi leader Tuuvi, who was pioneering in the old Hopi settlement at Munqapi, Mormons built a settlement there in 1873, and while it failed, they soon built "Tuba City" (named for Tuuvi) close by in the heart of a long-established Hopi farming area. The Mormons introduced the Hopis to silver dollars. Mormons brokered some Hopi relations with the outside world until 1903, when the United States, seeking to contain Mormon expansion, forcibly closed the Tuba City settlement.

The Hopi Agency—the local arm of the Bureau of Indian Affairs—was officially established in 1869, although initially it had little influence. In 1874, the agent established a small school, and annuity goods were distributed—the origins of Indian dependency on the government in many cases. At Orayvi, the annuities were refused, the Orayvis again rejecting any compromise of their sovereignty.

The 1870s mark another significant development: the establishment of the first trading post, at Keams Canyon. Thomas Keam, an English émigré, built the post into a major political and commercial presence over the next three decades. The Hopi Agency was manned only intermittently, so Keam was often the key intermediary with the outside world. In 1886, he drafted a petition to establish a boarding school, and in 1890 he arranged for the first visit to Washington by five principal Hopi leaders—Loololma of Orayvi; Simo and Aanawita of Walpi; Honani representing Songoopavi, and Polakaka of Hanoki—who met with President Benjamin Harrison.

In the late 1870s, the Hopi Agency had begun to assert a stronger presence, leading to demarcation by Executive Order of the "Hopi Reservation" in 1882, which neglected to include the growing settlement of Munqapi, as well as a great deal of traditional Hopi land. The reservation was created in part to halt Navajo and Mormon expansion, but the Executive Order contained the fateful language— at the time standard in such orders—"for the Hopi and such other Indians as the Secretary of the Interior may see fit to settle thereon" (see below).

Formal ethnography and museum collecting of Hopi crafts also began during this period. John Wesley Powell, who later headed the Smithsonian Institution's Bureau of American Ethnology, had passed through Hopi in 1870; in 1882 he sent Frank Hamilton Cushing, the famous early ethnographer of Zuni, and Victor and Cosmos Mindeleff to gather Hopi artifacts for the National Museum. And in 1885, Matilda Coxe Stevenson and her husband, James, came for the same purpose. Such expeditions and the subsequent dispatching of ethnologists, like Jesse Walter Fewkes, mark the earliest systematic collection of Hopi culture, including religious artifacts.

Alexander Stephen, a Scottish ethnologist, lived at First Mesa and Keams Canyon throughout the 1880s and early 1890s. Reverend H. R. Voth, Mennonite missionary to Orayvi, became increasingly interested in Hopi culture, publishing revealing accounts of esoteric rituals. He collected large quantities of artifacts for the Field Museum in Chicago and for the Fred Harvey Company, the tourist franchise on the Santa Fe Railway, which marketed Native crafts more widely than the local traders were able to do. Trader William Volz set up joint posts at Orayvi and Canyon Diablo, precisely to take advantage of the burgeoning market created by the railroad. Volz's Orayvi post was later taken over by Indian-trading magnate Lorenzo Hubbell, who also took over Keam's post when Keam returned to England in 1903. The railroad had been built through northern Arizona in 1882, but tourist interest in the Grand Canyon and the Hopi Snake Dance really developed in the 1890s.

Hopi exposure to the regional and national market systems thus really starts in the last two decades of the nineteenth century. The cooperation of ethnologists, museums, and traders in commodifying Hopi arts and crafts has continued into the present. And this same period witnesses the rise of serious opposition to United States control. In 1890, an order went out that all Hopi children must attend the Keams Canyon Boarding School. Many Orayvis resisted. So, Commissioner of Indian Affairs T. J. Morgan, attended by the United States Cavalry, visited. The government's allotment program, undertaken pursuant to the Dawes Severalty Act of 1887, attempted to divide up traditional land-holdings but encountered major opposition. Those the government came to call "Friendlies" sent a petition, organized by Stephen and Voth, to halt allotment. The "Hostiles" did not even sign the petition. At Orayvi, eleven resisters spent a year and a half in jail at Fort Wingate, inaugurating a series of political incarcerations that went on until the mid-1940s. Of those imprisoned in 1891, several were leaders of the Spider and Fire clans, including notably Lomahongiwma (Spider) and Yukiwma (Fire), who came to lead a growing "Hostile" faction at Orayvi. In 1894, nineteen Hostiles, including Lomahongiwma and Yukiwma, were sent to Alcatraz for one year.

In the 1890s day schools were constructed below the Hopi Mesas. In 1899, too, after a hiatus of some sixteen years (during which it was peripatetically administered by the Navajo agent at Fort Defiance), the Hopi Agency at Keams Canyon reopened in force under Charles S. Burton, who crusaded ardently against Hopi rituals and for forcible schooling of Hopi children. Crowds of tourists, often organized by Fred Harvey's "Indian Detours," increasingly appeared for the Snake Dance, accompanied by commercial photographers like Adam Clark Vroman, George Wharton James, and Sumner Matteson. Inspired partly by army captain John Gregory Bourke's first ethnography of Hopi, *The Snake Dance of the Moquis of Arizona*, published in 1884, the commodification of Hopi culture began in earnest.

This simultaneous conjuncture of military, civil, religious, and commercial challenges at Hopi was powerful. Not surprisingly, internal conflicts were exacerbated. Moreover, the last smallpox epidemic occurred in 1898–1899, resulting in a population decline of one-third at First and Second Mesas, though Orayvi was spared; as oral history records this was owing to vaccinations arranged by Tuuvi with the Mormons. All the social, cultural, economic, and demographic turmoil eventuated in the famous "split" of Orayvi in 1906. Fortified by "Hostile" migrants from Second Mesa, Orayvi's dissidents now significantly outnumbered Friendlies. The new *kikmongwi*, Tawakwaptiwa, led the Friendly faction, and he was very annoyed when Second Mesa Hostiles usurped some of his ceremonial prerogatives.[3] Things came to a head at the Snake Dance of 1906, and a day and a half later, the Friendlies, reinforced by allies from Munqapi, dragged the Hostiles out of the village. A pushing contest was arranged with Tawakwaptiwa and Yukiwma heading the contesting sides. The Hostiles lost and went to establish the new village of Hotvela. Shortly thereafter, government troops arrived and persuaded some to return to Orayvi (three years later they were forced out again and founded Paaqavi) and incarcerated others at Keams Canyon, Fort Huachuca in southern Arizona, and at Carlisle Indian School in Pennsylvania. Tawakwaptiwa and his closes allies were sent for three years to Sherman Institute, an Indian school in Riverside, California.

Orayvi was broken apart by a combination of internal and external pressures: a watershed event in Hopi history with ongoing ramifications. Hotvela grew into the most staunchly conservative village. The Third Mesa politico-ritual system gradually broke down. Orayvi shrank to scarcely a tenth of its former size, when Tawakwaptiwa, disillusioned after his experience at Sherman, gradually drove out all Christian converts and other "progressives" to

"New Oraibi," or Kiqötsmovi. Munqapi and Kiqötsmovi became large centers of Third Mesa population. The Second Mesa Hostiles were absorbed back into Songoopavi, where a separate area was set aside for them. Recently, antagonisms among the descendants of the Songoopavi factions have become so serious that some predict a splitting of that village.

The twentieth century has seen a gradual expansion of outside pressures, athough Hopi—perhaps more than any other Native American society— has retained a good deal of social and cultural sovereignty. Removed from the closest city by some eighty-five miles, surrounded by the large Navajo Reservation, and possessing no major natural resources to encourage colonization, Hopis have to some extent been buffered from modernization. The pace of change was fairly slow into the 1930s. A survey of the Hopi villages in 1922 recorded the great majority of people still principally dependent on the subsistence economy with minor additions of cash earned from work for the Hopi Agency, missions, traders, or from freighting goods to the railroad. Sales of crafts, however, began to increase. Traditionally, Katsina dolls were for internal consumption, as presents given by Katsinam at the Home Dance and Bean Dance to uninitiated girls, and they persist with great value in that context. While ethnologists and museums had collected Katsina dolls from the 1880s on, many Hopi men resisted carving dolls for sale, and some still do, citing this religious purpose. But when Tawakwaptiwa began to carve dolls for sale after he returned from Sherman, others followed suit, reasoning that if the *kikmongwi* could do it, so could they.

The 1930s marked another period of significant change. John Collier's appointment as Commissioner of Indian Affairs ushered in major reforms in Indian governance. The Indian Reorganization Act of 1934 led to elected "Tribal Councils." Highly controversial at Hopi, the Tribal Council was voted in at a referendum by a bare margin, and its legitimacy has been seriously questioned ever since. To begin with the council operated with some success; but the timing was bad. Severe overgrazing of the Navajo and Hopi Reservations led the government in the late 1930s to delineate "grazing districts" in the Hopi Reservation as established in 1882. Supposedly only for livestock management, "District Six," which included all the Hopi villages except Munqapi, became the de facto Hopi area, although it was one-fourth the size of the 1882 Hopi Reservation. Hopi livestock was severely culled, fomenting anger at Commissioner Collier. When it became clear that the Tribal Council was powerless to prevent stock reduction or to restore Hopi lands parceled into Navajo grazing districts, the council lost all support and folded in the early 1940s. During the same period, several traditionalists from Hotvela were incarcerated, ostensibly for refusing to serve in World War II. The governor of Kiqötsmovi, supposedly the most progressive village, was also jailed for resisting stock reduction.

Many Hopis served in the armed forces or otherwise assisted in the war effort. Expanded knowledge about the outside world brought further transformations within Hopi society. Veterans adopted some habits of the dominant society, including increased dependence on the money economy, wage work, and, unfortunately, alcohol. There is little evidence of drinking problems prior to World War II, and Hopi Agency reports into the 1920s consistently contrasted deliberate Hopi rejection of alcohol with its status as a serious problem in Navajo society. Empowered by their war experiences, Hopi men often came back unwilling to follow traditionalist leaders, whose own worldly knowledge was called into question. The demand for jobs in a subsistence-based reservation economy caused many to leave for work in Los Angeles, Albuquerque, and elsewhere. But they typically retained strong ties to their home villages, and upon retirement many returned. This pattern continues into the present. Phoenix has probably the largest concentration of urban Hopi residents with a formal organization. Nonetheless, an estimated 80 percent of Hopis still live on the reservation—in contrast to some other Indian reservations, where diasporas have completely altered the character of local communities.

The postwar period also saw the rise of a formally organized Traditionalist movement at Hopi, under the leadership of several who had been young Hostiles at the time of the Orayvi split, including Yukiwma's son Dan Katchongva (Qötshongva), and his supporter David Monongye (Manangya), with Thomas Banyacya (Paangaqwya), formerly a progressive and Bureau of Indian Affairs employee, as their spokesperson and translator. Producing a series of public statements, petitions, and documents, eventuating in a newsletter (*Techqua Ikachi*), a film of the same name, visits to the United Nations in New York, flamboyant Hollywood allies, and a Web site, this group attracted disproportionate interest in the outside world, even a cultlike following among some younger Whites.

Politically, the Traditionalists strongly opposed the Tribal Council, which had been restarted in the early 1950s at the behest of John Boyden, a lawyer who sought to represent the Hopis before the Indian Claims Commission. The commission was charged with compensating Indians monetarily for lands lost, not with restoring any lands. Hopi attachment to their traditional lands is justly famous, and many opposed the commission and continue to do so into the present, even following the award of five million dollars in the 1970s. Hopis long refused to accept this, reasoning that their land was not for sale at any price. Boyden was also interested in arranging contracts with energy companies that wanted to prospect on Hopi lands. To do so, he needed an official body that would represent the Hopi people. So he persuaded several Hopis to reorganize the council, though this was strongly opposed, even by some prime movers in the original council of the 1930s.

In fits and starts, the council grew, however, and since the 1970s, it has come to form the largest corporate organization with the largest source of local employment opportunities on the reservation. Many functions previously performed by the Hopi Agency have been taken over by the Tribal Council, or the "Hopi Tribe," as it is known locally. The council has built an extensive civil service that is largely independent of the elected council itself. Departments of Health, Education, and Natural Resources, with offices of Cultural Preservation, Water Resources, and Hopi Lands, as well as Hopi Tribal Court, are all institutions that Hopis rely upon, no matter what their feelings about the council proper. At present, Hotvela and Lower Munqapi are the only villages never to have sent a representative, although there has been much talk lately of their doing so. Hotvela, which long resisted modernization, finally witnessed the digging of water lines into the village in 1995–1996 over the objections of many of the older generation. But younger people prevailed, and Hotvela's elected "Board of Directors" has gained increasing standing in village affairs.

The 1960s, like the 1930s, was another decade of major change. The *Healing v. Jones* case—brought to settle the question of Hopi versus Navajo interests in the 1882 Hopi Reservation—effectively confirmed District Six as the sole Hopi Reservation. It did so by a revisionist interpretation of the fateful language of the Executive Order of 1882 "such other Indians as the Secretary of the Interior may see fit to settle thereon." After the decision, many Hopis who had eked out their livelihood herding sheep, began to switch to cattle or got out of livestock altogether. In response to the shortcomings of the Healing decision, Congress passed the Navajo-Hopi Land Settlement Act in 1974, restoring about half of the 1882 Reservation to Hopis in theory and requiring relocation of those Hopis and Navajos on the wrong side of the partition line. The subsequent history of Navajo relocation has been traumatic and staunchly contested by some, especially at Big Mountain, but seems to be nearing a conclusion with the recent acceptance by most Navajos remaining on "Hopi Partitioned Lands" of seventy-five-year homesite leases from the Hopi Tribe. Hopi access to lands awarded by Congress in 1974 has only recently begun to be realized. And aspects of the land dispute persist, especially in the 1934 Navajo Reservation surrounding the Hopi Reservation, where a court case to settle the tribes' respective interests is now in its third phase.

The building of metaled roads into the reservation in the 1960s and the acquisition of trucks and cars also signaled significant changes. The first motor vehicles appeared in the 1920s, but they were few and far between, and the clay and sand reservation roads were frequently impassable. With metaled roads, one could now commute the thirty-five miles to Keams Canyon from as far away as Third Mesa, for work at the police station, hospital, trading post, or agency. Further road building between Second Mesa and Winslow, and Third Mesa and Flagstaff, and exponential growth at Tuba City since the 1970s increased opportunities for (reasonably) local off-reservation employment. Mobility thus increased greatly during this period, as did modern house construction in village "suburbs." Several villages diminished as residential sites, becoming traditional centers to which people return for religious purposes and important social gatherings. Walpi, for example, was almost at the point of residential abandonment, until it was rebuilt by a Museum of Northern Arizona project led by archaeologist Charles Adams in the 1970s. Many First Mesa people have houses in Polacca and return to the mesa-top villages for ceremonies. Similarly, settlements below Supawlavi and Musangnuvi were built in the 1970s and 1980s, and Songoopavi, Hotvela, Paaqavi, and Munqapi have expanded laterally to include modern HUD housing in their outskirts.

Economic changes have come in several waves throughout the twentieth century. Money is the mode of exchange for most goods and services, although traditional patterns of sharing and exchange are very marked in ceremonial contexts and in public works at the village or extended-family levels. In 1960, despite the earlier stock reduction, many households maintained sheep as well as active farmlands. The following three decades saw a major decline in the traditional economy. Today, there is only one old-time Hopi sheepherder left, Victor Masayesva Sr. of Hotvela; interestingly enough, he is the father of Vernon, a Tribal Chairman in the early 1990s; Victor Jr., the internationally renowned filmmaker (whose best-known film is *Imagining Indians*); and LaVerne, an MIT, Chomsky-trained professor of linguistics at the University of Nevada.

Many households retain cattle, and raising beef for market, as well as domestic consumption, has become increasingly common. Off-reservation residence has declined somewhat with the expansion of local employment opportunities. The reservation cash economy is dominated by the public sector with little business development, except most notably in crafts. Traditionally, crafts were divided by gender and by mesa. Women's crafts were principally pottery and basketry. Men wove all cloth and carved and decorated ceremonial artifacts, including Katsina dolls. While pottery was made at all three mesas, women at Second and Third Mesas were only producing utility ware by the turn of the twentieth century; their craft specialization was focused on basketry—the distinctive coiled plaques of Second Mesa and the wicker plaques of Third Mesa. Earlier complex bichrome and polychrome pottery, found throughout Hopi ruins, was defunct until Hopi-Tewa potter Nampeyo resuscitated Sikyatki Polychrome designs at the instigation of trader Thomas Keam. This is perhaps the earliest, most direct influence of the market system on Hopi crafts and aesthetics: pottery for the trader quickly became a commodity for sale to tourists. In the 1930s the Museum of Northern Arizona began an annual Hopi crafts fair, which has had a significant influence in standardizing aesthetic norms in the emergent craft-art market. Later developments like Santa Fe's upscale "Indian Market" added to this trend.

The gender and mesa patterns of Hopi crafts persist, although there are exceptions, like Third Mesa potters Elizabeth White and Al Qoyawayma. The most lucrative crafts have been pottery and silver jewelry. Pottery is controlled by what one commentator calls a "cartel" at First Mesa, which strictly manages design styles and distribution.

Silverwork was undertaken by a few Hopi men in the earlier twentieth century, but really expanded with classes run by Fred Kabotie for veterans returning from World War II (see Pearlstone, this volume).

Commoditization of Katsina dolls has grown since the 1960s. At that point, dolls typically went for fifteen dollars apiece. That was still sufficient to encourage non-Hopis to encroach on the trade. The market has been glutted with so-called "Katsina" dolls carved by non-Hopi carvers (some even imported from the Far East). Today the great majority of dolls at a typical Southwest craft store are not made by Hopis, Zunis, or other Pueblo people, i.e., the people for whom Katsinam are genuine religious figures. Hopis have protested rampant bastardization and commercialization of their iconography by outsiders, but with little success. There are several effects. First and most obvious, the competition for Hopi dollmakers in general is an inroad into a previously exclusive market, cutting out sales. Second, and contrasting with the first point, this to some extent boosts prices for genuine Hopi dolls, whose craftsmanship is in most instances vastly superior to the knockoffs produced for the low-end tourist trade. There have also been aesthetic effects. The elaboration of carving techniques with sophisticated carpentry tools, producing details of costume, musculature, and action postures, involves a major "modernist" departure from the more static formalist style of older dolls. At first a response to a realist aesthetic among the buying non-Indian public (and encouraged at Indian schools), that aesthetic has now infiltrated Hopi values, and such styles appear in many dolls given on ceremonial occasions. At the same time, fine-grained stylistic elaboration has effected an upgrading of the market—especially for renowned carvers like Henry Shelton, Dennis Tewa, or Brian Honyuti—from "tourist art" to "fine art." More than a few Hopi carvers now command prices in the galleries of Santa Fe, Sedona, and Scottsdale that were previously only attained by master jeweler Charles Loloma or painter Dan Namingha. And, acting again in the reverse direction, the transition to ethnic "fine art" also revalues more "authentic" styles, boosting prices for older items, and encouraging

some carvers to resume using natural pigments and static postural forms: the "authentically primitive" acquires new value in this collectors' context. In the words of a Zuni elder discussing Fred Harvey's effect on indigenous crafts, Katsina dolls have moved "from ritual to retail."

At the turn of the millennium, Hopi society faces multiple influences and a babel of competing demands.[4] Some liken present times to the long-prophesied reappearance of *koyaanisqatsi*, the chaotic phase prior to emergence into the Fourth World. Hopi cultural and social sovereignty persist, but amid erosions—through land loss, declining language use among the younger generation, and acculturation to technology and the mores of the consumer society. Songoopavi is the only village to retain the complete traditional religious cycle intact (in spite of the theft, inspired by the collectors' market, of key religious objects in the late 1970s). The religious cycles at Musangnuvi, Supawlavi, and Walpi, and the Tewa cycle at Hanoki, persist strongly, but major elements (including the formerly all-important Wuwtsim initiations) have subsided over the last two decades. The continuance of time-honored values and practices remains striking, however, for an indigenous society entering the twenty-first century surrounded by the most powerful nation on earth with its bombardment of seductive images and values and its addiction to commodity consumption and the transience of the new. Katsina ceremonies continue to be very active on all three Hopi Mesas and serve as perhaps the fundamental ritual frame of Hopi religious thought and action. There is some evidence that this is owing to a renaissance since the 1960s, which came in part as a critique of the evident shallowness of new ways, and a proud reassertion of Hopi difference. Katsina dolls remain a key element in Katsina ceremonies and are still given as magical presents by personated Katsinam to young female relatives. And the art market for Hopi dolls is sustained by an authenticity of content and value that Hopi artisans consciously bring to their work, in consonance with an abiding Hopi philosophy passed on since the covenant with Maasaw at emergence into the Fourth World. ●

Neil David Sr.

Neil David Sr. is a Hopi artist based in Polacca, First Mesa, Hopi. The following are excerpts from an interview conducted at Hopi by Zena Pearlstone, July 25, 1997.

When I began as an artist, I carved for ceremonies, but my main concern was painting. After I served in the military, the Artist Hopid was formed [1973], and I devoted myself to painting through the Hopi Arts and Crafts Guild. For three to four years I painted every day and carved a doll a month. Artist Hopid dispersed in 1977–1978, and after that I started carving full time. Soon I got caught up in Koshari [Koyaalam] and began to carve only these Tewa clowns (fig. 1.6 and see fig. 3.8). I did this for five to six years.

Around 1983 I was approached by an agent, William Graven, who put up money for me to do bronze castings in Sedona (see fig. 3.52). At the same time I was working in lithography in Albuquerque. Graven also arranged for six, eight-inch, porcelain Katsina figurines to be made in Mexico across the border from El Paso (see fig. 3.55). Lowell Talashoma and I did the drawings for these figurines, including Crow Mother, Morning Katsina, Kooyemsi, and Koshari. They didn't sell well. A set of four collector plates with Katsinam followed (see figs. 3.54, 3.55). The unsold figurines and plates were bought by McGee at Keams Canyon. I went back to carving. Sometime during this period I switched to electric tools. I made action figures for a while, but the Koshari took over. I made the action figures primarily

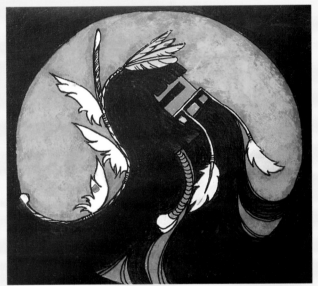

1.1

1.2

1.3

1.4

for collectors, but I would do them for ceremonies as well. I believe that all carvings are *tithu*. These days I am getting back to painting. In 1996 I showed only paintings.

Navajo shouldn't be carving Katsina-like figures at all. I have yet to see one that is accurate. It would be okay if they were accurate in their representation. Robert Chee [a Navajo carver] and Richard Grover [a member of the Walapai, a people located near Grand Canyon] both made accurate ones. My nephew, Kerry, who is half Navajo, also does accurate carvings. I also believe that it is all right for women to carve for economic reasons, again as long as they are not altering the representations. What else can they do? Times change, and I am not opposed to many of the corresponding changes at Hopi.

I am also not opposed to Katsina representations on tourist art. I am guilty of this myself, as I've made drawings for T-shirts and designs for note paper cubes. It bothers me that some ceremonies are closed. I think they should all be open to the public. Collectors should be able to see the dances. At the same time, there are things that are taboo. There are some Katsinam that I will not represent in carvings or paintings. It makes a difference what Katsinam are represented.

1.5

1.1 Angaktsina (Long-Hair Katsina), circa 1998. Acrylic on canvas. 25.4 x 25.4 cm. Photograph by Zena Pearlstone.

1.2 Angaktsina (Long-Hair Katsina), circa 1998. Watercolor on paper. 27.94 x 20.3 cm. Photograph by Zena Pearlstone.

1.3 Angwusnasomtaqa (Crow Mother Katsina), circa 1998. Felt pen on paper. 27.94 x 20.3 cm. Photograph by Zena Pearlstone.

1.4 Suyang'ephoya (Left-Handed Katsina), circa 1998. Oil on canvas. 17.8 x 12.7 cm. Photograph by Zena Pearlstone.

1.5 Angaktsina (Long-Hair Katsina), 1980s. Wood and feather. H: 14.5 cm. Collection of Doris and Jerry Selmer.

1.6 Koyaala *tihu*, 1990. Wood and pigment. H: 16.5 cm. Collection of Tom and Nancy Juda.

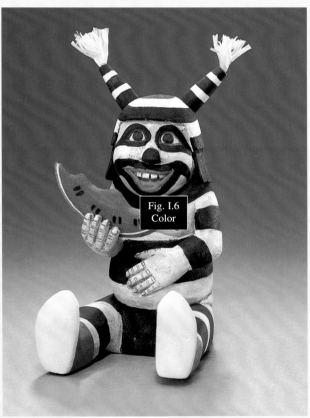

Fig. 1.6 Color

1.6

Diane Branam

Diane Branam is a Euro-American artist based in Arizona. Her statement given below is dated February 9, 1998.

I began working with wood in about 1987; I enjoyed it in my leisure moments. I was employed by U.S. West as an engineer at the time. I bought a handheld jigsaw to cut the first pieces that I made. With that and a belt sander, I was set, making my first compositions out on the patio. In 1995, after my husband and I had retired, we built a shop, and I graduated to a large scroll saw. That's when I really began. I had the time, equipment, place, and desire. I spent ten to twelve hours a day working on an assortment of "pieced" objects. I found out that there was a name for the process I had settled into, *intarsia*.

Living in the Southwest, it was natural to research the region's objects and art. With their beauty and color, Native American arts and crafts intrigued me from the start: silver contrasting with turquoise, colorful sand paintings, and, of course, the beautiful, colorful Katsinam. I wanted to achieve a lifelike figure and one as authentic as possible. I read every book that the library had on Katsinam and decided to try working one up using the intarsia method. I developed patterns that I could cut into puzzlelike pieces. Intarsia is usually done using the natural color of the wood, but I felt the colors of the Katsinam should be used. So I washed the colors onto the wood leaving the natural grain showing through. Each piece goes through four to six different sanding processes; when I'm satisfied with the smoothness, it is colored before it is reassembled—very much like a puzzle—on a backboard that holds it all together.

My patterns include the popular Eagle Dancer, Sun Katsina, Crow Mother, Mudhead, Wolf, Bear, and Hano Clown, to name just a few. The more I work with the Katsinam, the more engrossed in them I become. I can easily lose track of time, spending hours working one up and seeing it almost come to life before my eyes. It is a very satisfying endeavor. I feel my work is unique enough that it does not compete with the beautiful original Katsinam made by the Hopi and Zuni peoples. I admire their work and their cultural achievements, their love of our great Mother Earth. We should all take lessons from the original peoples of this land and take care of it as they have always tried to do by respecting all that we see and do. That is how I feel about their artwork; I love and respect it and only hope to broaden the awareness of its great beauty.

II.1 *Talava—Morning Singer,* 1999. Wood and pigment. H: 56 cm.

II.2 *Pong—Mountain Sheep,* 1999. Wood and pigment. H: 64 cm.

II.3 *Tawa Sun Kachina,* 1999. Wood and pigment. H: 58 cm.

II.4 *Jumping Mudheads,* 1998. Wood and pigment. H: 59 cm.

II.5 *Aholi—Chiefs Ltd.,* 1999. Wood and pigment. H: 58 cm.

11.1

11.2

11.3

11.4

11.5

3 The Contemporary Katsina

ZENA PEARLSTONE

> If you do not commodify your religion yourself, someone will do it for you.
>
> R. Laurence Moore,
> *Selling God: American Religion in the Marketplace of Culture*

Introduction

In the closing decades of the twentieth century, Hopi artist Dennis Numkena configures Katsina-like sets and costumes for a production of Mozart's *Magic Flute* (figs. 3.3A–D); Kermit Oliver, a non-Indian from Waco, Texas, designs a "Katsina"-patterned silk scarf for the French couture house Hermès of Paris, Inc. (fig. 3.2); an Albuquerque electronics store displays life-size "Koyaala" holding camcorders;[1] the director of the Hopi Cultural Preservation Office is asked by the United States Customs Service to inspect five crates from the Philippines marked "Hopi Kachina Doll" (figs. 3.4A–D); the Pyramid Collection markets mail-order, alabaster, "authentic" Katsina figures made in Italy (fig. 3.5); and a salesman in Phoenix receives a carving of a "Katsina" as an award for most sales of the year.[2]

Chronicled here is the story—or, more accurately, part of the story—of how Katsinam (plural of Katsina), the supernaturals of the Hopi, a small Pueblo nation living in a remote area of Arizona, became international symbols. The investigation follows the commodification of Katsina carvings and imagery by the Hopi themselves over approximately 150 years and the appropriation of Katsina imagery by non-Pueblo peoples, leading to its status at the end of the twentieth century. In this study a *commodity* is defined as "something which is exchanged in the market for money or other commodities" (Wood 1996, 258). The items surveyed range from critically acclaimed works of art to mass-produced tourist items. They are tied to an exceptional variety of sources and producers: Pueblo peoples of the American Southwest, non-Pueblo Native Americans, Euro-Americans, Europeans, and Asians. The entry

3.1A,B The Hopi villages, housing about sixty-five hundred people, are situated on or near three adjacent mesas in northeastern Arizona. All villages share a distinctive Hopi lifestyle, but each is autonomous. Photographs 1994–1995.

of Katsina and Katsina-like portrayals into the world marketplace and their proliferation over the past decades provide an ongoing juxtaposition of identities and interactions with individual threads becoming interwoven within a global whole. Involved are complex issues concerning the consequences of inter- and intracultural perception, commodification, definitions of sacred and secular, colonialist thought and postcolonial retort, all of which are applicable to many cultures worldwide. The Katsina representa tions provide an opportunity to examine a multitude of cultural attitudes that for both Pueblo and non-Pueblo peoples have been modified through time.

The world of business, proficient at exploiting the objects and ideas that capture public attention, has touched many Hopis. In this, the Hopi are not alone. "The period since the Second World War has…seen culture on a world scale increasingly dominated by the most consumption-oriented, and hence commodity producing, society in history" (Wood 1996, 274). Katsinam as exotic, supernatural, and colorful are amenable to commodification, and the demanding market that has been created ensures constantly changing and interacting Pueblo and non-Pueblo representations and meanings. Objects that were, in the nineteenth century, exclusively gifts are now also commodities and fine art. Today, Katsina carvings and objects that carry Katsina imagery can no longer be easily categorized as art, artifact, or commodity but "must now be merged into a single domain where the categories are seen

to inform one another rather than to compete in their claims for social primacy and cultural value" (Phillips and Steiner 1999, 16; see also Bourdieu 1984). Further, "commoditization lies at the complex intersection of temporal, cultural, and social factors" (Appadurai 1986, 15; see N. Thomas 1991, 27–30).

This study is also about mimesis and many attempts to tap into a spiritual, as well as an economic, bonanza. Walter Benjamin (1969), more than sixty years ago, called attention to the changes that "the age of mechanical reproduction" was bringing to art.

3.2 Kermit Oliver, scarf with "Katsina" patterns designed for the French couture house Hermès of Paris, Inc., 1992. Silk. 90 x 90 cm. Photograph courtesy of Hermès of Paris, Inc.

The original, he noted, is charged with authority, but authority becomes jeopardized when the authenticity of an object and its "historical testimony" are altered. "That which withers in the age of mechanical reproduction is the aura of the work of art" (Benjamin 1969, 223). Hillel Schwartz feels that Benjamin got it wrong. What actually withers, says Schwartz is not in the object but in ourselves, the "assurance of our own liveliness" (Schwartz 1996, 141). For the Hopis, the opinions of both Benjamin and Schwartz may be valid. Perceptions of older objects as well as of the self are altered as replications themselves are replicated. As Katsina representations move further from the Hopi art that is rooted in ritual, it is perhaps wise to question the functioning of the magical power of replication, "wherein the representation shares in or takes power from the represented" (Taussig 1993, 2).

This is a study, therefore, of Native American–Euro-American relations, of non-Pueblo perceptions of Katsinam, and of Pueblo perceptions altered by non-Pueblo views. While Katsinam have been the focus of much scholarly and popular attention, considered here for the first time are the effects of the images of the supernaturals as they attain worldwide recognition and become international "cultural" symbols. As opposed to Disney characters or Christian symbols such as the cross, which are intended to be public, the traditional Hopi view is that the "greatest respect that can be paid to their culture is not to know." Some Hopis continue to find any commercial representation of these supernaturals objectionable. All Hopis continue to react to both internal and external pressures, and the philosophy by which the Pueblos measure themselves is being modified. The people as well as the objects have all been transformed by a market economy over which they have little control. Most Hopis, who are today saddened by the loss of intellectual and cultural property, nonetheless see themselves as partially responsible for the present situation.

It should never be assumed that Hopis speak for all Pueblo peoples or that any one Hopi speaks for the entire population. Hopi is one of twenty Pueblo communities, and the different Pueblo groups have long maintained varying perspectives on Katsina commodification and representation. There are differences among the Pueblos, and frequently factions within a Pueblo. Members of the Rio Grande Pueblos, who generally oppose non-Indian viewing of Katsinam or Katsina imagery, can be seen in opposition to those at Hopi who are

supporting themselves by making Katsina figurines for a non-Pueblo market. At the same time there are traditionalists at Hopi who feel that some of their own people have blighted Hopi culture. Some members of each Pueblo Nation challenge traditional Western definitions of art and aesthetics by restricting the viewing of those objects considered most important by their own communities. Others challenge their own traditions by adapting ceremonial imagery for gallery sales and popular items. It would be naive, however, to assume that Hopi makers of Katsinam have manipulated commodity production solely for economic reasons. In this complex scenario there are many other factors to be considered, including self-identity, social relationships, and creativity. Investigated here are different Hopi readings of the objects in the marketplace, whether Pueblo or non-Pueblo made, as well as the attitudes of other Native Americans and Euro-Americans.

It is a sign of profound change that sacred, and in some Pueblos secret, beings can now be marketed, bypassing the Southwest entirely. In order to understand the power and success of the commodification, it is necessary to look beyond the Katsina images themselves. Katsina appropriation is enmeshed in the image of the American Southwest, a mystique that has been sold for more than a hundred years (see Babcock, this volume). The opening of the railroad in the 1880s and the consequent trading posts attracted willing buyers. Tourism and the controlled image of the Southwest—the latter referred to by Marta Weigle as "early ethnic theme park" (1989)—have transformed the supernatural Katsinam into logos. Katsinam no longer signify the spirituality of a people; they say "Southwest." Questions of who is buying and buying into the romantic mythology of the Southwest as timeless and sacred become pertinent with reference to Katsina and Katsina-imagery production.

The peoples and the products of the Southwest as foreign, as Other, fall under the universal lure of exoticism. "The possession of an exotic object offers…an imagined access to a world of difference, often constituted as an enhancement of the new owner's knowledge, power or wealth…. such objects may evoke curiosity, awe, fear, admiration, contempt or a combination of these responses. The exotic object may variously be labeled trophy or talisman, relic or specimen, rarity or trade sample, souvenir or kitsch, art or craft" (Phillips and Steiner 1999, 3). The population explosion in the Southwest throughout this century, the phenomenal growth of the tourist industry, the postmodern idea of experiencing the past (MacCannell 1989, x–xi), and the passion of Euro-Americans for folding Indians into "their" America have catapulted the Katsina, as perhaps the Southwest's most unique export, into world visibility. The term *Katsina* is familiar to a great number of people, not only in North America but in many places around the world. What a person understands by the term, however, varies greatly.

Background

You have to grow up in it before you can understand what it is.

> Michael Kabotie, quoted in Seymour,
> *When the Rainbow Touches Down*

Katsinam are an integral part of the lives of nearly all Pueblo groups, but most of these communities do not make Katsina imagery for an outside public.

3.3A–D Dennis Numkena, Katsina-inspired set designs for a production of Mozart's *Magic Flute*. Arizona State University, Lyric Opera Theater, 1982. Photographs courtesy of the artist.

3.4A–D Imitation Katsina doll carvings made in the Philippines. Collection of Andy P. Abeita, Council for Indigenous Arts and Culture, Albuquerque. Photographs by Zena Pearlstone, 2000.

Hopis have been and continue to be the preeminent Pueblo producers of Katsina imagery. They have also had the most open policy regarding visitors to Katsina ceremonies, allowing outsiders to view dancers for themselves.[3] Katsina carvings were made exclusively for ceremonies probably until the 1850s, at which time a couple of Hopi *tithu* (Katsina dolls or figurines, singular *tihu*) were sold or given to United States Army surgeons (see Bol and Wright, this volume).[4] Between 1869 and 1872 a number may have been purchased by John Wesley Powell (Kuwanwisiwma, this volume; Jenkins [Kuwanwisiwma] in Wade 1995, 31). By 1930 the sale of Katsina dolls was a significant Hopi source of income (Wade 1976, 72). Katsina-adorned pottery, jewelry, and other objects became important consumer items. The economy of Hopi is and has been for some time bound to its artists, and Katsina imagery is prevalent. Today, Katsina carvings are made for sale by hundreds of Hopi men and some

3.5 Figurine said to represent "Corn Katsina," manufactured in Italy after an original by Castagna, 1993. Alabaster and pigment. H: 18.5 cm. Private collection.

women, and if this practice is not condoned by all Hopis, it is accepted by most as an economic necessity. Hopi artists today also represent Katsinam in paintings, as gourd rattles and gourd banks, on jewelry, pottery, baskets, stained glass, and a variety of other tourist goods. Hopi artists supply carvings and other items with Katsina images to museums and galleries, and the objects are sold at tourist shops in the villages, around the country, and internationally. In 1994, one Hopi, Becky Masayesva, began a short-lived mail-order business that included Katsina figurines.

Non-Pueblo Indians and non-Indians invariably use Hopi Katsinam as the models for their productions. Many non-Pueblo people have never seen a Zuni Katsina and almost surely have never seen one from the Rio Grande Pueblos. Extremely few carvings from the Rio Grande are in public view. Hopi Katsinam are the ones familiar to people around the world. Hopi carvings are also more diverse than those from Zuni because, freed of the priesthood's prohibitions (see below), they changed more rapidly. Today, Hopi commercial carvings are available in a variety of styles and sizes.

Katsinam

Katsinam are the supernaturals, or "benevolent spirit beings" (A. Secakuku 1995, 3), of the Pueblo peoples of the American Southwest.[5] The term *Katsina* is used to refer to: (1) the hundreds of spirit beings who are associated with rain, clouds, and the dead—ancestors of Hopis, (2) the participants in the Katsina ceremonies who appear at eleven Hopi villages from December to July (fig. 3.6), and (3) the *tithu*, the wooden carvings that were and are given to young girls at ceremonies (fig. 3.7). Non-Pueblo people use the term *Katsina* for all of these categories, but the Hopi use it only for the supernaturals and the dance participants, not for the carved figures (see Whiteley, this volume). For the Hopi, the spirits and dancers are sacred, the latter at times forbidden to be seen by non-Indians. The *tithu* are described by Alph Secakuku as "personifications of the katsina spirits, originally created by the katsinam in their physical embodiment" (1995, 4). The exact number of Katsinam cannot be determined. Estimates range from about three hundred to five hundred. The number does not remain constant. New Katsinam can be added; others may fade from view and ceremonies, while some reappear decades later (David 1993). Further, the pantheon is different at each Hopi village (see Pearlstone 1995b).

The literature on Hopi religion and the Katsina beings is voluminous and now has a history of well over one hundred years.[6] Since the primary focus of this volume is Katsina commodification, no attempt is made to survey or summarize this literature. Even though no masks or sacred items, or photographs of sacred items, are displayed in this volume, the significance of Katsina appropriation cannot be appreciated without underscoring the centrality of the supernaturals and personators to Hopi life.

Scholars have often noted that Hopi culture can only be understood as a totality. All is interrelated, and trying to tease out one thread, like the meaning of Katsina, simply results in unraveling the whole. The concept of Katsina is one of extraordinary complexity, not easily explained even by Hopis. The intricacies are well summarized by Louis A. Hieb who probes the "layers of meaning" that indicate "the masked face" as "in part a symbolic means of defining and giving expression to a significant 'person' in Hopi moral space" (1994, 23–24).

> The katsina…can be both visible and invisible, material and immaterial. Because of their beneficence, Hopis call them "our friends" (*itaakwatsim*)…*katsina* refers to masked and painted impersonation, to the spiritual being impersonated, to the clouds, and to the dead. At the same time…these are but different expressions or manifestations of one "person," the *katsina*. [Hieb 1994, 25]

Hieb goes on to state that to fully define and understand the term it is also necessary to attend to Hopi religious texts and songs, religious specialists, the Hopi concept of time, kinship, and the complex iconography of the Katsina mask. He concludes that "the meaning of katsina in its full complexity and richness is…only fully comprehensible in the lives of Hopi people" (Hieb 1994, 25–32). E. Charles Adams explains that the Katsinam are not gods but spiritual intermediaries or messengers to the Hopi deities that visit the villages from December to July. They are embodied in the masks and the men who don them. They take the prayers sung in the katsina songs and uttered in the days spent preparing for the

3.6

public dance to the Hopi gods. This pantheon of gods controls the weather and the growth of the Hopi crops and ultimately holds the survival of the people in their collective hands.... It is vitally important that the prayers are performed and uttered correctly so that the gods will hear and honor them. [E. C. Adams 1991, 8]

The Katsina spirits reside around the villages, among other places, from the time of the winter solstice to late July. In midsummer, they return to "their spirit world" (A. Secakuku 1995, 4). According to Alfred F. Whiting (1964), they enter this spirit world by means of a ladder descending from the top of the San Franciso peaks. When called by priests during Soyalangw, the winter solstice ceremonial period, which begins the Katsina season, they ascend a ladder at the top of the San Francisco peaks and travel as clouds to the Hopi villages.

While, in general parlance, all the performers in Katsina ceremonies are labeled as Katsinam, the situation is much more complex. Some masked performers are gods rather than Katsinam. Others can be social dancers or caretakers (see David 1993; Seymour 1988, 226–27). Unmasked performers like social dancers and some so-called clowns are not considered to be Katsinam. One category of unmasked clown, the Koyaala (Paiyakyamu, Kossa, Koshare), is among the most frequently represented on carvings and other forms of art for sale (see David, Artist Profile 1, this volume; fig. 3.8). It is a sacred clown introduced from the Eastern Pueblos, probably coming to Hopi with the immigrant Tewa people. Because these clowns are ubiquitous on commercial products and generally considered to be Katsinam by the buying public, their representations have been included here.

Katsina masks are never referred to as such by Hopis, rather they are known as "friends." The "friend," the spirit of the Katsina, when worn is united with the spirit of man. Hopi Emory Sekaquaptewa feels that "what happens to a man when he is performer is that if he understands the essence of the kachina, when he dons the mask he loses his identity and actually becomes what he is representing" (1976, 39). Masks are among the most sacred Hopi possessions, never to be reproduced,

3.6 Fred Kabotie, *Kachinas Distributing Gifts*, circa 1937. Watercolor on paper. 37.5 x 54.6 cm. Collection of the Newark Museum, 37.222.

3.7 Kwasatyaqa (One with a Dress) *tihu*, early twentieth century. Wood and pigment. H: 8.3 cm. Private collection.

3.8 Neil David Sr., Koyaala *tihu*, 1980. Wood and pigment. H: 48.5 cm. Collection of Tom and Nancy Juda.

3.7

3.8

given to non-Hopis, or sold for economic gain. They are not to be seen by the uninitiated except at appropriate ceremonials. Nevertheless, over the years a substantial number have found their way into museum and private collections.

When Pueblo communities enlighten their young people at the initiations that take place during Powamuya (the February ceremonial season), they impart the knowledge that the Katsina participants are personators with a "spiritual essence" (E. Sekaquaptewa 1976, 38). This disclosure forces the initiates to rethink the sacred and profane in ways not appropriate for younger minds. The effect of this revelation is often shocking to the initiates (see D. Eggan 1943; Gill 1977). Edmund Nequatewa recalls his initiation around 1890:

> After a while the Kachina came. They were making all sorts of Kachina noises on the top of the kiva, and the man asked them to come in. The first one came in. I looked up. No masks; I recognize everyone of them! Of course I was then surprised that the men that I knew could make these sounds like the Kachina, and before that time I was afraid of the Kachina.... Then when everything is over, that is the time they tell you that you mustn't talk about it or tell anyone about it. If you do, a whole bunch of Kachina, more than you ever did see in your life, will come and put you to death with a cholla cactus. Then they get you pretty well threatened. Then you just have to behave yourself. Of course, if you are mischievous, any kid will think about what he wants to do, but he never would talk about it. [Seaman 1993, 32]

Similarly, Don Talayesva revealed the following in his autobiography. He was nine years old at the time of his initiation in 1899.

> When the Katcinas entered the kiva without masks, I had a great surprise. They were not spirits, but human beings. I recognized nearly every one of them and felt very unhappy, because I had been told all my life that the Katcinas were gods. I was especially shocked and angry when I saw all my uncles, fathers and clan brothers dancing as Katcinas. I felt the worst when I saw my own father—and whenever he glanced at me I turned my face away. When the dances were over the head

man told us with a stern face that we now knew who the Katcinas really were and that if we ever talked about this to uninitiated children we would get a thrashing even worse than the one we had received the night before. "A long time ago," said he, "a child was whipped to death for telling the secret." I felt sure that I would never tell. [Simmons 1942, 84]

Girls are initiated with the boys. Helen Sekaquaptewa found the experience equally upsetting. "It was quite an ordeal for me. When I went back to my home I wished I didn't know that a kachina was a man with a costume and a mask, when all the time I thought they were real magic" (H. Sekaquaptewa 1969, 29). Adult Pueblo women have told me that they still fear Katsinam. One was careful to find a watching place during a ceremony where she was sure the Katsinam would not come. Although these events are startling and frightening, observers do not believe that Hopi children remain disillusioned. Emory Sekaquaptewa has noted, "When it is revealed to him that the kachina is just an impersonation, an impersonation which possesses a spiritual essence, the child's security is not destroyed. Instead the experience strengthens the individual in another phase of his life in the community" (E. Sekaquaptewa 1976, 38). Sam Gill (1976, 54), drawing on the observations of Alfonso Ortiz, an anthropologist and Tewa, notes that children at their initiation begin their journey to the understanding that all things have "essence," or a sacred quality, as well as matter. The world cannot be fully understood without the knowledge that things are often not as they initially appear. For this study, it is critical to perceive the importance of Pueblo initiation because aspects of today's commodification of Katsinam threaten the secrecy required for uninitiated children.

Tithu

Tithu are the wooden carvings that are made by Hopi men and distributed by the Katsinam at Powamuy, the Bean Dance ceremony in February, and Nímaniw (Niman), the midsummer ceremony that closes the Katsina season (see Bol, this volume, for other ceremonies employing tithu).[7] Hopis and the public generally refer to them as "dolls." Tithu were probably among the first Hopi items to be commodified, and they continue to be a primary item made for sale. Only carvings made by Hopis can be *tithu*, although as discussed below, some of these may no longer be considered as such. Carvings made by non-Pueblo people are never *tithu*; Hopis generally refer to these items as "imitation Katsinam." Since *tithu* were first sold to Euro-Americans, the carved images have been transformed into new visual and formal configurations as both Pueblo (primarily Hopi) and non-Pueblo artists respond to a growing international market. Over time the archetypal staid, geometric figurines have been reborn as brightly colored monuments to activity and originality.

Tithu are given to girls until they are initiated at age eight or nine, and sometimes to baby boys (fig. 3.10). They are variously described by Hopis. Leigh J. Kuwanwisiwma (this volume) refers to them as "religious items, part of a girl's rite of passage." Ferrell Secakuku describes them as "the symbols of the spirits that carry and provide messages to other spiritual bodies for the Hopi people" (1996, 3). Other writers have referred to them as a prayer or blessing in three dimensions and note that they require respect (B. Wright 1989, 66; Teiwes 1991, 33; see Bol this volume). Alph Secakuku, curator of the exhibition *Following the Sun and Moon: Hopi Kachina Tradition*, which was held at the Heard Museum in Phoenix, describes them as follows:

The katsina spirits are the very important, meaningful, and beneficial counterpart in a relationship invaluable to the Hopi religious beliefs. Accordingly, we do not perceive the katsina dolls simply as carved figurines or brightly decorated objects. They have important meaning to us, the Hopi people: We believe that they are personifications of the katsina spirits, originally created by the katsinam in their physical embodiment. They are presented to females by the spirits as personalized gifts to award virtuous behavior and to publicly recognize special persons, such as brides, who are presented at the Niman ceremony.... In the Niman ceremony...[a]ll kinds of katsina dolls are presented to the females representing their different stages and ages. For example, a newborn receiving her first doll will be presented with a simple flat doll [fig. 3.9], while one who has been initiated into the katsina beliefs that year will receive an elaborately created doll. Finally, to symbolize special blessings for ideal motherhood, each bride of that year will receive a real, lifelike katsina doll. [A. Secakuku 1995, 3–5]

3.9A–C *Putskatithu* (flat dolls), 1980s. (A) Ted Puhuyesva, Hahay'iwùuti (Happy Mother) *tihu*. Wood, pigment, yarn, and feather. H: 21 cm. (B) Ted Puhuyesva, Sa'lakwmana (a Cloud Maiden) *tihu*. Wood, pigment, and feathers. H: 20 cm. (C) Hanomana *tihu*. Wood, pigment, and yarn. H: 15.3 cm. Collection of Jeannette and William O'Malley.

3.10 Photograph of a young Hopi girl holding a *tihu*. Courtesy of Museum of Northern Arizona Photo Archives, Emory Kopta Collection, MS 240-2-1350.

Reverence for these carvings is expressed by Milland Lomakema Sr., the director and manager of the Hopi Arts and Crafts Silvercraft Cooperative Guild.

> The katsinam that a girl receives reflect her growth, they both grow together. The first one that she gets is of one piece, comparable to a fetus. Then arms and legs are added. Katsinam of one piece will be given to girls at Winter Solstice ceremonies, and then at Nímaniw in July. They will have arms and legs reflecting the growth of the child. If the katsina figure has deformities so will the child. The "old ones" that were made at the turn of the twentieth century have big heads reflecting the physical proportions of children. [Personal communication, 1995; see fig. 3.7]

Similarly Leigh J. Kuwanwisiwma notes that "misrepresentations can have ill effects, the curse of imagery affects newborns. The first, flat doll that baby girls receive is Hahay'iwùuti, Happy Mother, who has all of the attributes of motherhood and thus allows the infants to grow and learn to talk properly and instills all the virtues of motherhood into them" (personal communication, 1997; see also Secakuku, this volume).

While *tithu* are items of extraordinary significance to the Hopi, they are not sacred in the way of the "faces" of the dancers; they are not supernaturals but rather gifts from the spirits. They are not secret or hidden, except from the young girls who will receive them as gifts, and anyone may look at or handle them. They are, however, as discussed by Spencer (this volume), considered by the Hopi as part of their cultural and intellectual property, and many Hopis believe that their manufacture should be restricted to Hopi or other Pueblo people.

There were, and there continue to be for some artists, restrictions on who could carve *tithu* and how this activity was to proceed. Alph Secakuku (personal communication, 1997), Clark Tenakhongva (see Artist Profile X, this volume), and Ramson Lomatewama (see Artist Profile V, this volume) feel that initiation is a crucial requirement for carvers. According to Secakuku anyone who carves and is not initiated is misrepresenting, as are men who do not belong to a clan or who do not have a Hopi mother. The right to carve, he notes, comes with these criteria, but in addition the man has to carry out his responsibilities (see Secakuku, this volume). For Lomatewama the

initiation process imparts the knowledge necessary for carving, and this advantage can be transferred to other art forms, in his case to representations in etched and stained glass (fig. 3.11).

Hopi Art [8]

> Several summers ago during a weekend arts and crafts show, I was impressed at how greatly business influences Native American art. Thousands of dollars changed hands during two days of selling.... Top prizes validated artists to collectors who bought award-winning pieces at astronomical prices. Some parents sold their children's artwork for unreasonable sums, suggesting to buyers that first pieces from a budding artist might be a worthwhile investment. A frenzy of buying blanketed the booths of art as hundreds of people clamored to see the Indians and their artwork. In all of this I wondered how my people's creative integrity would survive.

> Nora Naranjo-Morse,
> *Mud Woman: Poems from the Clay*

The majority of Hopi artists who commodify Katsina imagery produce *tithu*, or Katsina sculpture (fig. 3.12). The economic success of these carvings combined with the economic needs of Hopis have led many to explore alternate ways of capitalizing on Katsina imagery. Some Hopis have applied the imagery to objects more suited to their talents than carving. Others were inadvertently driven by circumstance to invent new ways of illustrating Katsinam. Still others were encouraged by outsiders to try nontraditional avenues. When Hopi and Zuni artists move away from Katsina carving and into other media, they feel less pressure to follow traditional form, and each sets his or her own boundaries (see Horse, Artist Profile VI, this volume). Today, Hopi artists produce Katsina imagery using many different materials. Representations can appear in paintings, as "soft" dolls of fabric, as gourd figures and banks, on jewelry, and as designs woven into baskets and applied to quilts.

Hopi Carving

At one time, all *tithu* production took place in the kiva during the weeks preceding the ceremony at which they were to be distributed. "Hopi children are raised with the belief that the kachinas carve their own dolls at their mountain home or in the kivas" (Lomatewama 1992, 22). Despite this belief some Hopi men felt that children could be present while the men were carving, but not while they were decorating their work (see Bol, this volume). Carvings were of cottonwood root, and they were colored with natural pigments. Carvers had a close relationship to their creations. This relationship, Milland Lomakema Sr. says, gives men a sense of identity. When natural pigments were used, even

blind men could apply the correct colors because color could be ascertained by the taste of the pigments (personal communication, 1995).

Today some Hopis continue to adhere to these traditions, but many do not. Most carving now is done in homes or studios, a change that Barton Wright sees as analogous to having Katsina manufacture shift to a factory from a church (1989, 71). Carving and decorating is, therefore, now carried out in front of children, although some artists indi-

3.11 Ramson Lomatewama, Katsina-like figure, 1998. Etched glass. H: 122 cm. Private collection.

3.12 H. Tewa, Qöqlö *tihu*, 1995. Wood and pigment. H: 30 cm. Private collection.

cated to me that they make an effort not to let their daughters or granddaughters see the *tithu* that will be presented to them in ceremonies. If a girl has seen the *tihu,* artists will at times exchange a carving for one by another artist, sometimes removing the base (Joseph Day, personal communication, 1999). *Tithu* to be given in ceremonies are made at any time of the year. Some artists' lives are so driven by economics or they may be so short of time that they will buy traditional dolls for ceremonies rather

than make them themselves (Joseph Day, personal communication, 1994; John Tanner, personal communication, 1995). Almost all, however, note that there are some katsinam they will not represent, but others carve the previously tabooed Chiefly Katsinam (Mongkatsinam). These Katsinam "belong to a particular clan group, and members of these groups often object to their representation and commercialization" (Breunig and Lomatuway'ma 1992, 11). At the same time, dolls, such as "White

3.13

3.14

Buffalo" and "Field Mouse," are made today that do not represent Katsinam (Wallis 1992, 49). Wright (this volume) details the changes in style and media over the years. Almost all *tithu* received by girls today are more elaborate than those of the early twentieth century, and occasionally even the so-called action figures are given out at ceremonies (see figs. 3.24–3.28).

In the past women did not make *tithu* or touch the shavings because this would interfere with their producing perfect children, but as early as the 1930s women were helping their husbands or other male family members with aspects of the production (John Tanner, personal communication, 1995). Today, a number of Hopi women have taken up carving (see Teiwes 1991). The most celebrated of these is perhaps Muriel Navasie Calnimptewa, the wife of Cecil Calnimptewa, a renowned Hopi carver. Muriel, who started carving her detailed miniature constructions

in 1975 (figs. 3.13–3.15), died in 1988 (Teiwes 1991, 96). Women's carvings are accepted by some liberal Hopis but not by traditionalists (note the views of Secakuku and David in this volume). Some of these women, perhaps all, have been asked to stop carving by leaders of the Katsina societies. One carver told me early in 1998 that she had acquiesced to such a request because she was convinced of the importance of this action (fig. 3.16). Other women, like Esther Jackson (Artist Profile III, this volume), feel that they have no choice but to continue carving because it is the only way they know to support their families (fig. 3.17). Marilyn Clashin of Polacca emphasizes that women carve for economic reasons and to have a sense of pride—many are single parents. They want to stay off welfare or to supplement their welfare payments. Old traditions continue to be rewritten for modern times. When Clashin, who was taught

3.13 Muriel Navasie Calnimptewa, Pangwu (Mountain Sheep Katsina) *tihu*, 1986. Wood and pigment. H: 11.5 cm. Collection of Tom and Nancy Juda.

3.14 Muriel Navasie Calnimptewa, Nangöysohu (Chasing Star Katsina) *tihu*, mid-1980s. Wood and pigment. H: 11.2 cm. Collection of Tom and Nancy Juda.

3.15 Muriel Navasie Calnimptewa, Palakwayo (Red Tail Hawk Katsina) *tihu*, mid-1980s. Wood and pigment. H: 18.3 cm. Collection of Tom and Nancy Juda.

3.15

by her godmother Loretta Yestewa, started carving Koyaala in 1988, no one said that she should not be doing this because she is a woman, but her family did tell her that she should not carve when she was pregnant because if anything went wrong with the carving it would affect her baby. "In the old days," she notes "men wouldn't carve when their wives were pregnant" (personal communication, 1995). Regina Naha also carves Koyaala, but she specializes in representing them engaged in non-Hopi activities (fig. 3.18A–D).

The discussion as to the primary use of *tithu*— whether as teaching tools, playthings, or wall deco-

rations—is an old one (see Bol, this volume), but it seems clear that they have all of these functions (figs. 3.19, 3.20). They are always teaching vehicles. "The importance placed on learning about katsinas for the child reflects the significance of katsinas to Hopi society" (E. C. Adams 1991, 6–7). While with some children, or within some families, one or another use may be emphasized, it is apparent that the use of dolls as playthings has changed dramatically over the years.

With the increasing commercialization and value of Hopi carvings, people today often try to keep the *tithu* in better condition than they did in the past.

3.16 Anonymous Hopi female artist, Angaktsinmana (White Corn Maiden) *tihu*, circa 1996. Wood and pigment. H: 23 cm. Private collection.

3.17 Esther Jackson, Poliimana (Butterfly Girl) *tihu*, 1998. Wood and pigment. H: 23 cm. Private collection.

3.18A–D Regina Naha, Koyaala *tihu*, 1990s. Wood and pigment. (A) Clown mending his shoe. H: 15.5 cm. (B) Clown dressed as Santa Claus. H: 17.5 cm. (C) Possibly a clown on a bucking bronco. H: 24 cm. (D) Clown with a turkey. H: 16.5 cm. Collection of Anne and Randy Joseph.

3.16

3.17

Helga Teiwes, for example, states that they "are seldom played with" (1991, 33). But many Hopis remember that in days past they were used so energetically that in some cases they fell apart and were thrown away (Breunig, personal communication, 1997; Bol, this volume; Wright, this volume). Emory Sekaquaptewa remembers seeing old and broken Katsina dolls in the trash. The discarding of the dolls, he says, mirrored the life cycle of being born, living, and returning to the earth (Page 1994, 105). Annabelle Nequatewa, a grandmother from Second Mesa, told me that when she was a girl, they would play with the dolls to the extent that the carvings would often lose their ears and legs. They would then be hung on the walls in this condition (personal communication, 1997). Leigh Jenkins [Kuwanwisiwma] recalls his mother telling him the same:

My mom told me, "I don't have any of my dolls, because we were allowed to play with them. We rolled around with them in the dirt, we played house with them, they were our babies, we role-played with them, we left them outside and they're gone." But today the dolls are carved so elaborately that people just put them on the wall. They won't allow the child to experience them. [Quoted in Wade 1995, 31]

As reminders of Hopi history and as symbols of growth and maturity in this difficult environment, *tithu* are honored, if not always considered sacred. They may have been battered, but they were supposed to remain in the family. "Children are not supposed to sell the kachina dolls that have been presented to them, for in doing so many Hopis believe that an

3.18A–D

epidemic disease may result which might kill many of the children" (Nequatewa 1948, 62). A young Hopi woman told me that she would never consider selling the *tithu* she had received as a youngster. Nevertheless with increasing economic concerns and carving prices rising, some families and individuals offer these dolls for sale, and there are always buyers who will pay top dollar for an object that was used in a ceremony.

Until recently, the only significant difference between *tithu* made for ceremonies and carvings made for sale was that the latter have increasingly been signed by the artist. Those made for ceremonies, as gifts from the Katsinam, are never signed. Over the past few decades certain classes of carvings have strayed so far from what is considered traditional that a schism has developed at Hopi as to which carvings should and should not be termed *tithu*. These changes have also generated a discussion about carvings as art.

The Hopis consulted for this volume often divide Katsina carvings into categories, but they do not necessarily agree as to what these categories should be. Alph Secakuku (this volume) notes four categories of carvings: old-style (simply carved; see fig. 3.7), traditional (more elaborate than old-style, but still not "lifelike"; fig. 3.22), one-piece (fig. 3.21A), and sculpture (see figs. 3.24–3.28). Secakuku sees the first three, whether made for ceremonies or for sale, as *tithu* but not the fourth. Sculptures are those carvings that some call "action figures"; they are characterized by exaggerated movement and can be either ultrarealistic or stylized; additionally they may incorporate narrative elements. Secakuku feels these fall too far from Hopi tradition to be included in the category of *tithu*. Jonathan Day, a Hopi artist, agrees that these new figures are "a different form of art than the ceremonial" (T. Bassman 1991, 48). Unlike Secakuku, Clark Tenakhongva (see Artist

3.19

3.19 *Tithu* decorating the walls of the home of Annabelle Nequatewa, Songoopavi, Second Mesa. Photograph by Zena Pearlstone, 1997.

3.20 A. C. Vroman, *"Interior of Hooker's House." Sichimovi* [Sitsomovi], *1902*. Seaver Center for Western History Research, Los Angeles County Museum of Natural History, v-554. Vroman's photograph illustrates the practice of hanging *tithu* on interior house walls.

3.21A,B (A) Tsa'kwayna (Zuni Warrior Katsina) *tihu*, 1930s. Wood and pigment. H: 22 cm. (B) Katsinmana (Katsina Maiden) *tihu*, 1940s. Wood and pigment. H: 19 cm. Private collection. The Tsa'kwayna figure on the left is a one-piece Katsina.

3.22 Monongya (Lizard Katsina) *tihu*, 1940s. Wood, pigment, feather, and string. H: 26 cm. Private collection.

3.20

Profile X, this volume) disdains the term "old-style," preferring the term "traditional" to refer both to older carvings and the ones that continue that convention. Tenakhongva today produces dolls in the so-called "new old-style," initiated around 1970 by Manfred Susunkewa (fig. 3.23).[9] This mode is seen, by the artists who employ it and their patrons, as continuing to convey the spirits of the Katsinam rather than creating a portrait of the dancers (Wallis 1992; Walsh 1993). "Traditional," for Tenakhongva, indicates the method of construction. He also differs from Secakuku in believing that anything carved by a Hopi is a *tihu*. Leigh J. Kuwanwisiwma (personal communication, 1997), like Tenakhongva, believes that all carvings made by Hopi are *tithu* and special, but "if made for sale they are missing something."

Many Hopis who want to embrace the belief that all Hopi carvings are *tithu* are having difficulty finding a place for the increasingly elaborate action figures. If they consider them *tithu*, it may be grudgingly. The concept of an art form driven by individual creativity rather than ceremonial tradition is Euro-American, rather than Hopi. The creators of action figures are caught between the distinction that Arnold Rubin makes between the twentieth-century Western artist whose efforts are "introspective, self-reflective and highly individual" and the non-Western artist whose efforts "serve the community as a whole"; in short, between two—or today more than two—worlds (1989, 18). Tenakhongva (Artist Profile X, this volume), who believes that all carvings are *tithu*, refers to the action carvings as the Michelangelo dolls, "detailed dolls with fine line carving," thus defining them as straddling two worlds.

Some Hopi scholars have more readily secularized the action figures than the Hopis themselves, perhaps because it is for them a more familiar situation.

3.21A,B

3.22

Barton Wright notes that the economic demands of the non-Indian market have "incorporated dolls into a sculptural milieu rather than an ethnic one and placed them in galleries devoted to fine art" (1989, 71). J. J. Brody discusses the transformation of Katsina images into what he calls "secular art objects," acknowledging the complex intercultural interactions over time (1994). He sees this transformation to another kind of art as "primarily a response to their formal, aesthetic qualities rather than to any local conditions which caused them to be created in the first place" (Brody 1994, 148). Noting the trend toward naturalism in Katsina carvings, Brody follows Wade (1976, 136) in stating that "most twentieth-century carvings represent kachina impersonators rather than the sacred personages themselves" (1994, 153), an observation now oft voiced at Hopi. It is as though, Brody states, "the objective is to render the most realistic possible human body masquerading as a kachina" (1994, 153). Brody traces the socially accepted norms for aesthetics throughout this century and feels that objects collected early for their iconic significance but seen as anti-art are now considered as highly aesthetic, while the "action

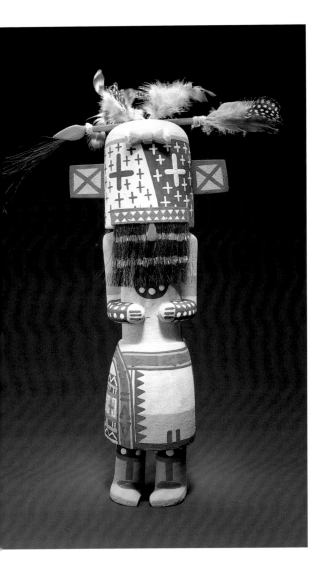

3.23 Manuel Denet Chavarria Jr., Eewiro (a type of Warrior Katsina) *tihu*. Wood and pigment. H: 42 cm. Private collection.

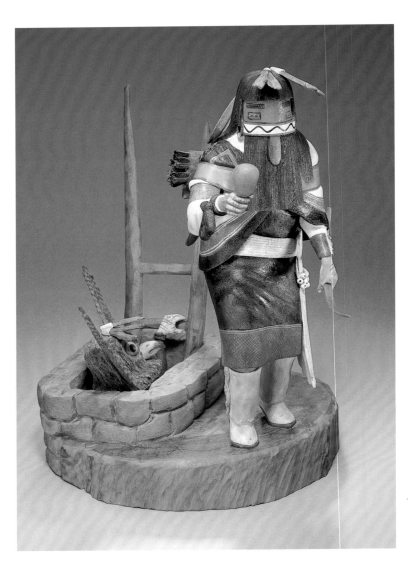

3.24 Cecil Calnimptewa, Hewtomana and Mongwu (Great Horned Owl Katsina) *tithu*, 1980s. Wood and pigment. H: 38.5 cm. Collection of Tom and Nancy Juda.

figures are 'kachina dancers' first, 'art' second, and two steps removed from the sacred" (Brody 1994, 155). Brody's analysis does not correspond with the feelings of some Hopis. As noted above, some are hesitant to describe these sometimes fanciful carvings as even one step removed from the sacred, feeling that any carving by an initiated Hopi carries Hopi spirituality.

Over the last few decades, however, action figures, made primarily for sale, have in numerous ways moved well beyond depictions of Katsina dancers and even further from the ceremonial *tihu*. Figures

are now commonly represented in dramatic poses, far beyond the limited and preprogrammed movements of the dancers. Artist James Fred noted this several years ago: "I have seen a lot of dolls that are doing certain motions that the kachinas don't do, such as the Long-Haired kachina. It rarely moves" (T. Bassman 1991, 53). In contrast to the dancers, some carvings today are best described as baroque in their complications, exaggerations, and abstractions. Details of feathers, costume, and body become increasingly elaborate. Bases, originally nonexistent (see Wright, this volume) have

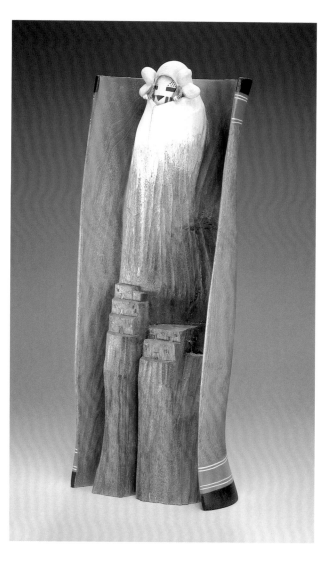

3.25 Wilmer Kaye, Nuvaktsinmana (Snow Maiden Katsina) *tihu*, 1980s. Wood and pigment. H: 40.5 cm. Collection of Tom and Nancy Juda.

3.26 Loren Phillips, "Supremes" Kwaakatsina (Eagle Katsina) *tihu*, 1980s. Wood and pigment. H: 44.5 cm. Collection of Tom and Nancy Juda.

developed into tableaux of their own, carrying narrative scenes, architecture, additional figures, and Katsina representations.

Theda Bassman (1994) has documented the changes from the 1970s to the early 1990s in the work of one of Hopi's most well-known artists Cecil Calnimptewa who, in addition to single Katsina representations, provides tableaux with two or more Katsinam, animals, and clowns. In one tableau, Suyang'ephoya (Left-Handed Katsina) crawls on his knees, beard and cloak blowing in the breeze, while a bear about twice his size looms on a rock behind (T. Bassman 1994, 79). In another, Kwaakatsina (Eagle Katsina) shelters a muscular Kooyemsi

(Mudhead Katsina), under his enormous wings (T. Bassman 1994, 77). In yet another (fig. 3.24), Mongwu (Great Horned Owl Katsina) emerges from a kiva while Hewtomana dances in the plaza (T. Bassman 1991, 16–17).

Other artists employ similar concepts. Neil David Sr. replaces the abdomen and legs of Angwusnasomtaqa (Crow Mother Katsina) with bas relief Hopi symbols on unpainted wood (T. Bassman 1991, 45). Wilmer Kaye's Nuvaktsinmana (Snow Maiden Katsina; fig. 3.25) is architectonic. Her small head tops an amorphous torso that merges into a pueblo; all of this is surrounded by a semicircular screen carrying the designs of her

3.27 Loren Phillips, So'yoko (a female Ogre Katsina) *tihu*, 1989. Wood and pigment. H: 25 cm. Collection of Tom and Nancy Juda.

3.28 Alvin James Sr., "Makya," Kaasayle *tihu* with watermelon, 1989. Wood and pigment. H: 54.5 cm. Collection of Tom and Nancy Juda.

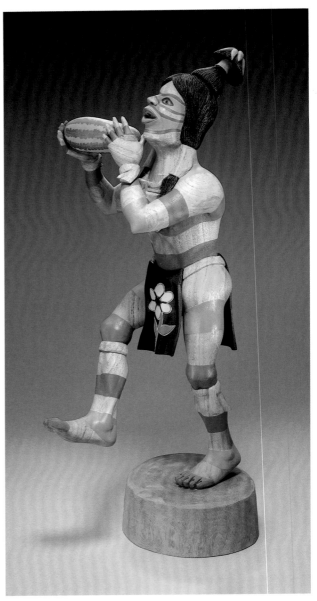

clothing (T. Bassman 1991, 96). Kwaakatsina (Eagle Katsina), in a representation by Loren Phillips (fig. 3.26), is dwarfed by a bird twice as tall and three times as wide (T. Bassman 1991, 118, see also fig. 3.27). These sculptures have evolved greatly since the 1970s when Hopi artist Alvin James Sr., also known as "Makya" (fig. 3.28), was criticized by the elders for taking "his carvings beyond the realm of being simply dolls…and instead [modeling] them after the men who dance in the ceremonies." At the time the elders may have feared that such accuracy would be an affront to the supernaturals and that uninitiated children would guess that the Katsina participants were really men (Wade 1976, 136). Given this attitude more than twenty years ago, it is not surprising that some Hopis today try to separate the dramatic carvings from *tithu*.

Hopi carvers are far from unified in their feelings about whether these dramatic objects should be considered as art, and the subject has generated much discussion in the villages and in published interviews. James Fred does not believe that carving has become an art form because it has always been art (T. Bassman 1991, 52), but John Fredericks does not consider himself an artist (T. Bassman 1991, 63). Others think there has been change. Neil David Sr. relates that "[a]s an artist I see that Kachina dolls have become an art form and I enjoy the public wanting to learn more about our culture and I like to share my knowledge with people" (T. Bassman 1991, 43). Orin Poley asserts that "dolls have evolved from a religious form to an art form" (T. Bassman 1991, 133). Seeing them as art does not mean that they do not encompass traditional values. Silas Roy feels that "[t]he carvings are like art. It's nothing to be worshiped," but then he notes that "I never burn [the shavings].… They are sacred. The elders say that when you are making dolls it's like making your kids, and the shavings and the small pieces must never be burned" (T. Bassman 1991,146).

Although some carvers see and describe their work as modern art, other Hopis only see the display of traditional figures removed from Hopi ways. It is often difficult for Hopis raised with Pueblo ideas of material culture to comprehend the Western concept of artists trying to solve a set of problems. Bennetta Jules-Rosette points out that scholars, too, have difficulty seeing this art in a new context (1984, 230). Discussing examples of African tourist art as signs that through commercialization become objects of "symbolic exchange," she cautions that it is a mistake to try to understand the artwork "as a

deviation from traditional forms rather than an object emerging within a new social context." Art made for outsiders is defined by social change, and its importance (discussed below for Hopis) has received more attention in the years since Jules-Rosette's study. For some investigators, as well as some Hopis, however, the tendency remains to see these artworks as digressions, a frame of reference probably even more difficult to relinquish when the art has religious significance. The debate concerning the negative effects of commercialization on the native art of the Southwest is an old one and has been active for well over one hundred years.

Carvers in Two Worlds

The booming art and tourist markets for Katsina figurines may be more viable economically than culturally, and many artists live with anxiety about breaking from tradition.[10] They question whether they are artists simply churning out commodities or Hopis continuing their Native American identity. "You're not even supposed to sell your Kachina dolls," explains Laurence Martin Dallas. "It's like selling your children, but people have to make a living" (T. Bassman 1991, 32). When Alvin James Sr., "Makya," was told that Hopi culture does not permit the selling of Katsina carvings, he decided that he would stop making them and turn to images of unmasked social dancers such as White Buffalo, clowns (see fig. 3.28), or Butterfly Maidens (T. Bassman 1991, 91). Ramson Lomatewama speaks of preparing himself "mentally and emotionally.… It is not the monetary benefits, nor the prestige that is important. It is the belief that my creations, the kachina dolls that I carve, are manifestations of my attitudes toward life itself. And, if I radiate those positive feelings, somehow or other, my carvings will become the vehicle for those feelings to be carried and further radiated in someone else's life" (Lomatewama 1992, 24). Lomatewama (see Artist Profile V, this volume) thinks of his art as a healing process, a way for others to benefit from his experience.

Many of the Hopi artists who produce the elaborate objects viable in the contemporary marketplace insist on traditional methods of manufacture even if they know from the start that their carvings will be sold. In interviews with Theda Bassman (1991), they report that they chant the appropriate songs and pray to the figurines while they are carving. Some will not carve Katsinam that they have not seen dance (Joseph Day, personal communication,

1997). Many assert that they would never burn the wood shavings (David and Tenakhongva, see Artist Profiles I, x, this volume; Lomatewama 1992, 23). Some (Ronald Honyouti, Wilmer Kaye) state their belief that the figures have souls and spirits and that once begun the figures must be completed (T. Bassman 1991, 80, 96). Von Monongya believes that the carving "has a soul once it is finished but not while he is working on it" (T. Bassman 1991, 101). Many artists eschew working in metal. According to Laurence Martin Dallas "cutting up a doll like that. It's just like cutting up a kachina. You wouldn't cut off the head of a kachina" (T. Bassman 1991, 30, 32). Neil David Sr. regrets casting Katsinam in bronze "since fire should never touch a doll" and does not think he would do this again (T. Bassman 1991, 42).

Ellen Reisland, who worked with Hopi artists at Gallery 10 in Scottsdale for ten years, notes how they set boundaries and censor themselves. She was impressed with the extent of their sense of cultural responsibility and emphasized that it should not be assumed that artists who live at Hopi are more concerned about the integrity of their work than those who do not (fig. 3.29). The following is from an interview I conducted in 1995 when Reisland was still at the gallery:

> Much of the Native American population, most commonly out of New Mexico, although Hopi more and more, who are college educated, have lived off the reservation for many years, and live somewhat with the old ways and are torn. A lot of people will actually go back and live there [at Hopi]. They will decide that what's happening for them in their career off the reservation out in the real world is too much of a compromise. There's a lot of social criticism and pressure to come back and support their people and the culture and traditions. And so there is a lot of anxiety within themselves, and especially at Hopi where there are so many different political factions. They are having trouble deciding what is the old way and what isn't the old way and what is good enough to pass muster.... In my position in an art gallery I spend a lot of time trying to buffer some of those anxieties that our artists feel—whether they're just churning stuff out for commercial purposes or whether the art is really happening within their identity as a Native American.... They feel responsible not just to themselves as artists but to how

Hopi are looked upon by the outside— not just the Anglo culture but other Native American groups.

When one artist began to work with a wood other than the traditional cottonwood, because the latter was increasingly difficult to obtain in large blocks, Reisland relates, he was concerned about the integrity of his work, whether this would make it less Hopi. As Reisland notes, living on or away from the Pueblo is not a measure of credibility, but artists living away from Hopi will sometimes compare their work with that of Pueblo residents.

3.29 Quanhoyeoma, an off-Reservation Hopi artist, Tasapkatsinmuy Kwa'am (grandfather role of Navajo Katsinam) *tihu*, 1995. Wood and pigment. H: 30 cm. Private collection.

Gerry Quotskuyva (see Artist Profile VIII, this volume) feels that there is a commonality in the work produced by artists who live at Hopi, as opposed to those who do not. Conversely, there are artists who rationalize the sale of carvings by trying to make their work "less Hopi," or perhaps less religious, by subtly altering details of the carving or by leaving off special symbols.[11] Others omit the body painting of the dancers or symbols on the masks. Further, Hopis "have adopted the rationalization that an inexact rendering of a sacred art will not be taken as an insult by the supernaturals" (Wade 1976, 146).

It is a mistake, however, to presume that all artists are aware of the issues and controversies that swirl around the villages and the art world. One artist living at Hopi, who has been carving for some time and sells through an East Coast gallery, was alarmed when I mentioned that some Hopis objected to the selling of Katsina carvings. Despite the fact that he lives at Hopi, he was not aware of this sentiment. There is a segment of the Hopi population that is still relatively isolated, does not spend much time away from the villages, and may not read well, thus not even following issues in the *Tutuveni*, the Hopi newspaper. The well-paid and well-known artists get the lion's share of attention, but they are not the only Hopis who are selling to the public. In addition, those at Hopi who are opposed to commercial carving generally keep a low profile—as is the Hopi way—and they are aware that even though they would like the selling to stop, they are at a loss to suggest substitute livelihoods.

Today, hundreds of Hopi men and some Hopi women carve Katsinam for sale. It would be difficult to overestimate the effect that the outside world has on this work, these "entangled objects" (N. Thomas 1991).[12] Many Hopi artists buy the materials that they need at Tsakurshovi, a shop on Second Mesa run by Joseph Day and his Hopi wife, Janice. Artists, well aware of the vagaries of the market, will often ask the Days and other shop owners what Euro-American buyers want, so that the market becomes further shaped by non-Hopi taste (Joseph Day, personal communication, 1994). Buyers, Barton Wright has noted, exert pressures to restrict the repertoire by asking for a limited variety (1989, 71). Artists whose work is in demand will often carve only when they have a commission; some are under contract to galleries and collectors. Joseph Day has been influential in promoting the "new old-style" (Walsh 1993; Tenakhongva, see Artist Profile X, this volume). Juried exhibitions in Santa Fe, Gallup,

Flagstaff and other locations move the art market. Artists try to copy what is successful. Categories in which art is judged may highlight cultural differences and, if determined by Euro-Americans, incorporate standards unacceptable to the Hopi. At one juried Santa Fe Indian Market contest, the Indians would not accept sculpture with burnt wood or acrylic paints in the traditional category, and the entries had to be rearranged (Alph Secakuku, personal communication, 1997). Disagreements about categories are long-standing (John Tanner, personal communication, 1995).

Books on Katsinam written and published by non-Indians (sometimes with illustrations by Hopi artists) further influence the market. Katsinam most requested are the ones that buyers are familiar with from the available books. Artists may look to the illustrations for stylistic ideas. Until the publication of Alph Secakuku's *Following the Sun and Moon* in 1995, the book most frequently referred to by both patrons and artists was Barton Wright's *Kachinas: A Hopi Artist's Documentary*, which has been in print since 1973. Before this, Jesse Walter Fewkes's *Hopi Katcinas Drawn by Native Artists* ([1903] 1969) was frequently used as a reference.

Successful artists may be forced to operate in a world where values are directly opposite to traditional Pueblo values. Euro-American society rewards those who are competitive, individualistic, and ambitious, those who stand out because of their unique qualities. The outside art world is one that deals in celebrities, and it elevates successful Pueblo artists to this status. All of these characteristics, as Edwin Wade (1976) notes, are in contrast to the admired Pueblo attributes of communality and a lack of assertiveness. Perhaps most disruptive, Wade suggests, is that outsiders encourage artists to be spokesmen for their communities before they have earned that right in Pueblo terms. Artistic success has inadvertently upset the Pueblo ideology of egalitarianism and challenged the "concept of limited good," which is based on the idea that there is a finite amount of wealth, good fortune, status, and fame for a community. If any one person gets more than his or her share, then the social and economic balance is upset. Innovations move the artist further away from his community and are threatening to traditionalists (Wade 1976, 28–35, 150–78). "The Indian artist must conform to the image of a good man prescribed by his society, and at the same time live up to the role of a sophisticated, westernized art market participant" (Wade 1976, 151).[13]

Imbalances can lead to envy from the artists' neighbors, as in Euro-American society, but also to distrust, ostracism, and accusations of witchcraft. While financial inequality can sometimes be remedied by putting money back into the community, this behavior addresses only one aspect of the situation. Pueblo people have had to adapt to these changes, and Edwin Wade reports that by the 1970s they were beginning to accept the fact of inequality, that some people were going to make more money, claim more attention, and form a class of their own (1976, 192). Some artists by this period could lead relatively normal lives, but in the twenty-plus years since Wade wrote, Hopis have become even more accustomed to a classed society where some artists are extremely wealthy. In this respect Hopis have become a mirror of the world around them. This does not mean, however, that the fear of increasingly rapid change is no longer present. And it does not mean that all successful artists are comfortable with the spotlight that the outside world has shone upon them.

Painting

Painted Katsina forms can be traced back to the precontact period when masklike images were applied to rock art and pottery (E. C. Adams 1991, 21). Katsina images are also evident in the fourteenth- to sixteenth-century kiva murals at Awat'ovi and Kawaika-a just east of First Mesa (Smith 1952, 1980). The earliest Hopi paintings created for nonceremonial purposes are probably those commissioned and published by Jesse Walter Fewkes ([1903] 1969) a century ago (figs. 3.30A,B). To learn more about Hopi religious beliefs, Fewkes asked a number of Hopi artists to produce paintings of Katsinam.

> To facilitate the painting the author provided the artists with paper, pencils, brushes, and pigments; he left the execution of the work wholly to the Indians, no suggestion being made save the name of the god whose representation was desired. They carried the materials to the mesa, and in a few days returned with a half-dozen paintings which were found to be so good that they were encouraged to continue the work. [Fewkes (1903) 1969, 16]

Fewkes's primary concern was with purity; he did not want the images to be tainted with non-Pueblo influence. This concern largely determined the choice of his artists. In choosing White Bear (Kutcahonauu), Fewkes noted: "This Hopi had picked up a slight knowledge of English at the Keams Canyon school, and while his method of drawing may have been somewhat influenced by instruction there, this modifying influence is believed to be very slight, as the figures themselves show" ([1903] 1969, 15). Other artists were Homovi, White Bear's uncle, and Winuta, both of whom Fewkes assures us were not influenced by outside sources. Other artists were asked to identify the figures and sometimes "made critical suggestions which were of great value regarding the fidelity of the work and embodied information which is incorporated in the exposition of the collection" (Fewkes [1903] 1969, 16).

Unlike the Katsina carvings of the late nineteenth century, which are geometric and static (see Bol, this volume), the Katsina paintings made for Fewkes are often quite animated, foreshadowing the action Katsina carvings of the second half of the twentieth century.[14] While maintaining the proportions of the contemporaneous *tithu*—large heads and relatively small bodies—Fewkes's artists seem to have relied on the memory of Katsina dancers for poses. Barton Wright (personal communication, 1998) has noted that Fewkes's artists may have been influenced by the religious paintings of their era, and indeed, the works do resemble the supernaturals painted on cloth screens at the time (Stephen 1936, pl. 11; Broder 1978, figs. 1.9), as well as those on dance wands (e.g., Broder 1978, fig.1.6).

To promote feedback, Fewkes encouraged people to examine the pictures, but during this process he noted that: "some person circulated a report that it was sorcery to make these pictures, and this gossip sorely troubled the painters and seriously hampered them in their work, but the author was able to persuade the artists and the more intelligent visitors that no harm would come to them on account of the collection" (Fewkes [1903] 1969, 16). Despite the fact that some individuals had been selling Katsina carvings since the 1860s, Hopis appear to have been divided on the acceptability of two-dimensional representations.

The negative reaction to Fewkes's paintings led to a hiatus in painted Katsinam. Oil paintings and watercolors were occasionally done at Hopi in the following years, but painting did not really reemerge for a generation, and then it was in Santa Fe (Brody 1997, 37).[15] There, in 1917 or earlier, Hopi artist Fred Kabotie sold pictures of single Katsinam to his teachers at the Indian School (Kabotie and Belknap 1977, 28–29; Seymour 1988, 238), and watercolors of multiple Katsinam followed (Dunn 1968, 53).

Kabotie and fellow Hopi Otis Polelonema, also in Santa Fe, were the first commercial painters to represent Katsinam, and they influenced others to do the same—Raymond Naha, Waldo Mootzka, Peter Shelton, and Michael Kabotie, Fred's son, who learned to paint by watching men in his father's studio from the time he was a small boy (Snodgrass 1968, 90; Brody 1971, 109–11). These artists were actively painting from the 1930s to the 1960s. In the 1970s, a number of artists formed the Artist Hopid, an international modernist movement (Broder 1978; Brody 1979, 1994). Edwin Wade feels that throughout this period Hopis were more tolerant of Katsina-ceremony commercial paintings than other Pueblos because "Hopi has had a longer period of exposure to the commercializing effects of the Indian art market,…[and] Hopi religious rituals have been studied so assiduously and documented so thoroughly that it has become almost pointless for the pueblo to persist in their secrecy" (1976, 138–39).

Many Hopi today distinguish between sculptural representations of Katsinam and two-dimensional representations. Despite the representations on kiva murals, now four hundred to seven hundred years old, two-dimensional imagery is not seen by all as an aspect of the culture. Thus, some Hopi are accepting of painted Katsinam by non-Pueblo people and women as long as the representations are accurate

3.30A,B Illustrations by Hopi artists for Jesse Walter Fewkes, *Hopi Katcinas Drawn by Native Artists,* 1903, pls. XL, XLI.

3.31 Michael Kabotie
"Lomawywesa," *Rain-Spirits*,
1984. Lithograph.
55.5 x 74.5 cm.
Private collection.

3.32 James Campus,
Kooyemsi Katsina at a Hopi
village, 1994. Colored pencil
on paper. 27.9 x 20.3 cm.
Author's collection.

3.33 Lamaoya (Burt
Nicholas), dream catcher
with Katsina image, 1995.
Animal hide, pigment,
string, feathers, and beads.
H: 62.2 cm. Private collection.

3.34A–D Cliff Bahnimptewa, (A) Nata'aska (Black Ogre Katsina), (B) Taatangaya (a type of moth), (C) Àykatsina (Rattle Katsina), (D) Tsorpo-syaqahöntaqa (A Katsina associated with the Raider Katsinam to the clowns). Illustrations from Barton Wright, *Kachinas: A Hopi Artist's Documentary* (Arizona: Northland Publishing and the Heard Museum: 1973), 78, 86, 122, 118. Reproduced with permission of the publisher.

3.34A

3.34B

3.34C

3.34D

(Alph Secakuku, personal communication, 1997; Leigh J. Kuwanwisiwma, personal communication, 1997). Despite this tolerant attitude, paintings of Katsinam have not been common, although their numbers have increased. Annie Acker noted in the early 1990s, "Originally, [when] I went to the Hopi reservation to study Hopi painting…I was unable to meet any Hopi artists who were living on the reservation and were currently painting. All the painters I knew, or heard of, were no longer painting…. Those who were currently painting lived off the reservation" (Acker 1993, 2).

In tourist and gift stores generally away from Hopi, one can find some paintings of Katsinam by Hopi artists. Both Neil David Sr. and Michael Kabotie

(fig. 3.31), past members of Artists Hopid, have returned to painting, but David still devotes much time to sculpture and Kabotie to jewelry. Meanwhile, a new generation of painters including Jenelle Numken and Carliss Sinquah has emerged. In 1995 Lamaoya (Burt Nicholas) was selling dream catchers adorned with painted Katsinam (fig. 3.33) along with *tithu* from a shop on Second Mesa. Boys will sometimes sell their drawings. I bought the one illustrated here (fig. 3.32) at Walpi in 1994 from then ten-year-old James Campus, who may be tapping into an old practice. Fred Kabotie says that when he was a boy drawing Katsinam with charcoal on walls or scratching them on rocks in abandoned houses was play (1977, 8; see also Seymour 1988, 242).

3.35 Dan Namingha, *Dream State 24,* 1997. Acrylic on canvas. 127 x 101.6 cm. © Dan Namingha. Photograph courtesy of Niman Fine Art.

3.36 Dan Namingha, *Emergence,* 1985. Acrylic on canvas. 202.2 x 203.2 cm. National Aeronautics and Space Administration

3.35

Since the time of Jesse Walter Fewkes's publication (1903), several Hopi artists have provided drawings of Katsinam to illustrate books. Cliff Bahnimptewa from Old Orayvi, Third Mesa, did the paintings for Barton Wright's *Kachinas: A Hopi Artist's Documentary* (1973). Wright (1973, 4) notes that "while he is not a professional artist his paintings are realistic renderings of single dancers in which each figure appears as if in a performance. His full figure renditions convey with immediacy and effectiveness the Hopi Kachina Dancers" (figs. 3.34A–D). Neil David Sr. did the illustrations for *Kachinas: Spirit Beings of the Hopi*, published in 1993, and Michael Lacapa is the author and illustrator of children's books that at times feature Katsinam.

One of the best-known Hopi artists working today is Hopi-Tewa painter and sculptor Dan Namingha. Namingha, who was raised in the First Mesa village of Polacca, is the great-great-grandson of famed potter Nampeyo, whose designs influenced him (Clay 1988, 48). Today he lives near Santa Fe and owns a prestigious Santa Fe gallery that features his work, which has been described by one writer as "a seamless union of tribal and mainstream modernist thought that interprets the dynamics of modern existence" (Deats 1998, 35). His paintings often draw on Hopi subject matter and Katsina imagery (fig. 3.35), but he is careful to protect the sanctity of the Katsinam and the privacy of the Hopi by allowing only distilled glimpses or by rearranging

3.36

elements to give the illusion of masked performers (e.g., *Kachina Symbolism,* 1992; Deats 1998). Jane Wilson describes one of his works, *Dream State 17,* as "his vision of various Kachina images floating back and forth in space and time" (1994). The strong colors and patterns in Namingha's work lead people to associate them with jazz. Scale, depth, and boundaries are mobile and interactive in a style that draws on much of the abstract and expressionist art of the late nineteenth and twentieth centuries.

Invited by the National Aeronautics and Space Administration (NASA) to witness the launch of the space shuttle Discovery in 1985, Namingha was the first Native American to join a NASA art team—those artists invited to launches and asked to donate an artwork inspired by the event to NASA. Namingha,

who flew to Florida the day after participating in a Katsina ceremony at Hopi, saw parallels between the ancient culture and the launch (Hait 1986). His painting *Emergence* (1985) combines the Hero Twins (Palöngawhoya and Pöqangwhoya) and the Sun Katsina (Taawakatsina) with an astronaut floating in space (fig. 3.36). Namingha explains that he "had just come from an ancient ceremony that was about being connected to the cosmos, the planets, stars, moon and sun" (J. Wilson 1994, 16B).

Painter and sculptor Gregory Lomayesva, however, who also successfully depicts Katsina-like images, has come under fire from the Hopi (figs. 3.37, 3.38). According to Lomayesva, "[t]he Hopi tribe freaked. They said, 'You're doing things that look like kachinas, but they're not.'" Lomayesva,

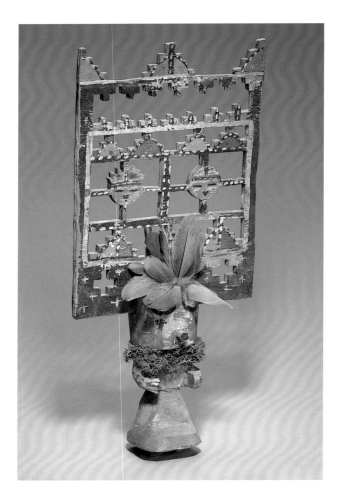

3.37 Gregory Lomayesva, a sculpture representing a Katsina-like figure, 1996. Wood, pigment, feathers, and leather. H: 48 cm. Private collection.

3.38 Gregory Lomayesva, a sculpture representing a Katsina-like figure, 1997. Wood, pigment, feathers, and leather. H: 43.2 cm. Private collection.

who has a non-Hopi mother, and is thus not considered Hopi, says that he created "something that was similar in look and form [to Katsinam] but wasn't sacrilegious. The dolls I do are abstract, contemporary sculpture." He asks that his works not be called Katsinam, but they are frequently labeled as such, particularly in gallery advertisements. "I don't feel comfortable assimilating a spiritual, very powerful being and selling it." He thinks of himself not as a Hopi painter of Katsinam but as a "contemporary artist of Hopi heritage" (Indyke 1997, 48).

Gourd Rattles

The Katsina gourd rattles of the Nequatewa family, which were the original impetus for this study, began as a reinvention of the ceremonial gourd

rattle and soon after became a new commodity. When Edmund (Eddie) Nequatewa, of Songoopavi, Second Mesa, was preparing his costume for a night dance one day in the early 1960s, he gave his gourd rattle the face of a Kooyemsi instead of applying the usual whitewash or simple design. His wife, Annabelle, recalls that he gave that particular rattle to his children, but sometime later it was sold.[16]

3.40A–C Edmund Nequatewa, (A) Hemiskatsina (Home Dancer), 1980s. Gourd, cottonwood, feathers, and paint. H: 38.1 cm. Fowler Museum of Cultural History, x90.669. (B) Kokopölmana, 1980s. Gourd, cottonwood, and paint. H: 21.6 cm. Fowler Museum of Cultural History, x90.677. (C) Mongwu (Great Horned Owl Katsina), 1987. Gourd, Cottonwood, feathers, and paint. H: 25 cm. Fowler Museum of Cultural History, x87.40.

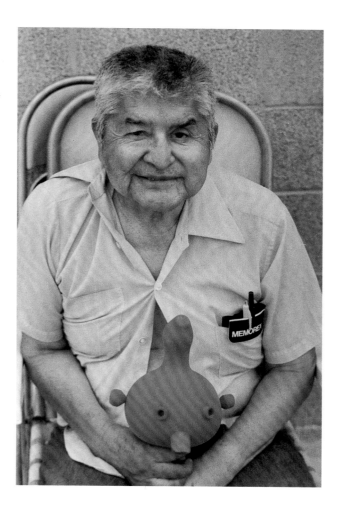

3.39 Edmund (Eddie) Nequatewa holding one of his Mudhead Katsina gourd rattles, circa 1980.

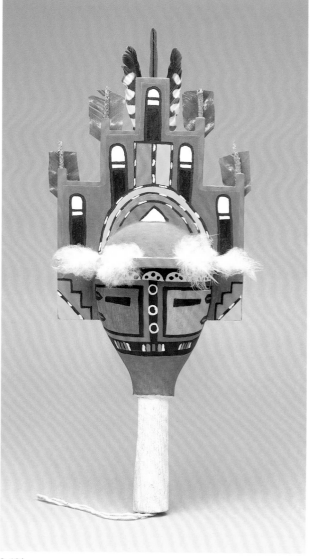

3.40A

3.40B

3.40C

3.41A,B

3.41A,B Merrill Nequatewa, Ogre Katsina gourd rattles. (A) Nata'aska (Black Ogre Katsina), 1994. Wood and pigment. H: 36 cm. (B) Qötsa Wiharu (White Ogre Katsina), 1994. Wood and pigment. H: 41 cm. Courtesy of the Natural History Museum of Los Angeles County, Hearst Native American Art Endowment Purchase, FP.4.96-15, FP.4.96-14. Photograph by Dick Meier.

3.42 Ferrill Nequatewa, Kwaakatsina (Eagle Katsina), 1995. Gourd, pigment, fur, feathers, and wood H: 40.5 cm. Private collection.

3.43 Merrill Nequatewa, Nata'aska (Black Ogre Katsina) bank, 1980s. Gourd, wood, and pigment. H: 60 cm. Courtesy of the Natural History Museum of Los Angeles County, Gift of Richard and Margo Mehagian, F.A.3656.98-2. Photograph by Dick Meier.

3.44 Merrill Nequatewa, Qötsa Wiharu (White Ogre Katsina) bank, 1980s. Gourd, wood, and pigment. H: 51 cm. Courtesy of the Natural History Museum of Los Angeles County, Gift of Richard and Margo Mehagian, F.A.3656.98-1. Photograph by Dick Meier.

3.42

3.43

3.44

3.45

Its manufacture marks the beginning of a new art form (figs. 3.39, 3.40A–C; see also Appendix, pp. 182–85). After the creation of the original Kooyemsi gourd rattle, Eddie made both *tithu* and rattles. Despite his skill and the potential market, chances are that only a handful of Katsina gourd rattles would ever have been made if Eddie had not had a stroke in 1973, and if he had not met Richard Mehagian. The stroke paralyzed his left arm, and he was forced to stop making *tithu*. He could, however, continue to make gourd rattles by standing the gourd in a vice. A few years later he began to work with Richard and his wife, Margo, dealers in Indian art and owners of Kopavi International in Sedona, Arizona.

Gourds are difficult to grow at Hopi, and when Eddie met the Mehagians, he was buying most of his from Santo Domingo Pueblo at about five dollars apiece. Mehagian found that California gourd farmers would sell them for twenty-five to fifty cents if purchased in large quantities. Richard, Eddie, and later Eddie's sons would discuss the shape of the gourds and the most suitable Katsina that each could provide. The sons, twins Merrill and Ferrill (sometimes spelled Merrell and Ferrell), began making gourd rattles around 1984, when they were twenty-seven, and Eddie's younger son, Edward, began in about 1986 when he was twenty-four. Eddie's sons inherited his talent and his skills (fig. 3.41A,B). It is difficult for an outsider to distinguish one hand from another. When shown photographs of rattles in collections, the Nequatewas themselves were not always sure of the artist.

The gourds were cleaned. Old ones sometimes had to be boiled and scraped or sanded. The seeds were removed and the preferred rattling material added. The handle and other substantial attachments, such as ears, nose, beak, eyes, and horns,

3.45 Left: Stacy Talahaftewa, Koyaala rattle, early 1990s. Gourd, wood, pigment, and leather. H: 27.3 cm. Private collection.Right: Merrill Nequatewa, Paatangkatsina (Squash Katsina) piggy bank, 1990s. Gourd, pigment, and wood. H: 65.5.

3.46 Unidentified Navajo female artist, Tasapkatsinmana-like gourd rattle, 1980s. Gourd, wood, and pigment. H: 38 cm. Private collection.

3.47 Robert Rivera, gourds with Katsina-like images. Courtesy of Adagio Galleries, Palm Springs, California.

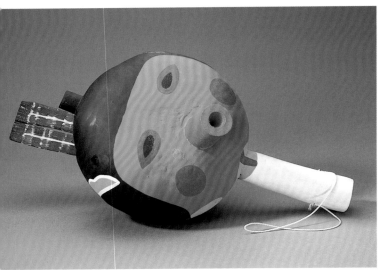

3.46

were fashioned from cottonwood root. The gourd and attachments were then whitewashed, painted, and finally decorated with feathers, string, and whatever else was needed. Eddie initiated two forms of gourd rattles, head only or head and torso. Both types bring together the Hopi traditions of *tithu* and painted gourd rattles. Gourd rattles are used in kiva ceremonies, in most men's dances to mark rhythm, and by Katsinam to note a response or an appreciation (Parsons 1939, 384). Eddie's original Kooyemsi rattle may have been the only one used in a ceremony. Most of the constructions are clearly not meant to be rattled; pieces fly off if they are shaken too vigorously. But Eddie's rattles are nonetheless well constructed and carefully formulated, bringing together a sense of history and a sense of humor. The shape of the gourd is the primary determination of which Katsina is to be represented, but Eddie

3.47

seems as well to have had personal leanings. Clowns—Koyaala and Kooyemsi—were selected most often.

The work of Eddie and his sons remains distinguished compared to today's large body of imitators, in part because of its humor. Everyone who knew Eddie talked foremost about his sense of humor, and the drollery in his art is unquestionable. Gourds provide exquisite material for noses, and Eddie exploits this, enhancing their effect with expressive eyes. Added noses, ears, and mouths are skillfully placed. Clowns' eyes sparkle, a Broadface Katsina (Wuyaqqötö) smirks, bird Katsinam seem coquettish. Rattles of other artists when compared with those made by the Nequatewas often appear technically competent but lacking in personality. The Nequatewas, however, were circumspect in the liberties they took, always careful to portray Katsinam accurately in the traditional manner. Merrill told me that one Kooyemsi could not have been made by a member of his family because it was rendered incorrectly.

In the mid-1980s Eddie branched out into Katsina gourd banks. This art form was directed at a commercial market, and as with rattles he began with the clown forms. These objects, too, were taken up by the twins (figs. 3.43–3.45). After Eddie's death, Merrill and Ferrill began to make gourd Katsina figures, combining two small gourds and adding appendages (fig. 3.42). Merrill continued to make these and other gourd forms until his death in a car accident, January 25, 1996. Edward had died earlier in a car accident in 1991. Ferrill continues to produce a few gourd rattles. In the case of Eddie Nequatewa, economic need and artistic creativity transformed Katsina representation into a new genre derived from Hopi tradition. The Nequatewas' creations are of such whimsy and character that they reaffirm the Hopi spirit.

Economic success does not go unnoticed, and even before Eddie's death, gourd rattles and spin-offs in the form of endearing animals could be seen in Hopi stores. Over the years these have increased in number and are now being produced by Hopis and non-Hopis at and away from the villages (fig. 3.46). No gourd artist, however, has matched the skill of the Nequatewas. The most prolific artist representing Katsina-like forms with gourds is the Euro-American Robert Rivera (fig. 3.47). Beginning in 1975, Rivera fashioned a career out of decorating gourds with a variety of Indian motifs and designs; these are sold today in elegant galleries in Santa Fe, Scottsdale, and Palm Springs. He calls one series of "prehistoric Kachinas" Kiva Spirits. A set from the mid-1990s he calls his Rainbow Kachina series.

Jewelry

Margaret Wright documents the early years of Hopi silversmithing and notes that by 1906 Hopi men from all three mesas were engaged in this art (1989, 11–34). A unique Hopi style developed in the late 1930s. The overlay style, now synonymous with Hopi jewelry, developed out of a project sponsored in 1938 by Museum of Northern Arizona founders, Harold Colton and Mary Russell Ferrell Colton, who encouraged Hopi artists to develop their own distinctive jewelry. To help Hopis create jewelry that was distinguishable from that of Navajos and Zunis, the Coltons with the assistance of their staff collected designs from baskets, ceramics, and textiles and distributed these to Hopi silversmiths (Cirillo 1992, 97; M. Wright 1989). Hopi silverwork overlay is made by soldering two pieces of silver together. The one on top has a section cut out leaving a negative design, the inside of which is oxidized to make it appear black (fig. 3.49). The silver is often textured with a hand tool.

Silversmithing stopped during World War II. In the summer of 1946, Dr. Willard Beatty, the director of education for the Indian Service, visited an exhibition of Hopi arts and crafts at Songoopavi and conceived the idea of establishing a silvercraft school for Hopi veterans under the G.I. Bill of Rights. Fred Kabotie agreed to act as director of design along with his other duties as art instructor at Hopi High School, and Paul Saufkie served as head craftsman. Saufkie had previously worked with the Coltons interpreting Hopi designs in silver. Shortly after the first class completed its training in January 1949, its members organized the Hopi Silvercraft Guild. In 1962 the Guild constructed a permanent building near Songoopavi, Second Mesa, which provides work space and classes for Hopi silversmiths. The Guild was renamed the Hopi Arts and Crafts Silvercraft Cooperative Guild. It furnishes material to the artists and buys back their finished work (Cirillo 1992, 98).

Paul Saufkie first worked in silver in the 1920s (M. Wright 1989, 26). Charles Loloma and Preston Monongye were innovators in the use of figures in jewelry. Monongye achieved impressive detail in his work as seen in a Sa'lakwmana (Cirillo 1992, pl. 156) where the costume, including earrings and bead necklace, are carefully rendered (fig. 3.48). Today Katsina imagery appears on a wide variety of silver jewelry including bolo ties, belt buckles, bracelets, pins, earrings, necklaces, and rings made by both men and women. Verma Nequatewa, Charles Loloma's niece and protégée, has crafted bracelets with abstract Katsina faces in Loloma's style and also pendants based on specific Katsinam (see Artist Profile XII, this volume). Unlike Monongye, she notes that she only rarely tries to depict a specific Katsina but rather aims to illustrate in a general way their "strength, beauty and presence." Some artists such as Phil Poseyesva specialize in one Katsina, in Poseyesva's case Mountain Sheep Katsina (Pàngwkatsina).

Several artists, including Perry Fred, Verden Mansfield, and Jack Nequatewa, have adopted a narrative style that usually features dancing figures, thereby paralleling developments in Katsina carving. Concha belts are particularly well suited to this representation and give artists an opportunity to depict an array of Katsina ceremonies. Those of Roy Talahaftewa are particularly complex (fig. 3.50). Each concha features a dancing Katsina in the plaza framed by the Pueblo architecture and clouds (Cirillo 1992, pl. 93).

3.50 Roy Talahaftewa, sterling-silver-overlay concha belt. Photograph by Michel Monteaux.

3.48 Preston Monongye, silver bolo with Sa'lakwmana (a Cloud Maiden). Photograph by Michel Monteaux.

3.49 Lendrick Lomayestewa, silver concha belt depicting Qöqlö'vitu (a pair of Qöqlö). Photograph by Zena Pearlstone, 2000.

Other Hopi Katsina Representations

In the late 1960s or early 1970s a dealer cast Henry Shelton's *Snake Dancer* in bronze (Wright, this volume). Other artists followed (fig. 3.51, 3.52). In 1983 Neil David Sr. had some of his Katsina dolls cast in bronze but was "disturbed that the original piece becomes colored by the flame" (T. Bassman 1991, 42; see also T. Bassman 1997, 92). Around the same time, Lowell Talashoma Sr. also had some carvings cast in bronze. "I've done very

good carvings in the bronze. The wood has more warmth and life in it, but the bronze looks good too" (T. Bassman 1991, 154; see also Bromberg 1986, 30). David and Talashoma also did drawings for a set of six, eight-inch porcelain Katsina images. These were marketed through American Indian Life and Legends and advertised in publications like *Archaeology* (37, no. 2 [1984]: 8), but at eighty-five dollars apiece, they did not sell well (fig. 3.55). David followed these with a set of four collector

3.51 Ronald Honyouti, Sowi'ingwkatsina (Deer Katsina), mid- to late 1980s. Cast bronze. H: 25 cm. Collection of Tom and Nancy Juda.

3.52 Neil David Sr., Angaktsina (Long-Hair Katsina), 1983. Cast bronze and pigment. H: 49 cm. Collection of Tom and Nancy Juda.

plates with Katsina representations (fig. 3.53, 3.54). The unsold figurines and plates were bought by Bruce McGee, then manager of the Arts and Crafts store at Keams Canyon, and David went back to carving (see fig. 3. 8 and Artist Profile 1, this volume).

Several Hopi women have taken up cloth-doll making, but Vernette Thomas is the only one, to my knowledge, to make Katsina forms (fig. 3.56, 3.57). She credits her cloth-doll making, which began in the early 1980s, to her late son, Quinton, who she

says told her one day to make dolls. Despite the fact that she had never thought about making dolls, and in fact disliked sewing, she has been producing cloth Katsinam and clowns since that time and supports her five children with this work (T. Bassman 1997, 86, fig. p. 83). These soft dolls are occasionally used in ceremonies (Alph Secakuku, personal communication, 1995).

The ceremonial *tablitas* (headdresses) worn by women at the summer Butterfly Dances—prayers

3.53 Neil David Sr., collector plate with an image of Talavaykatsina (Morning Katsina), 1985. Diam: 21.8 cm. Private collection.

3.54 Certificate of authenticity accompanying the plate by Neil David illustrated in fig. 3.53.

3.55 American Life and Legends advertisement for a set of six, eight-inch porcelain Katsina images drawn by Neil David Sr. and Lowell Talashoma Sr.

3.56

3.57

3.56 Vernette Thomas, popular art representing Hehey'amuy Taaha'am (uncle to the Hehey'akatsinam), 1994. Cloth. H: 49.5 cm. Private collection.

3.57 Vernette Thomas, popular art representing Hewtomana, circa 1997. Cloth. H: 49 cm. Private collection.

3.58 *Tablita*, 1950s. Wood, pigment, leather, cord, and corn husk. H: 40 cm. Private collection.

3.58

3.59

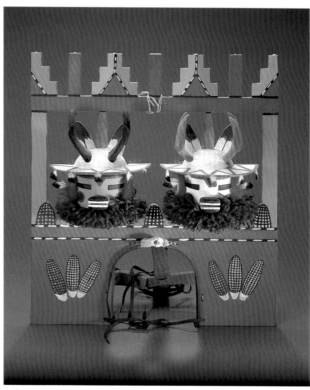

3.60

3.61

3.59 Leroy Kewanimptewa, *Tablita* with Qa'ötiyo Katsina (Corn Boy Katsina), 1995. H: 62 cm. Private collection. This example was made at the collector's request.

3.60 *Tablita*, 1990s. Wood, pigment, yarn, leather, feathers, shoelace, corn husk, and string. H: 47 cm. Private collection.

3.61 *Tablita*, 1980s. Wood, pigment, foam, and string. H: 45.5 cm. Private collection.

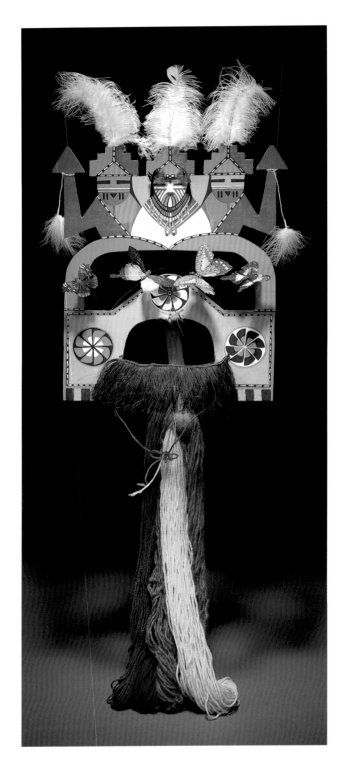

3.63

3.64

3.62 *Tablita*, 1990s. Wood, pigment, yarn, animal hair, leather, feathers, and cord. H: 53 cm. Private collection.

3.63 Basket with Wakaskatsina (Cow Katsina), Second Mesa, 1940s. Plant fiber. Diam: 25.5 cm. Private collection.

3.64 Annabelle Nequatewa, basket with Pöqangwhoya (Warrior Katsina) and ears of corn, 2000. Plant fiber. Diam: 17 cm. Private collection.

3.65A–C

3.66A,B

3.65A–C (A) Basket with
Hiilili (a Whipper Katsina),
1986. Plant fiber. Diam:
40 cm. Private collection.
(B) Jolene Lomatska
Lomayaktawa, basket with

Taawakatsina (Sun Katsina),
1990s. Plant fiber. Diam:
41.2 cm. (C) Basket with
Palhikwmana (Moisture
Drink Maiden), 1990s.
Plant fiber. Diam: 34.2 cm.

3.66A,B (A) Basket with
Kwarurnakvuhooli (a Hooli
with feathers for ears), 1920s.
Plant fiber. Diam: 38 cm.
(B) Basket with Sa'lakwmana
(a Cloud Maiden), 1930s.
Plant fiber. Diam: 43 cm.
Private collection.

3.68 Arthur Yowytewa, Paaqavi, Third Mesa, dance wands with images of Kookopölmana't (a pair of Kookopölö Maidens). Wood, paint, feathers, plant materials. H: 40.6 cm. Private collection.

3.67 Hopi jar, 1880. Pottery pigmented black, brown, and orange-red with six Katsina figures. H: 44.5 cm. Courtesy of the Southwest Museum, Los Angeles, acc. no. 421.G.191, photo no. CS.15425.

3.69 Hopi Tiles with Katsina Imagery. Ceramic pigmented in red and black. H: 15.3–15.6 cm. Courtesy of the Southwest Museum, Los Angeles, 30.L.110 (top left), 30.L.101 (top right), 30.L.89 (bottom left), 30.L.94 (bottom right); photo no. 15420. Photograph by Larry Reynolds.

for rain and a good harvest—increasingly employ three-dimensional Katsinam as the central image (figs. 3.58–3.62). The *tablitas* are usually carved by the girl's partner as a gift to her, and Hopi women have told me that they keep all that they have worn. They are not frequently available for sale. E. C. Parsons notes that formerly only girls past puberty took part in these ceremonies (in Stephen 1936, 147 n.). Both boys and girls had to disclose names of their sweethearts, and the girl's partner had to furnish her entire costume.

Katsinam have appeared on baskets for at least a hundred years. Helga Teiwes thinks that the earliest were woven into wicker plaques on Third Mesa, probably at Orayvi (1996, 160–61). The first Katsina image known to have been woven on a basket is Sa'lakwmana. Today, Katsina representations are acknowledged as a selling feature (figs. 3.63–3.66). "On Second Mesa, weavers speak openly about the fact that large coiled baskets with Katsina figures and eagles can be sold for more money because they are especially sought by collectors" (Teiwes 1996, 63).

3.70 Imogene Tewa, quilt with Pàngwkatsinam (Ram Katsinam), circa 1998. Cloth and pigment, 124.5 x 99 cm. Private collection.

3.71 Eldon Kewanyama, light switch plate with Palhikwmana (Moisture Drink Maiden), 1998. Wood and pigment. H. 24.6 cm. Private collection.

3.72 Hopi-drawn watch face, circa 1995. Metal, pigment, and leather. Private collection.

Ruby Saufkie, a Second Mesa weaver, thinks that "figurative designs like deer, turtles and Katsina figures (particularly Mudheads) sell better than geometric designs." Large coiled deep baskets with Katsinam are made only for the collector market (Teiwes 1996, 63–64, 99). Bertha Wadsworth of Songoopavi began making basketry Katsina figurines in 1988.

Over the years Katsina images have also appeared as decoration on pottery and tiles (figs. 3.67, 3.69). Tom Polacca, a grandson of Nampeyo, developed a style of pottery new to Hopi called sgraffito where animals and Katsinam are carved on pots. The effect is produced by cutting away parts of the surface layer in order to expose a different colored surface. Polacca taught his daughters, Elvira Naha Nampeyo, and Carla Claw Nampeyo, his son, Gary Polacca Nampeyo, and his son-in-law, Marty Naha, the technique, and today all make sgraffito pots for sale (T. Bassman 1997, 74).

Quilting was introduced to the Hopi by Mennonite missionaries, probably in the 1890s (Davis 1997, 44). Quilts today are made at Hopi for home use, gifts, and for sale (fig. 3.70). They have come to be used in certain rituals, especially the Baby Naming ceremony. A number of women, including Susie Archambeau, Imogene Tewa, Erma Tewa, Elsie Talashoma, Joanne Quotskuyva, and Janice Dennis, paint Katsina designs on their quilt blocks with an oil-based fabric paint, a practice dating to at least the 1950s (Davis 1997, 78, 93).

The marketability of Katsina and other ceremonial imagery is evident to the Hopi themselves, and with time an increasing number find more ways to display it (fig. 3.68). Ramson Lomatewama has been incorporating Katsina imagery into stained glass (see fig. 3.11), and Eldon Kewanyama has used it in light switch plates (fig. 3.71). Some Hopi have provided designs for inexpensive tourist items. Anthony Honanie does the illustrations for watch faces (fig. 3.72), and Neil David Sr. has designed T-shirts and notepaper cubes.

Other Pueblos

> Pueblo culture…has a long homogeneous history behind it, and we have special need of this knowledge of it because the cultural life of these peoples is so at variance with that of the rest of North America.
>
> Ruth Benedict, *Patterns of Culture*

The Hopi people see themselves as more closely related to other Pueblo groups than to other Native Americans or to non-Indians. "The Pueblos form a unit in comparison with neighboring groups," and they share religious and behavioral practices (F. Eggan 1979, 224). There are, however, significant differences among the Hopi and their Pueblo neighbors regarding the behavior of Katsina participants, the secrecy of Katsina ceremonies, and the use of Katsina imagery. Some Hopis feel that they do not always completely understand some practices at other Pueblos, but they always regard them with

3.73 J. D. Roybal, Koyaala and Skunks, 1960s. Lithograph. 32 x 43.5 cm. Private collection. Roybal is from San Ildefonso Pueblo.

respect. This recognition can be seen in opposition to Hopi feelings about much of the behavior of non-Pueblo peoples who appropriate Hopi or other Pueblo ceremonies and visual culture.

In contrast to Hopis, the inhabitants of the Pueblos that line the Rio Grande in New Mexico are opposed to non-Indians viewing Katsina ceremonies or Katsina imagery, and by the 1880s they had effectively cut off access by outsiders to their Katsina imagery (Brody 1994, 149).[17] Most Rio Grande communities continue to impose these restrictions on outsiders. Cynthia Chavez, who

was raised at San Felipe Pueblo, has written of the climate there.

At a young age, San Felipe Pueblo members are instructed in the ways of secrecy through observation and verbal reminders. There are certain subjects one should never discuss, illustrate or ask questions about. Many are related to the closed ceremonies of the Pueblo; however, any type of ceremonial information may be considered private. Any individual who grows up in the San Felipe

3.74 Helen Hardin, *Recurrence of Spiritual Elements*, 1973. Acrylic on board. 61 x 50.8 cm. © Helen Hardin, 1973. Photograph © Cradoc Bagshaw 2001. All rights reserved.

community and wishes to be creative is cognizant of the limitations placed on what they produce. [1997, 16]

Joseph H. Suina, a resident of Cochiti Pueblo, feels that the very survival of Pueblo peoples has rested with this inwardness: "The credit for maintaining a rich native religion for more than 300 years of intercultural relations must be given to the most important weapon: secrecy" (1992, 61). Chavez notes, however, that "Pueblo members who grow up outside of the Pueblo community may not be indoctrinated to adhere to secrecy" and that "[t]here are always individuals who choose to go beyond what is considered acceptable" (1997, 16 n.). Most Rio Grande artists, however, hold to the restrictions. When the boundaries are crossed, consequences are expected to be dire.

Commercial carvings of Katsinam by Rio Grande peoples are, therefore, rare. Occasionally artists from the Rio Grande Pueblos will paint Katsinam, Katsina-like imagery, or Koyaala (fig. 3.73). Helen Hardin (1943–1984) of Santa Clara Pueblo, although

a practicing Catholic, painted the culture of her childhood (fig. 3.74). Katsinam "provided Hardin with her richest imagery and her most unfailing inspiration; they were a constant in her career, and she could not imagine being without them" (Scott 1989, 46). One reviewer describes her work as "a spiritual escape from the world of reality. The figures and events are not earthbound persons but, are spirit people, emerging in a kind of supernatural world. They are filled with religious concepts handed down through generations by the Pueblo Indians" (Wilks 1978, 67). Pablita Velarde, Hardin's mother, believed that Hardin may have contracted the cancer that took her life because she painted Katsinam (Scott 1989, 53).

Artists at the Pueblos of Laguna and Acoma, considered members of the Western Pueblo Group—which includes Hopi and Zuni—rather than the Rio Grande Pueblos, at times make Katsina carvings (fig. 3.76). Edwin Wade notes that they are (or were) made at Laguna but that most of the carvers are "migrants from Hopi" (1976, 136). E. Charles Adams (1991, 6) points to the existence of Acoma

3.75 Yvonne Lewis, miniature Kooyemsi tree, circa 1994. Toothpicks and tree branches. H: 10.5 cm. Private collection.

3.76 Katsina, Acoma Pueblo, 1990s. H: 38 cm. Wood, pigment, feathers, yarn, and beads. Private collection. This piece was made for sale.

carvings that have been used inside the community but have appeared for sale (see Harvey 1963b).

Non-Hopi Pueblo artists who wish to make commercial items with Katsina imagery will sometimes circumvent the restrictions of their communities by using Hopi Katsinam rather than their own. Yvonne Louis, whose father was Hopi and mother Laguna, spent her early years at Paguate, near Laguna. She began carving around 1984 and since 1989 has been doing miniatures. Her tiny figures, often Kooyemsi or Koyaala, are constructed from toothpicks and mounted on branches like a tree (fig. 3.75). Louis uses both Hopi and Zuni figures but is not allowed to represent those from Acoma or Laguna "at the risk

of being disenrolled or shunned by the tribe" (this according to a biography issued by Andrews Pueblo Pottery and Art Gallery, Albuquerque, in 1992).

The case of the Zuni in New Mexico is more complex than that of the Rio Grande communities. Unlike the Rio Grande Pueblos, Zunis have not barred outsiders from all Katsina ceremonies, and they have not stopped producing Katsina imagery, but community and religious leaders have placed restrictions on the representation and sale of Katsinam (see B. Wright 1989, 70). Zuni attempts to carve commercially have sometimes been accompanied by subterfuge and severe social disapproval. "[A]t one period not even a painting of the kachinas was

3.77A,B Zuni Katsinam. (A, LEFT) Shalako, 1900–1935. Wood, pigment, hair, muslin, wool, and deerskin. H: 114.3 cm. (B, CENTER) Wakashi (Cow Katsina), circa 1920. Wood, pigment, calf hide, hair, and beads. H: 26.7 cm. Courtesy of the Southwest

Museum, Los Angeles, (A) 648.G.84, photograph by Larry Reynolds; (B) 648.G.93, photograph by Don Meyer.

3.78 (RIGHT) Tiffany Tsabetsaye, Messenger. Wood and pigment. H: 21.6 cm. Collection of Sunshine Studio, Santa Fe.

allowed to be made under the threat of ostracism from the pueblo. Any doll that was sold was delivered to buyers after store hours in plainly wrapped packages, and those who bought such dolls found that they could not display them without fear of losing other Zuni customers" (B. Wright 1989, 70–71). Similarly, in 1968, when Zuni artist Duane Dishta made a number of figurines for sale, he kept his identity secret. When his activities eventually became public knowledge, he stopped this production "in the face of village disapproval" (B. Wright 1985, 4). Many Zuni people have therefore resisted making Katsinam and other ceremonial items for sale.

There are Zuni carvings in museum collections dating from the turn of the twentieth century, but they are rare compared with Hopi examples, and there is less information about them available. Nonetheless, they have been studied (see B. Wright 1985, 2–3). They look different than those of Hopis. While Hopis render all the detail through paint and carving, Zunis only paint the areas not covered by

the clothing, which they make separately (figs. 3.77A,B). Zunis dress the figurines in miniature costumes, including moccasins, with the garments "decorated with bits of cloth sewn on to show the designs of kilts and sashes." Coral and turquoise bracelets, necklaces, and pendants ornament the figurines, which hold tiny ceremonial objects (B. Wright 1989, 70).

Restrictions at Zuni, however, are not consistent, and their severity, at least in the last few decades, has waxed and waned. E. Charles Adams documents that six Zuni carvings were available for sale in 1991, and Ellen Reisland notes that they were actively being made in 1995 (personal communication, 1995); but at this writing in 1998, figurines for sale are forbidden by the Tribal Council, and there are none in the Pueblo. Nevertheless, some Zuni carvers, presumably driven by economic necessity or perhaps disagreement with tribal authorities, provide Katsina carvings to trading posts a few miles from the reservation boundary or even sell

3.79

3.80

them privately at the Pueblo. Officials know about these carvings but sometimes simply dismiss them as of no consequence (James Ostler, personal communication, 1994). Some Zuni artists who produced Katsina carvings for sale in the 1990s, like Tiffany Tsabetsaye, have been influenced by Hopis (fig. 3.78). Tsabetsaye carves in the sculptural style initiated by Wilmer Kaye around 1980 and adopted by many Hopi carvers. Ben Seciwa, however, continues in the traditional Zuni style (fig. 3.79), dressing his figures and adorning them with jewelry (see T. Bassman 1996,14–15).

Like Hopis, some Zunis consider two-dimensional representations of Katsina imagery more abstract and less controversial than the three-dimensional figurines. At least some Zunis feel that if the artwork does not threaten traditional ceremonials, then it is not necessary to restrict its manufacture (James Ostler, personal communication, 1994). Paintings of Katsinam were the subject of an exhibition held in 1994 at the A:shiwi A:wan Museum and Heritage

Center at Zuni Pueblo. Featured was the work of Filbert Bowannie, Ronnie Cachini, Duane Dishta, Phil Hughte, Chris Natachu, Eldred Sanchez, Patrick Sanchez, and Alex Seowtewa.[18] Today, Zuni paintings can be found in galleries and tourist stores throughout the Southwest, but this was not always the case. Barton Wright believes that "[t]he resistance to painting anything of a ceremonial nature…not only curtailed the representation of all ceremonial material" but also "deprived or seriously hampered the Zuni themselves in the exploration of creative avenues. For while the Zuni abound in gifted crafts-people who work in metal and stone, the number who have produced two-dimensional art of note is disproportionately small" (1985, 2–3).

Barbara Tedlock recounts the unusual case of Phil Hughte's Sa'lako mural at the Indian Pueblo Cultural Center in Albuquerque (1995, 166–67). The mural was painted over in 1981 when the governors of other New Mexico Pueblos found it objection-able because it depicted a religious scene. The Zuni

3.79 Ben Seciwa, Zuni Katsina, 1970s. Wood, cotton, yarn, animal hide, feathers, and pigment. H: 44.5 cm. Private collection.

3.80 Phil Hughte, *Cow Kachinas, Cows, and Calves*, 1993. Acrylic on canvas. 40.6 x 50.8 cm. Collection of James Ostler. Photograph © 2000 Dale W. Anderson.

3.81 Filbert Bowannie, Saiyatasha (Rain Priest of the North or Long Horn) and his deputy, Hututu, 1995. Watercolor on paper. 56.8 x 54.3 cm. Private collection.

3.81

governor, who had not been at the decision-making meeting, later issued a statement: "We [Zunis] were never contacted or consulted. We support the painting. We don't see any problems with it. The tribe gave its consent to the painting before it was done, and so did the Pueblo Council. It's not something anyone has ever complained about. Everyone in the tribe sees the Shalako during several days of ceremonies and even non-Indian people are allowed to see it during our ceremonies" (Ehn 1981, A-6, quoted in B. Tedlock 1995, 167). Today, the number of Zuni commercial painters remains small, especially compared with the number of Zuni creating jewelry and carving fetishes. When the Zuni paint, however, they are more likely than the Hopi to paint Katsinam. This may be because Zuni feel restricted in Katsina carving and use painting as an outlet for one of the most familiar aspects of their culture (figs. 3.80, 3.81).

As noted above, Zuni painter, Duane Dishta, has been representing Katsinam since the 1960s

(fig. 3.82). A set of his watercolors painted in 1966 is used to illustrate Barton Wright's *Kachinas of the Zuni* (1985). Dishta has continued to paint Katsinam, and in 1990 he won first prize at the Gallup Inter-Tribal Indian Ceremonial for a drum painted to depict the Katsinam associated with the four seasons (T. Bassman 1996, 98). Dishta, whose mother has some Hopi ancestry and who was inspired by the Hopi artists Roy Naha and Neil David Sr., will sometimes paint Hopi Katsinam, as in his *Spirits Coming from the Anasazi Ruins*, which illustrates both Hopi and Zuni Katsinam (T. Bassman 1996, 75, 88). "I paint in a very traditional way," states Dishta, "and I am inspired by my belief in my religion" (A:shiwi A:wan 1994).

A great many Zunis make jewelry, some estimate 30 percent of the population (fig. 3.83). Zunis have been jewelers for about one hundred years and began setting stones in the current Zuni fashion around 1940 (Adair 1944, 28; Ostler, Rodee, and Nahohai 1996, 57). While jewelry is crucial to the Zuni economy—about 99 percent is bought by outsiders—Zuni potter Milford Nahohai thinks the designs are still Zuni controlled. Some see jewelry as a statement about being Zuni. The tightly fitting pieces are "a metaphor for Zuni society where the members are held tightly together with minimal restraint and where each member depends on every other member to hold his or her position to make the whole work." Unlike the world outside, the Zuni do not compartmentalize into "costume jewelry, keepsake jewelry and, investment jewelry" (Ostler, Rodee, and Nahohai 1996, 30–31, 134).

A number of Zuni jewelers represent ceremonial figures and Katsinam. Frequently seen are Knifewing and Rainbow Man, figures who are important in

3.82 Duane Dishta, He li li, 1986. Oil on canvas. 30.5 x 23 cm. Private collection.

Zuni traditions but are not Katsinam and lack the power of the latter (figs. 3.84A,B, 3.85A,B). Jewelers may use "these beings in their work at first before venturing on to the more powerful and potentially controversial beings" (Ostler, Rodee, and Nahohai 1996, 88). Large, complex Katsina images are constructed by jeweler Ed Beyuka generally as bolo ties

or standing figures. He is adept at intricate details like the baskets that some Katsinam carry (to put bad children in) and the hand-fashioned drums he uses as bolo tips (Ostler, Rodee, and Nahohai 1996, 90–91; T. Bassman 1996, 35, 50; see B. Wright 1985, 27). Forty years ago, Kathryn Sikorski considered Katsina images the finest examples of Zuni inlay.

3.83 Zuni pin with Kokosho (Good or Beautiful), 1981. Silver, mother of pearl, and turquoise. H: 4.4 cm. Private collection.

3.84A,B (A) Roger and Eva Cellicion, antelope-head pendant, 1990s. Silver with tortoise shell and abalone shell inlay. H: 8 cm. (B) Leonard Martza, Ahmetolela Okya (Rainbow Man Dancer) pendant, 1990s. Silver with turquoise inlay. H: 8.7 cm. Private collection.

3.85A,B (A) Zuni Katsina bolo, 1990s. Silver, turquoise, and leather. L: 28 cm. (B) Valentino Laweeka, bolo with Saiyatasha (Rain Priest of the North), 1990s. Silver, turquoise, and leather. L: 29.5 cm. Private collection.

3.86 Andrea Lonjose Shirley, Wolf Katsina pin. Silver, mother-of-pearl, turquoise, and coral. Photograph © 2000 Dale W. Anderson.

3.83

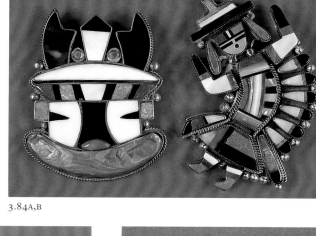

3.84A,B

3.85A,B

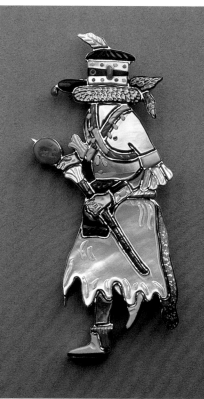

3.86

"The most beautiful inlays...are of ceremonial dancers or their masks. The inlay makers take great pains to make these realistic, using orange shell for faces and hands, green turquoise for leafy collars and iridescent gray abalone shell for fur. The lines of small details such as fingers and feathers may be engraved to make the figures still more life like" (Sikorski 1958, 11). Zuni jewelers will, on occasion, represent Hopi Katsinam and the Hopi version of the Kooyemsi.

While Ostler, Rodee, and Nahohai feel that it is "not considered proper for a woman to make kachina jewelry," a number of Zuni women have done so (1996, 91). In fact, the most elaborate production of Zuni Katsina imagery in jewelry involved two women, one Zuni and one Navajo. In the 1980s Bill Harmsen commissioned 130 metal Katsinam from Zuni Ida Poblano, who created the mosaic inlay Katsinam, and Mary Morgan, a Navajo silversmith who made the silver settings under the guidance of Jim Turpen (B. Wright 1988, x–xi, 4–7). One of the most prolific woman jewelers using Katsina imagery is Andrea Lonjose Shirley (fig. 3.86) who constructs intricately designed pins (Ostler, Rodee, and Nahohai 1996, 31; T. and M. Bassman 1992, 28, 34; T. Bassman 1996, 47).

Los Angeles jeweler Michael Horse, whose ancestry includes Zuni, Apache, Latino, and European, began using Katsina imagery in jewelry in 1973 (see Artist Profile VI, this volume). For him, there is a difference between carving Katsinam and representing them in other materials. He draws his images from both Hopi and Zuni Katsinam but creates what he calls "contemporary images" or "stylized figures." Sometimes, his representations are generic: "I do contemporary versions, but they are not any particular Katsina." He emphasizes that he only works with the Katsinam that "he knows" and that there are some that he can not represent. "There are certain Katsinas that my clan has nothing to do with that I can't do.... There are certain ones I won't do.... I try to be very respectful.... I ask permission" (Horse, personal communication, 1994).

Non-Pueblo Appropriation and Imitation

Tourism in Indian country is far more complicated than either a simple declensionist construction or the Shangri-la view that it is replacing.

Hal K. Rothman, *Reopening the American West*

Non-Pueblo Artists

There are hundreds of artists—non-Pueblo Indians and non-Indians—who have appropriated and capitalized on the selling power of Hopi Katsina imagery (figs. 3.88, 3.89).[19] Their work is pervasive in Southwest art and tourist shops. Only a few are considered here. Interpretations of Katsina imagery range from fairly accurate reproductions to sketchy resemblances (fig. 3.87). Diane Branam, who constructs wooden Katsina-like images in the intarsia method (see Artist Profile II, this volume), aims "to achieve a lifelike figure and one as authentic as possible" (see also Duarte 1998). In contrast, painter Poteet Victory (see Artist Profile XI, this volume) never tries "to reproduce specific Katsinas," instead depicting his own interpretation. These non-Pueblo artists bring to their work varying degrees of understanding of Hopi culture. Some are well acquainted with Pueblo life, others have never visited Hopi.

The artists interviewed for this project all express respect for the Hopi. Jeweler David Freeland (see Artist Profile IV, this volume) states that he began using Katsina-like imagery "to honor the Hopi." Non-Pueblo artists are drawn to Katsina imagery by what they see as the beauty of the Katsinam (Diane Branam and John Farnsworth, see Artist Profiles II VII, this volume) or because of the spirituality of the supernaturals. Painter Tom Perkinson notes: "When I came to New Mexico, I felt the spiritual impact of the katsina image, and because I was deeply moved by it, the katsina image became a central theme of my work."[20]

Some artists are aware of potential infringement. Christopher Pardell (see Artist Profile IX, this volume) who combines bronze, pewter, and gold for his sculptures, states: "Sensitive to the beliefs of the Hopi and Zuni, I hold that only *they* can make true katsinas, and in any event, certainly not in metal. I wanted to create figures depicting, not the katsinas themselves, but Native Americans [dancing] the katsinas as they do in ceremonials." Jean Healey (see Artist Profile XIII, this volume) did not crochet Katsina-like figures when she was first asked because she "knew that some members of the Hopi nation objected to anyone, including their own people, selling Katsina representations, and [she] didn't want to offend anyone." Painter John Farnsworth (see Artist Profile VII, this volume) notes that he is "not trying to replicate or imitate Katsinas" but rather to report on them. These artists, therefore, knowingly or instinctively feel the need to remove themselves somewhat from the Hopi domain.

Sculptor Charlie Pratt, who lives in Santa Fe, is one of several artists who have made life-size Katsina-like representations. Raised in southwestern Oklahoma by a grandfather who was half-French and half-Cheyenne, Pratt was attracted to bronze sculptures as a teenager, and when he got a job in an automobile body shop, he transformed discarded car parts into sculpture. Pratt works directly with metal (usually bronze or brass), welding it into shape with an acetylene torch (Pearson 1989, 96, 98). Southwest influence led him to masked dancers with removable masks made of brass, leather, or bronze. His *Corn Dancer* of patinaed and welded

brass is ninety-six inches tall; it was modeled after Hopi examples (fig. 3.90). When it was displayed at a Gallup Inter-Tribal Indian Ceremonial, some Hopis noticed the figure without its mask and insisted that the mask be permanently returned to the figure (Pratt, personal communication, 1997; Pearson 1989, 100).[21] Another Pratt sculpture is a forty-five-inch, welded brass Mudhead-like image wearing a wristwatch and consuming a Snickers bar and a Pepsi (Pearson 1989, 98).

Large images in wood are made by Ralph Gallagher, a sculptor of Irish ancestry married to a Navajo. His four-foot, wooden Katsina-like sculptures

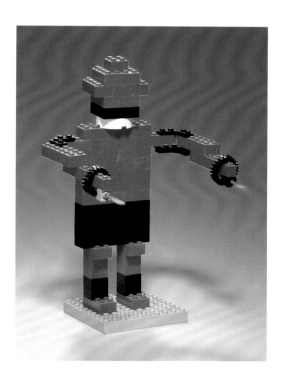

3.87 Hayden and Cary Speck, Lego Katsina-like figure, 1990s. Plastic Lego blocks. H: 23.5 cm. Private collection. Euro-American children Hayden and Cary Speck were inspired to create a Katsina-like figure of their own invention using Lego blocks. Private collection.

3.88 Bookends with Hopi-style Katsina figure. Museum of Indian Arts and Culture/Laboratory of Anthropology, Museum of New Mexico, Bequest of Margaret Moses, 50230/12. Photograph by Blair Clark.

3.89 Gourd with Katsina imagery purchased at a Las Vegas, Nevada, flea market, 1993. Private collection.

appear to be influenced by cigar-store Indian figures (fig. 3.91). In 1994, large metal Katsina-like forms by Tony Price stood at Biosphere 2 in Oracle, Arizona, north of Tucson (fig. 3.92). Tom Perkinson, a Euro-American artist, who sells his work through a Santa Fe gallery, describes his style of painting with Katsina-like imagery as "visionary." His work is rooted in Surrealism but investigates "Southwestern subject matter, including Native American art, sand paintings, pottery, weaving, Kachina figures, and the bright colors and drama of Native American dances and ceremonies." He starts his paintings and then allows a "state of flow" to occur, looking for figures to appear that can be developed in a chosen direction. Perkinson sees his "visionary paintings as an exploration of universal spirituality and the balance of nature," alluding to symmetry and "achieving a harmonious balance" between forms and figures. He strives "to create mystery that becomes convincing to the viewer. One can step into this world, and investigate his or her own imagination, subconscious, and spiritual reality" (artist's statement, provided by Deborah Hudgins Fine Art and Rio Grande Gallery, Santa Fe, August 1996).

Perkinson claims that he would do his paintings whether they sold or not because of the inner reward that he receives (personal communication,

1997), but George Aiazzi of Sparks, Nevada, carves Katsina-like figures that he does not even attempt to sell. "I'm not a Hopi and I don't know if it's all right for me to be doing this…. I shy away from [Hopis] because I don't want to infringe." Aiazzi, who uses only cottonwood root, plans to carve every Katsina image he can find. His business card reads "'Hopi Inspired' kachinas by G. Bahana." *Bahana* is the Hopi word for Europeans and Euro-Americans. Aiazzi notes one problem of the non-Hopi sculptor: "The pictures in the books only show them from the front. That makes it hard to carve the backs" (McCune 1993).

Upscale Southwest shops abound with Katsina-like objects or Katsina imagery that adorns lamps, mirrors, and items of furniture (fig. 3.93). Greg Gowen, who sells his pieces through Gowen Arts in Albuquerque, and Kathy Kohl, who sells through the Mescalero Trading Post, both make large copper masks with Katsina-like features.[22] Other artists use pressed paper or gourds. Many construct jewelry. Ruben M. Gallegos, a native of northern New Mexico, produces what he calls "eggshell art" (fig. 3.94). Katsina-like images are hand painted onto eggshells, which are sometimes attached to a base as one item in a tableau. These works, Gallegos tells us, reflect his "style in both the Indian and Spanish heritage."

3.90

3.91

3.90 Charlie Pratt, Corn Dancer, circa 1989. Patinated, welded brass. H: 243.9 cm. Photograph © Jerry Jacka

3.91 Ralph Gallagher, figure resembling Sun Katsina standing in front of a Santa Fe shop. Photograph by Zena Pearlstone, 1995.

3.92 Tony Price, *Rockette Nuclear Kachina*, 1994. This sculpture was created to stand in front of Biosphere 2 in Oracle, Arizona, north of Tucson. It has since been removed.

3.93 Katsina-influenced decorative object. Collection of Richard C. Trexler.

3.94 Ruben M. Gallegos, Katsina-like images painted on eggshell, circa 1990. Eggshell and pigment. H: 7 cm. Private collection.

One Native American artist appears sensitive to the Hopis' wishes that the term *Katsina* not be used by outsiders. Kenneth Banks, a Kumeyaai/Diegueno from Southern California created a limited edition of two shadow box figures—Yellow Corn Girl and Morning Singer—"cast in wood pulp and gypsum, individually hand painted, lavishly decorated with feathers and attractively framed in a blond hardwood." Banks calls his figures Shadow Box Messengers.[23]

Navajo

Most offensive to the majority of Hopis are non-Pueblo made objects that mimic their carvings. The Hopis see the Navajo as the worst offenders in this category. Milland Lomakema Sr. believes that the Navajo were the first to appropriate Hopi imagery, thus beginning the present ubiquitous Katsina imitation (personal communication, 1995). *Tithu* carving, as noted, has special significance for Hopi men. Even if made for sale, Hopi carvers feel a religious kinship with these objects and emphasize that only those who have participated in ceremonies can truly re-create the dancers. Carving of Katsina figures, many note, cannot be learned from books. Some Hopi have no objection to Navajo production as long as the portrayals are accurate and respectful (David, see Artist Profile 1, this volume), but they

seldom are. The history of Navajo "Katsina" production provides the clearest window onto the complexities of today's Southwest tourist market.

Navajo Katsina-like figurines by now have a history of about fifty years. Labeled "kachina curios" by Barry Walsh (1994, 6), these items were first made by Navajos for tourists in the 1950s (fig. 3.95). In 1957 Paul Coze noted that "Of the thousands [of imitation Katsina figurines] sold every year at roadside stands, few are the ritual dolls made by [Pueblo] carvers; most are turned out by Indian employees of white men" (1957, 222). Production may have increased in 1973 when a Euro-American dealer in Gallup showed the just-published *Kachinas: A Hopi Artist's Documentary* by Barton Wright to some Navajo and suggested they copy the figures (Bromberg 1986, 57).

These imitations were sold for quite a while before they began to attract media attention. Two articles appearing in the *Indian Trader* in 1980 indicate that at the time, the trade in non-Hopi carvings was still not well publicized. The first article, which appeared in August 1980, noted the "booming kachina business." The second appeared in the following issue (September) with the confession that the reporters had "managed to miss what may be the biggest story...that a sizable percentage of the

3.92

3.93

3.94

kachina doll market is not made up of Hopi crafted dolls at all, but rather of the imitation figures produced by non-Hopi carvers." They further reported that many retailers around the country were unaware that they were buying non-Hopi products. Surveying shops in Tucson, they did not find anyone overtly claiming that the Navajo work was Hopi but did notice that there were "a number of stores that sell the two dolls side by side without plainly labeling their different origins" (fig. 3.96).[24]

The number of Navajo-made figurines jumped dramatically between 1992 and 1994 when individual production was supplemented by the output of five doll-making factories, which opened in western New Mexico (figs. 3.97, 3.98A,B). The factories, all Euro-American owned with Navajo workers, include Kachina Traders and the Kachina Connection in Thoreau and Traveling Traders and Inter-Tribal Traders in Milan. Several more have started operations since then, including Powwow Traders in Holbrook, Arizona. Steve Roberts, manager of a Thoreau, New Mexico, factory, says that these "'largely machine-cut' products can be turned out in two and one half hours compared with months for a Hopi carving" (Shaffer and Donovan 1994, A11). Mike Ross, owner of Kachina Traders, says that his factory employs about thirty to thirty-five Navajos at a time (Walsh 1994, 6). Each worker produces eighty to one hundred carvings a day, and in addition the owners buy pieces from Navajos who make them at home. In 1994 Walsh estimated that over one hundred thousand carvings a year were produced. Today the total would be well beyond that number.

The huge number of Navajo-made figures on the market these days cannot be missed. Large trading posts in the Southwest carry staggering numbers of these carvings, and more are shipped out to stores around the country. It is probably safe to say that

3.95 Commercial Katsina-like figure. Museum of Indian Arts and Culture/ Laboratory of Anthropology, Museum of New Mexico, Gift of Byron Harvey III, 25571/12. Photograph by Blair Clark.

3.96 Navajo balsawood figure, pre-1972. Museum of Indian Arts and Culture/ Laboratory of Anthropology, Museum of New Mexico, Bequest of P. Stockton, 46144/12. Photograph by Blair Clark.

3.97 Imitation Katsina *tihu* manufactured in a Euro-American doll-making factory using Navajo labor, 1990s. Wood, leather, synthetic fur, and feathers. H: 29 cm. Private collection.

there is hardly a business catering to tourists in the Southwest that does not carry them. Unlike the marketing of 1980, the biases in advertising are now often blatant (Hall 1996). Signs scream "We sell Hopi Kachina Dolls," but inside there are two and the remainder are Navajo. Tom Hall has been told that Hopi and Navajo practice the same religion and that Hopi works are more expensive because of the wood used. Most of us who shop or ask questions in the Southwest have heard similar stories. Often the salesperson has no idea of Katsina history or of the differences between Hopi and Navajo religion and art. Tourists, if they are aware at all of the issue, are commonly bewildered.

Most of the mass-produced pieces retail for twenty-five to one hundred dollars, but some are more expensive. Barry Walsh (1994) reported six-foot-tall eagle figures at Inter-Tribal Traders for over two thousand dollars. Often they are sold by the inch. In the mid-1990s Tasia, a wholesale mail order company located in Tucson, sold four-inch dolls for twenty-five dollars, eight-inch dolls for forty dollars, and up to twenty-four-inch figures for one hundred and seventy dollars (fig. 3.99). The figures bear only a superficial resemblance to Hopi products and would not be mistaken for them by knowledgeable purchasers. The factory products are hurriedly and awkwardly constructed. Unlike Hopi carvings, which are usually sensitive to the human figure, these "carvings" simply cover a central shaft with paint, fur, feathers, and some leather clothing (fig. 3.100). A large number of personages can be represented by changing the heads, the colors, and the handheld items. Fur and leather rarely appear on *tithu*. The leather—generally in the form of fringes—gives these figurines a Plains cast that their makers presumably

think allows the buyer to be more comfortable with their "Indianness." The figurines with removable masks further distance these objects from those made by the Hopi and add to Hopi discomfort.

These objects do not fall comfortably into any of the categories of fakes, forgeries, or copies. When directly questioned, few will try to pass them off as Pueblo made. Sellers will, however, play on the public's lack of understanding of Indians and the differences among them. Many people remain ignorant of the fact that certain images and objects may be felt to be the exclusive property of one or a few Indian nations. What the Navajos and Euro-Americans in the business play on is the name *Katsina*, for even a brief comparison of Hopi carvings with Navajo mass-produced figurines would reveal the enormous differences. Navajos can be accused of "copying" in only the most general sense. The term *Katsina*, however, and a vague facsimile of a

3.98A,B. Navajo workers in a New Mexico "Katsina" factory. (A) woodworking station—workers attach bodies to bases. (B) pigmenting station. Photographs by Barry Walsh, 1994.

Hopi product are enough to separate tourists from their dollars.

Hopis see in these carvings an affront to their religion, the usurpation of private supernaturals, and betrayals of confidential information. In addition, they see inaccurate representations and sloppy workmanship. Ivan Sydney, a former Hopi tribal chairman, finds it "upsetting to see the Navajo dolls being sold in the arts and crafts stores. Their facial markings are out of order. Their feathers are not placed right. To us, that's very serious. It's like creating a baby doll with an amputated leg" (Donovan 1987, 4). Vernell Vaughn of Polacca underscores how foreign they look to Hopis, "Navajo dolls look like aliens to me." Verlinda Adams of Polacca cites their lack of authenticity, "If they are going to copy our dolls, the Navajos should at least do it right" (Walsh 1994). Wallace Hyeoma, a carver from Songoopavi, feels that "Navajos shouldn't be making kachina dolls. They don't believe in kachinas and kachinas are not part of their culture. If they are going to carve, they should do their own gods, the Yeiis."[25] Hopi leaders were appalled that a factory in Thoreau, New Mexico, advertised on the radio for Katsina painters, sanders, carvers, and dressers.[26]

Other Hopis object but lay the blame on the Hopi themselves. Herman Lewis, a Hopi Katsina priest at First Mesa for more than five decades, felt that "the crass commercialization has occurred because Hopis started selling their own dolls." But if he cannot stop his own from selling the dolls, he would like to see non-Hopis stop the practice (Guthrie 1987). Kuwanwisiwma (this volume) addresses some of the complexities of these concerns.

Henry Gatewood II, a Navajo woodcarver living in Chandler, Arizona, has argued that Katsina dolls are not exclusively Hopi—wooden dolls, he feels, could be Yeibichais (Navajo spiritual beings) or from Zuni or Laguna. "There are all types of dolls carved from cottonwood root. And when it comes to Indian art, tribal blood does not decree what one can create. It's like the Navajo saying 'I'm a silversmith so you Hopis can't be.' These days anything is art. If it's done right, anyone should be allowed to pursue it." Gatewood states that he learned about Katsinam from his Hopi friends and always marks his as being made by a Navajo (Guthrie 1987, 2).

The issue is fueled by the long history of Hopi/Navajo antagonisms over land and resource rights. The Navajo Nation in geography and population is much larger than that of the Hopi, which it surrounds. In the late 1980s the Hopi Cultural Preservation Office raised the issue of cultural property and tribal rights with regard to Navajo Katsina-like figurines. Hopis argue that they have proprietary rights to their own culture; Navajos have no tradition of Katsinam and are therefore encroaching on Hopi culture. Hopis also note that mass production of

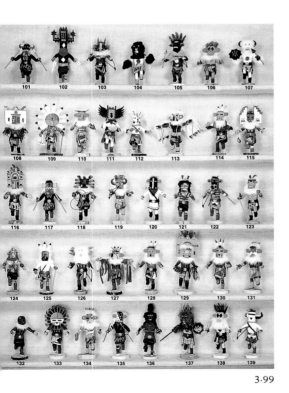

3.99 "Katsina" selection from Tasia, a wholesale mail-order company, mid-1990s. As is common, these "Katsina" figures are priced by the inch.

3.100 Factory-made "Katsina" figures for sale at the Gallup Inter-Tribal Indian Ceremonial. Photograph by Zena Pearlstone, 1994.

3.99   3.100

Katsinam is neither traditional nor authentic. The Hopi view is conservative, seeing a people's tradition as culturally exclusive.[27] Paul D. Gonzales from San Ildefonso Pueblo addresses the issue with a Rio Grande perspective. "The only way to maintain the sanctity of any religious object or cultural artifact is not to reproduce it for sale to the general public. The individual tribal member…has a responsibility to the community to honor the religious practices of one's tribe.... Any Indian person who uses images from another tribe must make it his or her responsibility to understand how and why those images are used and understand when one is crossing the line. When an artist crosses the line he should do it with the full understanding that his or her action is sacrilegious according to the tribe that uses the images in ceremony" (Gonzales 1996, 30–31). Deirdre Evans-Pritchard terms these Pueblo positions a "nostalgic view of tradition," given today's ethnographic complexities (1990, 123 n. 18).

Navajos see it differently. A common view is that Pueblo Katsinam are now part of the common Southwest Indian heritage and therefore open to all for economic purposes. The issue is compounded by the artistic history of the two peoples, for the Navajo, much more than the Pueblos, have long been known for their eclecticism in absorbing the art forms and techniques of other cultures (see Evans-Pritchard 1990, 123 n. 18). Hopis speaking to this issue point out that they do not make or use Navajo Yeibichai figures in their art. The Hopi, in fact, seldom draw on the art of any other Native People.[28]

It is common for Navajos to see the making of Katsina-like figures as simply a livelihood. Duane Beyal, who was assistant to former Navajo president Peterson Zah, voices the opinion of many Navajo when he says: "All the Navajos want to do is earn a living." Further he thinks that if anyone should be blamed it is the non-Indians who have set up the factories (Shaffer and Donovan 1994, 11). One of these non-Indians, Mike Ross, counters with the fact that they are providing jobs that would not be available otherwise. His father, Bob Ross, owner of Inter-Tribal Traders, states that: "we fill a need in the wholesale market for an inexpensive doll of consistent quality." He is opposed, however, to selling them as Hopi products (Walsh 1994, 7–8).

The popularity of the Navajo figures is certainly tied to their price. When the cost of Hopi carvings soared, many tourists and some collectors found them outside of their price range and were attracted to the less-expensive representations. Unless tourists are at Hopi or an art gallery, Navajo figures are the ones that they are more likely to see. Even museum gift shops, nowadays, at times carry non-Pueblo, Katsina-like carvings and, unfortunately, sometimes identify them as Hopi. Navajo carvings can be found at shops about an hour's drive from Hopi at prices far lower than the Hopi pieces sold in the villages.

The sales of these carvings may also underscore an authenticity communicated through repetition. Christopher Steiner, writing about West African tourist art, notes that multiple images, like Navajo carvings, are common in the marketplace (1999). If presented with an image frequently enough, the buyer may eventually code it as "what is most desirable to collect." Today, since Navajo carvings are one of the most frequently encountered items in the Southwest, they can quickly become associated with "Indian Katsina" or "Southwest Indians." Seen repeatedly, these mass-produced images may come to seem more authentic than the less-available originals on which they are loosely based. Further, for some tourists, these immobile images may seem more like the pictures they have seen of early twentieth-century Hopi *tithu* than do many of the complex Hopi carvings of today, thus further increasing their seeming authenticity. "Tourist arts," Steiner argues, "are structured around heavily redundant messages," and tourists are looking for "the forms they already know." Like stacks of a bestseller in a bookstore window or a supermarket display of oranges or crackers, the objects are appealing partly because their large numbers speak to familiarity. Wholesaler Erik Bromberg's thoughts of twenty years ago, which are echoed by some dealers today, may, in fact, be the reverse of the truth. Bromberg feels that "Navaho dolls are suitable for people, especially tourists, who are just looking for a souvenir and to whom authenticity is not that important."[29] Perhaps, Steiner suggests, these dolls are suitable because some tourists see them as defining authenticity.

An economic assessment of Navajo carvings on the market is not available, but some dealers feel that Hopi sales have not suffered despite the increased Navajo production. John Kennedy, a wholesaler of Navajo figures in Gallup, thinks that the Hopi are selling all they make and that others are addressing the extra demand. A number of Hopi carvers whose work is in the moderate range, around one hundred dollars, told me that they sell Katsinam as fast as they can make them (see Jackson, Artist Profile III, this volume). This does not mean that all Hopi carvings sell this well. In 1987 Jim Turpen, manager of Tobe Turpen's in Gallup, felt that the market for Hopi Katsinam had not changed. He said that he would carry more Hopi carvings if he could get them, but most Hopi sell directly to their own sources (Donovan 1987, 5). A few mail-order companies told me that they, too, would rather sell Hopi, than Navajo, products but that there are marketing problems (Pearlstone, forthcoming). Janice Jackson of Simply Southwest said they get theirs from the Navajos because they cannot get a steady supply from the Hopi (personal communication, 1995). Even Becky Masayesva, the founder of a short-lived Hopi mail-order company, said that she could not get the Hopi artists to do carvings on time and therefore did not have enough to sell (personal communication, 1995).

Many Hopis, however, are convinced that imitation art—including jewelry and to a lesser extent pottery, baskets, and carvings—is hurting them economically (fig. 3.101). The situation became more public in November of 1993 when the Hopi hosted a seminar on "Fakes, Imitation and Fraud in the Indian Arts and Crafts Market" for about fifty Arizona and western New Mexico artists, business leaders, collectors, dealers, and media members. At this gathering, the Arizona Attorney General's Office reported on cases of consumer fraud. In February 1996 Hopi leaders asked the Arizona legislature to make it a violation of Arizona's Consumer Fraud Act to sell any item purported to be the work of one tribe when it is made by members of another tribe. Then Hopi Chairman Ferrell Secakuku noted that Hopis take special exception to the sale of Katsina dolls that others claim to be authentically Hopi. "Kachina" he stated

is a traditional Hopi word that has been used for centuries. We consider it [Katsina] to be the intellectual property and part of the heritage of the Hopi people. Our people have occupied the vast region of the southwest for tens of thousands of years and today reside in villages continuously inhabited for at least one thousand years. We view ourselves as the first inhabitants of these lands and continue to practice a cultural and religious lifeway that is ancient and still in its original form.[30]

The bill was defeated in April 1996 in the Arizona House of Representatives. Some House members were concerned about state involvement with "tribal affairs." Senator James Henderson, a Navajo Democrat from Window Rock, felt that the bill singled out Navajo factory workers. Representative Jack C. Jackson, also a Navajo Democrat from Window Rock, thought the bill discriminated against both Hopis and Navajos who married outside of their nation. "This bill would deny these children the chance to practice whichever tribal customs they choose" (McBride 1996, 23). An amendment that

3.101 *Hopi Tutuveni,* October 11, 1996, vol. 6, no. 1. In February of 1996 the Hopis asked the Arizona legislature to make it a violation of Arizona's Consumer fraud Act to sell any item purported to be the work of one tribe when it was made by members of another. The bill was defeated in April 1996

3.102 Brochure published by the Hopi Foundation, January 1996, warning consumers of imitation Hopi arts and crafts items on the market. © 1995 The Hopi Foundation.

3.101

3.102

would have marked it a violation of the consumer fraud act to sell falsely identified Native American products was defeated the following month. The amendment would have allowed retailers or customers to bypass the Attorney General's Office if suing for damages (McBride 1996; Joseph 1996a).

Around this time, the Hopi Foundation published a brochure entitled "Buyer Beware of Fake and Imitation Hopi Arts and Crafts" (fig. 3.102). It was first released in January 1996 in Scottsdale during the Super Bowl and provided to shops and galleries on and off the Hopi Reservation. The brochure states that "The Hopi are the true owners of their cultural heritage. Only the Hopi and their Pueblo relatives have esoteric manifestations called Kachinas within their culture. The challenge for the Hopi is to protect and preserve Hopi culture, arts, crafts and individual trademarks." Sections are titled "Owners of an Ancient Cultural Heritage," "Trademark: 'The Individual Mark or Signature,'" and "What the Buyer Can Do." Boxed messages note that "100,000 imitation and fake Kachinas are placed into the stream of the Indian art market each year," and "Kachina dolls are mass produced in factories by non-Hopis.... Beware."[31]

The brochure, in addition to emphasizing issues of cultural property and consumer fraud, also points out the economic importance of art to the Pueblo. "Fake and imitation arts and crafts hurt the self

employment status of the Hopi. It literally erodes the economic self determination and self reliance of the entire tribe." It is thus of interest that the appearance of the brochure coincided with the threat of a federal budget cut, a time when Hopis were feeling pressured to absorb more tourist dollars (Masayesva 1996). The Hopi must increasingly juggle the issues of cultural property and economic concern, each clearly of paramount importance (Joseph 1996b). For a people who have resisted providing services for tourists (see Rivera 1990, 142–77), it is revealing that Wayne Taylor Jr., Hopi chairman as of December 1997, has promised to develop a program for tourism. Richard Tewa, acting director of economic development, has said that tourism is the "only real economic development tool in the reservation" (Beyal 1998, 21–22).

In the late 1980s, mass-produced Navajo figurines began to find their way out of the Southwest through mail-order catalogs (fig. 3.103). This fad peaked in the mid-1990s when about eight companies were marketing the figurines. Today, in 2000, there is, to the best of my knowledge, only one company still selling these figures. Most Navajo figurines sold through mail-order range between seventy and one hundred and sixty dollars, and are hand assembled of mass-produced parts. When I asked some company spokespeople if they had had input from the Pueblos, all said no. William McCarthy, spokesman for the

3.103 Page from the Southwest Indian Foundation catalog, Christmas 1993.

3.104 In 1988 a company called Kachina Country USA advertised a "Doll of the Month Club" where participants would receive a different "Navajo Kachina doll" each month. This advertisement appeared in *The Indian Trader*, September 1998: 20.

3.103

3.104

Southwest Indian Foundation, the largest marketer of these items, told me that they had never had feedback from Hopis but that everyone knows Hopis are just generally unhappy with Katsina sales (personal communication, 1995). Navajo carvers, he argued, were simply economically motivated, and he could not understand why anyone would object since Indians were profiting from the sales. There is, however, on file at the Hopi Cultural Preservation Office a copy of a letter from Leigh J. Kuwanwisiwma, the office's director, to the Southwest Indian Foundation protesting the sale of Navajo-made figurines as "a gross misrepresentation of genuinely Hopi carved dolls."[32] In 1998 a company called Kachina Country USA (Milan, New Mexico) advertised a "Doll of the Month Club" through which doll collectors are encouraged "to start or complete [a] collection of hand-made Navajo Kachina dolls.... [which] will be rushed to your door." The advertisement concludes by reassuring potential purchasers that "[a]ll dolls are hand-signed by the artist including their tribes' census number to insure their authenticity!!"(fig. 3.104).[33]

The Navajo carvings, no matter how they are sold, represent a limited number of beings, not surprisingly those that can be easily identified by a non-Pueblo audience. Eagle is the most popular of the non-Pueblo made figurines, followed by Sun (fig. 3.105). Others for sale include Ogre, Corn

Dancer, Wolf, Buffalo, Rainbow, and clowns. Within each category the items are often more or less identical. The repetitive quality of the imagery echoes the stereotype that as all Indians are the same, so are their products. Despite their sameness, items are marketed as "unique" as well as "authentic," "timeless" as well as "contemporary."

The most pressing aspect of uniqueness is the signature. Both makers and sellers have learned that Euro-American purchasers value individuality, and thus signatures are a boon for sales. But signing of the Navajo figures sometimes seems almost an in-joke among carvers and marketers. Marks often cannot be read, or they are emblems. One is signed "9B." While the act of signing is emphasized, the persons presumably doing the signing—the artists—are never identified. The mail-order companies and manufacturers, although they have no qualms about identifying the artists as Navajo, will never reveal the names of these artists. In part, they are afraid of losing their workers, but also there is often more than one person involved in the manufacture. In contrast, Hopi carvings for sale are always clearly identified, sometimes with the artist's village and clan as well as his or her name.

By the mid-1990s the Navajo-made items had become prominent in gift and tourist stores outside of the Pueblo homelands. Far from the Southwest, figures called "Kachinas" were being made, sold,

EAGLE DANCER KACHINA
To traditional Native Americans of the southwest, Kachinas are spirit beings. Eagle Dancer has a special connection with the sun and sky, representing the eagle who carries prayers upward to the creator and brings back moisture for the crops. Each figure is hand-carved from native wood and meticulously decorated with feathers, leather and paint. Navajo artists add their own touches to make each Kachina unique. 10-12" tall; signed by the artist.
#7606 $75

3.105 Eagle is the most popular of the non-Pueblo made "Katsina" figures. This one was advertised in the Simply Southwest mail-order catalogue in the fall of 1994.

3.106 This "Certificate of Authenticity" accompanied a Katsina-like figure that was purchased in 1995 from a Navajo selling carvings from his pick-up truck in Los Angeles's San Fernando Valley. Private collection.

and bought by non-Pueblo people. The following examples indicate the widespread network. A letter dated January 26, 1994, from Diamond B Kachina Sales in Gallup, New Mexico, to Buffalo Barry's Indian Art in Worcester, Massachusetts, says in part: "I sell high quality Kachina dolls made by members of the Navajo Tribe. Each doll is shipped with a certificate of authenticity and story card" (fig. 3.106; Barry Walsh, personal communication, 1997). The certificates of authenticity state that the figures are "Kachinas" and made by a Navajo and sometimes have initials, presumably of the artist. Around the same time a woman in Ellsworth, Maine, established the Native American Collector's Guild, a "Katsina"-of-the-every-other-month-club. While the picture on the brochure is of a Navajo-made product, part of the copy reads "Every kachina doll is individually handcrafted by the Pueblo Indians so styles vary from Indian to Indian and Village to Village." In 1996, as a promotion for a book called *The Spirit World*, Time/Life Books offered the first fifty orderers a free "Kachina Doll." The brochure carried the following garbled copy:

> For the Navajo people, the spirits played an amazingly direct role in everyday life. When a community wished to invoke the power of a certain spirit, one of the tribesman would don a costume associated with that spirit...

and become instantly imbued with its super-natural power. Such a man was called a Kachina Dancer. For centuries, Navajo artisans have carved dolls based on the dozens of spirits represented by Kachina Dancers... each one believed to possess and transmit the power of its patron spirit.

Hopis were fortunately able to intervene before Time/Life made good on this offer.

The volume of Navajo carvings was reported to increase during the summer of 1998. Merchandisers had become aware of the widening European market (fig. 3.107). "The usually reserved Hopi people" were described as "fighting mad." Milland Lomakema Sr. noted that "[p]ractically every Hopi is concerned" (Cart 1998, A5). Leigh J. Kuwanwisiwma reported that Hopis were again seeking legislation to protect them from Navajo and other imitations (Donovan 1998, 5). Mass-produced Navajo figures are only the most prolific aspect of the Navajo market in "Katsinam." A number of Navajo carvers make individual items (fig. 3.108A,B). There are some Navajo master carvers such as Robert Chee whose work has earned the respect of Hopis like Neil David Sr. (see Artisti Profile 1). Some, like David's nephew, Kerry Lyle David, have both Hopi and Navajo ancestry. Other Hopis object to all non-Pueblo carvings. When a Navajo carving

THE INDIAN TRADER, SEPTEMBER, 1998 Page 5

The controversy heats up over Navajo dolls

BY BILL DONOVAN

WINDOW ROCK — Ever since the late 1970s, Navajos have been churning out dolls by the thousands that Hopi tribal leaders say are nothing more than "rip-offs" of the more celebrated Hopi kachinas.

Selling for prices that are a fraction of what people would pay for Hopi kachinas and costing Hopi craftsmen countless sales a year, Hopi officials have now begun fighting back, asking state and federal officials to implement legislation that would stop the Navajos from carving the imitation kachinas.

There are federal and state laws, said Leigh Jenkins, director of the Hopi Tribe's cultural preservation office, that protect Native American craftspeople from cheap imported copies that are made overseas by people who make less than a dollar a day in wages.

"We're asking for similar legislation that would protect tribes from imitations made by members of other tribes," he said. "If the Navajos want to carve something, why don't they carve Yeis, which have a religious significance in their traditions."

Yeis, which are Navajo dieties, are used in Navajo rugs and sandpaintings and a few Navajos do carve them. But there really is no big demand in the carving market today for Yeis as compared to kachinas.

The Navajo Tribe itself has stayed out of the dispute, with Navajo leaders saying that the tribe has no authority to tell its members what they can and cannot carve or make.

No one knows just how many Navajos are carving dolls that look a lot like kachinas but several "factories" have been set up in the eastern portion of the reservation with the Navajo imitations being produced in an assembly-type operation. And dealers admit that the Navajo dolls have basically taken over as the mainstay in the cheap, touristy market where the Navajo dolls go for as little as $10 and the average price is in the $50 and below range.

At the same time, cheap kachinas can cost about $100 and the more expensive ones go up to the thousands.

For the Hopis, kachinas are sacred religious objects, modeled after tribal dieties, and carved by Hopi men to give to women or for children, to remind them what the dieties look like during the time of the year when no ceremonies are done.

See DOLLS on page 6

A HOPI-CARVED EAGLE KACHINA

A NAVAJO-CARVED EAGLE DOLL

3.107 During the summer of 1998, Hopis again sought legislation to protect themselves from Navajos and other imitators of *tithu*. This article appeared in *The Indian Trader*, September 1998.

3.108A,B Nate Jacobs,
Katsina-like figures. Wood
and pigment. Photographs
courtesy of the artist.

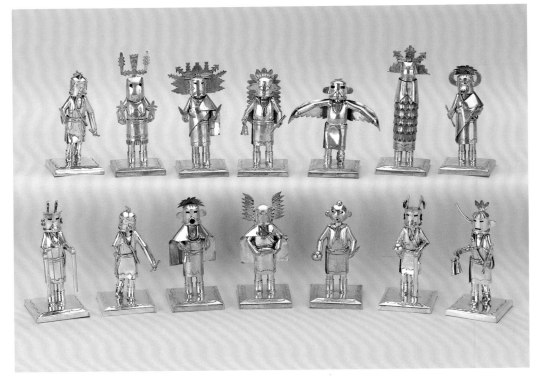

3.109 Navajo carving signed
"F. Chee '97" influenced by
the stylized figures of Wilmer
Kaye. Wood and pigment.
H: 37.5 cm. Private collection.

3.110 Jeffrey Castillo
(Navajo). Katsina-like
figures, 1980s. Handcrafted
silver. H (range): 10–12.7 cm.
Private collection.

won first prize at a judged competition in 1996, the artist was criticized by some for not having the "right" to do such a work (Gonzales 1996, 30). Other Navajos carve works of lesser status. They will frequently copy the styles of Hopi carvers of like abilities so that, unlike the factory-produced "Katsinam," which are easy to identify as such, it sometimes becomes virtually impossible to tell Hopi from Navajo products. In the past years there have been many Hopi and Navajo carvings influenced by the slim, stylized figures of Wilmer Kaye. This style is appealing to carvers because the bodies can be carved sparingly and there are no protruding limbs; therefore, they can be made fairly quickly. The labeling can be vague, as it is on the bottom of one such carving, "Prayer Long Hair Kachina by F. Chee '97" (fig. 3.109). There is no way of identifying this as non-Hopi or as Navajo unless the buyer happens to know that Chee is a Navajo name or unless it was labeled Navajo by the seller. Some Hopis feel that Navajos are selling such carvings by claiming that they are Hopi made (McBride 1996, 23).

Other Navajos paint Katsina images. One work by Ernest Franklin, which took first place in both the realistic painting category and the best of paintings at the 1995 Gallup Inter-Tribal Indian Ceremonial, caused a stir. Five Hopi tribal officials and elders protested the work, *Sacred Clowns*, which represents a Koyaala and Kooyemsi tug of war.[34] Franklin was criticized in the Hopi *Tutuveni* for doing the picture, and the Ceremonial was criticized for giving the award (Joseph 1995). Clifton Ami, a First Mesa council representative, was "dismayed [at seeing] a Navajo using Pueblo traditions and culture to win him honors and prestige. Navajos take advantage of foreign cultures and traditions to advance themselves." Leigh J. Kuwanwisiwma, director of the Hopi Cultural Preservation Office, equated the painting with the Marvel comic book, the Ezra Brooks liquor decanters (see fig. 3.134), and the movie *Dark Wind* as another instance of "Navajos appropriating Hopi culture without the permission of the Hopi and Tewa people" (Joseph 1995, 6). The director of the Ceremony said that no offense was intended and that the Hopi he had consulted were not offended.[35] Still other Navajos have turned their metal-working abilities to Katsina-like images (fig. 3.110). Three-dimensional silver images have become common and range from small—a few inches in height—to works like those of Lloyd Long, which can be several feet tall. Navajo jewelers like Ric Charlie integrate Katsina forms in pins and bolo ties.

It is easy to oversimplify this situation. Hopi-Navajo relations are long-standing and of enormous complexity (see Whiteley, this volume). The two Nations continue to have bitter conflicts, but at the same time there is a long history of intermarriage and cross-cultural friendships. There are probably some Hopi who teach their Navajo friends how to carve. Clearly there are Navajo who disdain the Hopi and do not care if they are profiting from Hopi imagery. Others are respectful of Katsinam but feel that the imagery is public property. To malign all Navajo regarding carving sales is a disservice to them and to ourselves. I was surprised to learn that well-informed Navajos living on or near the Navajo reservation were, until talking to me, totally unaware of the "Katsina controversy."

Souvenir Items

Navajo figure carvings are only a fraction of the many mass-produced items vying for tourist dollars. There are now dozens if not hundreds of objects bearing Katsina-like imagery marketed mainly through the tourist stores of the Southwest. Images of Katsina-like beings now occupy a marketing niche that most Americans usually reserve for the likes of Disney characters. For dining there are cups, coasters, placemats, and salsa labels (figs. 3.111A–C); for wearing, skirts, shirts, hats, jackets, and ties (figs. 3.112A–O); for adornment, earrings, bolo ties, pendants, and rings; for correspondence, postcards, notepaper, and pens; for household use, keychains, mouse pads, wrapping paper, and picture frames (figs. 3.113A–K, 3.114); for Christmas, tree ornaments and stockings. Almost all of these are designed, manufactured, and sold by non-Hopis capitalizing on the marketability of Katsina-like imagery. A few are Hopi designed; as noted earlier, Neil David Sr. has provided illustrations for notepaper cubes and T-shirts (see Artist Profile 1, this volume) and Anthony Honanie for wristwatches.

Mass-marketed items date back at least to the 1950s. The activity book *Kachina Dolls Cut and Color* (Albuquerque: Eukabi Publishers), with drawings by Eugene H. Bischoff and text by Kay Bischoff, was first published in 1950 (revised edition 1951; fig. 3.115). The book contains twenty-one color-coded drawings and a note from the authors that after coloring they should be cut out and mounted on cardboard for "a nice collection of Kachina paper dolls." The Bischoffs say that they "received valuable help from Chief Joe Secakuku, a Hopi Indian who markets Kachina dolls for the tourist

3.111A

3.111A–C Cups (C), coasters (B), and placemats in a variety of styles are available at a large number of tourist stores around the Southwest. The labels on jars of salsa produced by Goldwater's Foods of Arizona (A) feature Katsina-like imagery.

3.112A–O Practically any item of jewelry or outerwear can be found with "Katsina" imagery, including iron-on patches (A), earrings (B), button covers (C), and T-shirts (D–I). A Flagstaff company manufactures fabric (O) in a number of styles and colors. The shirt seen here (K) was homemade from such fabric. Private collection.

3.111B

3.112A

3.111C

3.112B

3.112C

3.112D

3.112E

3.112F

3.112G

3.112H

3.112I

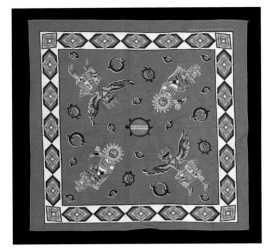

3.112J

3.112K

3.112L

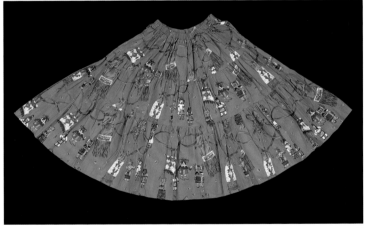

3.112M

3.112N

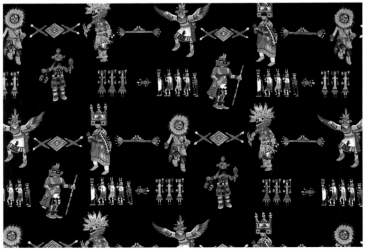

3.112O

3.113A

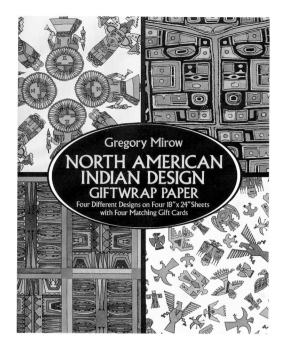

3.113B

3.113C

3.113D

3.113A–J Household items
with "Katsina" imagery,
including oven mitts (A),
gift wraps (B), note cubes (C),
magnets (D), light switch
plates (E), frames (F),
snow globes (G), pens (H),
decorative tiles (I), and night-
lights (J). Private collection.

3.113E

3.113F

3.113G

3.113H

3.113I

3.114A–C (A) Charles L.
Talawepi, Napkin Holder
with Crow Mother Katsina,
1980s. Wood and pigment.
H: 12.8 cm. (B) Tissue Box
with Snow Katsina Maiden,
1980s. Yarn. H: 15 cm.
(C) Todd Hoyungowa, Pencil
Holder, 1980s. Wood and
pigment. H: 12.5 cm. Private
collection.

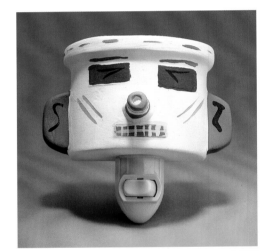

3.113J

3.114A–C

3.115 Eugene H. Bischoff
and Kay Bischoff, *Kachina
Dolls Cut and Color*
(Albuquerque: Eukabi
Publishers, 1950).

3.116 A. G. Smith and Josie
Hazen, *Cut and Make Kachina
Dolls* (New York: Dover
Publications, Inc., 1992).

3.117 With the "Kachina
Doll Kit" the buyer can
assemble his or her own
"Katsina" from the provided
pieces. The results are similar
to the factory-assembled
"Katsina" figures available
in tourist stores. This kit is
manufactured by Edge of
Extinction, Inc.

trade." The "punch-out" tradition has been continued by Dover Publications, Inc., New York (fig. 3.116), which currently markets *Cut and Make Kachina Dolls* (1992) and, more devastating to the Hopi, *Kachina Punch-Out Masks* (1995), both by A. G. Smith and Josie Hazen. Other Dover items in the "Katsina business" include a booklet of six "Katsina" doll postcards (1991), *North American Indian Design Giftwrap Paper* designed by Gregory Mirow (1993; fig. 3.113B), and *Authentic Kachina Stickers* (1996). In a letter to the president of Dover Publications, Inc., dated July 13, 1994, Leigh J. Kuwanwisiwma stated that "The Hopi have repeatedly and strongly objected to the production of kachina masks by non-Hopi people [which are] viewed as highly offensive to the Hopi and our kachina religion." The Cultural Preservation Office, on behalf of the Hopi people, requested an immediate cessation to the advertising and selling of such items. The president of Dover Publications, Inc., Hayward Cirker, responded on August 4, 1994, as follows: "may I ask whether your request that we stop publishing Kachina material in the public domain because of a religious objection would extend to similar situations which might arise from Catholics, Protestants, Islamics and Jews? This is important to us because on such matters we must act on the basis of broad policy rather than individual requests."[36]

Also in the do-it-yourself category is a "Kachina Doll Kit" (fig. 3.117), from which the buyer can assemble his or her own "Katsina," manufactured by a company with the memorable name Edge of Extinction, Inc., in Norco, California. Edge of Extinction provides pieces for "Morning Singer Katsina" but supplies information from Barton Wright (1977, 43) for the "Silent Warrior."

Goldwater's Foods of Arizona bottles some of the Goldwaters' "favorite family recipes" with Katsina-like masks on the labels of Sedona Red Salsa, Bisbee Barbeque Sauce, and Paradise Pineapple Salsa (see fig. 3.111A). The labels inform that, "The Kachinas depicted...represent spirits of the Hopi Indian tribe of northern Arizona." In 1994 Ty Ross, Barry Goldwater's grandson, issued a series of "Soft Spirit Kachinas" (Soft Spirit Inc., Phoenix, Arizona), which are softish, slightly sticky (probably a result of the recycled plastic) log-shaped objects with a Katsina-like image drawn on (fig. 3.118). The tag reads: "My kachinas are a soft inspiration of these forms [a reference to the *tithu* that Barry Goldwater collected; see Goldwater 1969; B. Wright 1975] that represent virtues passed down to all of us." On one the copy continues: "I am the Owl. I represent knowledge and wisdom. Through learning you may become successful, popular and powerful. I play marbles only after I have finished my homework." Alas, however, Mr. Ross has not given us an imitation Great Horned Owl Katsina, but rather an imitation of Qöqlö, the Second Mesa Katsina, who in this case wears old Euro-American clothing. The confusion no doubt arose because Qöqlö shares with Great Horned Owl wings at the sides of the headdress.

3.115

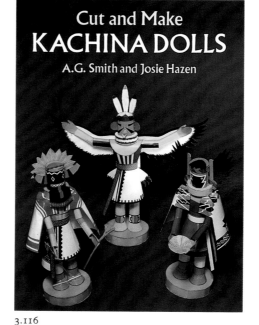

3.116

3.117

Hopi artists have occasionally contributed to these souvenir items, as noted previously. Anthony Honanie painted the Morning Singer Katsina image that appears as the face on watches manufactured by Red Stone in Tucson. The insert quotes him as saying that "[t]raditional Indian cultural subjects are my best expression of my sincere feelings as an artist." In the mid-1990s someone took Hopi painter Waldo Mootzka's (1903–1941) *Bean Dance* and reproduced a detail on computer mouse pads and refrigerator magnets (see fig. 3.113D).

Mass-produced items are today made all over the world. Katsina-like potholders are made in the Philippines (fig. 3.113A), tiles with pictures of Katsina-like beings at a kiva come from Sri Lanka (fig. 3.113I), ten-color, Katsina-like ballpoint pens

3.118

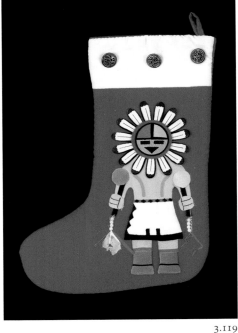

3.119

3.118 Ty Ross, "Soft Spirit Kachinas," 1994. Cloth. H (left): 34 cm; (right): 36 cm. Private collection.

3.119 Christmas stocking made in China, 1990s. Cotton, buttons, beads, and feathers. H: 36 cm. Private collection. Purchased at the Phoenix airport just after Christmas 1996.

3.120A,B Wrought-iron "Katsina" forms made in Mexico and sold through a store in Flagstaff. Photograph by Zena Pearlstone, 1994.

3.121 "Katsina" needlework kit purchased in 1995 from a general gift shop in Tucson. Paper and plastic. H: 27.8 cm. Private collection.

3.122 Margaret Parrott, Playing Cards with "Katsina" Designs. Private collection. © Margaret Parrott

3.123 Frame by Aquatique of San Francisco, 1993. Paper and plastic. H: 20.5 cm. Private collection.

3.124A–H Notecards and postcards with "Katsina" designs. Private collection.

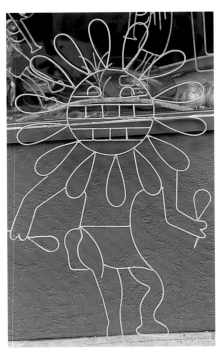

3.120A

3.120B

(fig. 3.113H) are from Taiwan, and a being resembling Sun Katsina is sewn onto a bright red Christmas stocking made in China (fig. 3.119). Wrought-iron "Katsina" forms in varying sizes are made in Mexico and sold through a Flagstaff store (fig. 3.120A,B). Most of the items, however, are made in the greater Southwest. These include Canyon Crafts Fine Art Needlework (Phoenix), which provides needlework patterns for a variety of Katsina-like images (fig. 3.121); Arroyo Enterprises of Scottsdale, which makes cloisonné/enamel earrings; Bag O'Beans (see fig. 1.1), which provides a Katsina-like image on the bag for Hopi Blue Popcorn (Reno, Nevada); absorbent coasters from Sandstone Creations (Phoenix); playing cards by Margaret Parrott, Albuquerque (fig. 3.122); a picture frame (fig. 3.123) produced in 1993 by

3.121

3.122

3.123

3.124A

3.124B

3.124C

3.124D

3.124E

3.124F

3.124G

3.124H

Aquatique (San Francisco); Seal-A-Letter stationery from Modern Color Creations (Mesa, Arizona); notepaper from Saga Inc. (Albuquerque); a fan pull made by Famous Fan Accessories (Richardson, Texas); stickers from Arbor International (Phoenix); and rubber stamps by Stampin' Designer (Albuquerque). Notecards and postcards are produced in Albuquerque, Santa Fe, Taos, Phoenix, Tucson, Flagstaff, Scottsdale, Tempe, Denver, Boulder, Pacific Palisades (California), Petaluma (California), and Salt Lake City (figs. 3.124A–H).

Like the figures on Navajo carvings, most of these images are far removed from the look of Hopi carvings. Unlike Navajo carvings, however, most of these items are not freestanding sculpture, and most lack any semblance of being handmade, a claim highly touted for Navajo carvings no matter how little truth it contains. In general, those who benefit from the sale of these items are not Hopi. Some of the Hopis with whom I spoke do not perceive these items as a major economic threat in the way that they see the Navajo figures. Many of these tourist items are so far removed from *tithu* and the appearance of performers that they are given little importance. And some Hopis, as noted, are not opposed to these forms of tourist art. It is impossible to argue, however, that this great wash of items has no effect. They play into concepts of trivialization and manifest "cutesification" of Hopi imagery as they caricature spiritual imagery in the most mundane of contexts. Like the continued representation of romanticized Indians in advertising and popular culture, they perpetuate stereotypes (Pearlstone 1995a).

Unlike Euro-American religious imagery, which is also packaged for consumers, mass-marketed merchandise bearing Katsina imagery is sold mainly in non-Hopi stores and purchased almost exclusively by non-Hopis. Designing and packaging are done by people who know little or nothing about the subject. The copy on labels is seldom accurate and often presents painfully garbled versions of actual situations. Contrasting items featuring Katsina-like imagery with those that are sometimes referred to as "Christian kitsch" or "Jesus junk" is revealing. As opposed to the Hopi situation, the commodification of Christianity is commonplace and has an ancient history (McDannell 1995, 6–8; Moore 1994, 7). Most Christians have no objection to commercialized religious imagery unless it becomes extreme, as in cases like Andres Serrano's *Piss Christ* (1988), or when used by nonreligious rock bands (Elisabeth Cameron, personal communication, 1998).[37]

Further, one study indicates that 97 percent of those shopping at Christian bookstores, where much of this material is sold, are Christians who attend church once a week or more (McDannell 1995, 256). Unlike Hopis, Christians employ commercialized items as markers: "Christians use religious goods to tell themselves and the world around them that they are Christians.… Religious objects also signal who is in the group and who is not" (McDannell 1995, 45).

Hopis would hardly need such items to identify themselves, and even though some distinctions between sacred and profane are becoming increasingly blurred, as discussed previously, the great outlay of popular items is not marketed to them.[38] Occasionally members of the Hopi nation can be seen wearing T-shirts, wristwatches, or buttons with Katsina-like images (fig. 3.125), but no one would profit if this were the directed audience. However, when Catholic imagery in the form of Mexican-American saints is reproduced on T-shirts, the situations find common ground. According to McDannell there are various reasons why non-Catholics buy these T-shirts—fashion or nostalgia for example—but the images that sell best to non-Catholics are those that "have never been commonplace in American culture" and thus "carry with them the aura of the exotic" (1995, 62–63).

3.125 A pin proclaiming "I'm Hopi and proud of it." Plastic, paper, and metal. Diam: 5.6 cm. Private collection.

3.126A

3.126B

3.126C

Popular Culture

In the cities of the Southwest, Katsina-like images appear to hover in the air, jump off walls, and fill store windows (fig. 3.126A–D). It is impossible to avoid them. Trading posts and tourist stores use life-size cutouts of Katsina-like forms and flash neon outlines as come-ons. Some U-Haul moving trucks feature a representation of Hopi Eagle Katsina (fig. 3.127). "Kachina" appears as a street name and as part of hundreds of business titles. The Flagstaff Arizona phone directory includes Kachina Auto Salvage, Kachina Dental Studio, Kachina House Cleaning, Kachina Refrigeration & Mechanical, and Kachina Waste Water Co-Op. "Kachina" is taken as an organizational name. A Phoenix Suns Promotional Event in 1994 was sponsored by the "Flagstaff Kacinas." "The Kacinas are the Sports Committee for the Flagstaff Chamber of Commerce. Their objectives include increasing awareness of the Phoenix Cardinals and Phoenix Suns Training Camp held in Flagstaff."[39] In the 1960s the Hopi Tribal Council attempted unsuccessfully to copyright the name *Katsina*, in part, to stop this kind of degradation (Clemmer 1995, 328 n. 93). Today, more than thirty years later, the term is used ever more widely.

The Bank of America in a Phoenix suburb retains a stained-glass window with a Katsina-like image, the last reminder of the original bank's "Katsina theme" when "Katsina" images were also

3.127 Eagle "Katsina" on a U-Haul truck spotted in Los Angeles. Photograph by Elisabeth Cameron, 1996.

3.128 Stained glass "Katsina," Bank of America, Scottsdale, Arizona. Photograph by Zena Pearlstone, 1994.

3.129 Kachina Square in Flagstaff features its name on a large stained glass "Katsina" elevated in the middle of the parking lot. Photograph by Zena Pearlstone, 1998.

3.126A–D Katsina imagery is everywhere in the city of Gallup. Stores often advertise their wares by displaying large "Katsina" paintings or cutouts. Photographs by Zena Pearlstone, 1994.

3.130 Sign in front of Southwestern Style Lighting, Albuquerque. Two masked figures help a Koyaala-like being hang a light fixture. Photograph by Zena Pearlstone, 1994.

featured on checks (fig. 3.128). The Arizona Bank in Tucson continues to display Katsina-like figures on signage around its branches. Kachina Square in Flagstaff features its name alongside a large stained-glass Katsina look-alike, elevated in the middle of the parking lot (fig. 3.129). Southwestern Style Lighting in Albuquerque has a large sign in front of the store showing two masked figures helping a Koyaala-like being hang a light fixture (fig. 3.130). Ultimate Electronics in Albuquerque has life-size Koyaala-like figures using cameras and camcorders in a center display.

In Gallup, New Mexico, the "Indian Capital of the World" where Indian-made products bring in more than seventy million dollars a year in retail sales (Norrell 1995a, B1), "Katsina" murals or illustrations appear to cover almost every wall (fig. 3.131A–C). In the mid-1990s highly visible billboards with "Kooyemsi" and "Koyaala" advertising a Toyota dealership and a trading post, towered over the city (fig. 3.132A,B). Indian designs, including Katsina-like forms, on wooden "tepees" have been a fixture in the city for some time (fig. 3.133). The "tepees," with designs painted by Navajo Charlie Hafen, stand at Gallup Indian Plaza and have been the subject of protest by Native Americans. Interviewed at the time of one of the demonstrations, Mr. Hafen argued that he did not know what all the fuss was about and pointed out that Katsinam and Navajo Yeibichais had been used by Indians in items for

3.126D

3.127

3.128

3.129

3.130

117

3.131A

3.131B

COST + 10%

RETAIL 50%

3.131C

sale for decades. "I've got a good idea of what is sacred. They're not used on the teepees," he said. Adding fuel to the controversy, activists accused Mohammed Ayscheh, who owns the Plaza, of exploiting Indian culture and said that he "should use his own culture as an attraction and host caravan tents and camel rides." "That sounds very racist to me," responded Mr. Hafen (Norrell 1995b, B1).

Interestingly, two of the most painful instances of appropriation did not originate in the Southwest. In both cases, the damage was so extreme that Hopis felt forced to intercede. In 1971 the Ezra Brooks Distilling Company of Frankfort, Kentucky, issued its seventy-third in a series of commemorative collectible whisky bottles, a Katsina-like image that was sold only in Arizona (fig. 3.134, bottle on the right). In an advertisement that ran in the *Arizona Republic* on October 26, 1971, the bottle was described as "an authentic replica of the unique Hopi Indian Kachina Doll, complete with colorful headdress, mask and costume." Despite this billing of authenticity, the figure does not correspond to any known Katsina and seems rather to be an accumulation of elements that the designers saw as distinctive. It was identifiable enough, however, to enrage Hopis, who learned about the bottles when a shipment arrived in Winslow, Arizona, where many Hopis shop. Two days before the advertisement appeared, a Hopi official was quoted as saying that the Hopis, who had previously been successful in stopping a winery from using "Kachina" bottles, were considering filing suit against the distillery. The spokesman noted that "the act is sacrilegious in the eyes of the Hopis. It would be the same as though the distillery

3.131A–C Murals on store walls are common in Gallup, New Mexico, the "Indian Capital of the World." Photographs by Zena Pearlstone, 1994.

3.132A,B Highly visible billboards on which Koyaalam and Kooyemsi are used to sell merchandise hover over Gallup, New Mexico. Photographs by Zena Pearlstone, 1994.

used images of Jesus Christ." Clarence Hamilton, then Hopi council chairman, said that "using the Kachina doll for whiskey is going too far." The distillery agreed to Hopi demands by arranging for television coverage of Barry Goldwater and then Arizona Senator Harold Giss smashing the mold while Ezra Brooks officials looked on. In the intervening weeks the bottles, which were priced at $15.99, had become collectors' items and were selling for up to $500. In the following years, however, at least five additional "Katsina" commemorative bottles were issued by Ezra Brooks.[40]

Twenty years later, a similar incident rocked the Pueblo (see Youvella, pp.180–81, this volume). The March 1992 issue of Marvel Comics (1, no. 6), *NFL Superpro: The Kachinas Sing of Doom*, unfolds an inane plot featuring two groups of Hopis— "'hostiles' who advocate isolationism" and "'friendlies' who want dealings with the outside"—plus non-Hopi hired mafia thugs who dress as "Katsinam" and wield spears, knives, chain saws, and metal bows and arrows. The Hopis are represented as running a gambling casino, which they do not have, and are dressed in traditional Navajo rather than Hopi clothing. The Katsina Hee'e'e (Mother Katsina who leads the Powamuy ceremony Katsina procession) always danced—as are all Katsinam—by a man, is seen in the comic as a woman. In addition, this Katsina and another are pictured having their masks knocked off, revealing the human faces underneath.[41] "When I saw this thing, I was so angry that I couldn't even think" said the director of the Hopi Cultural

3.132A

3.132B

3.133 Wooden "tepee" at the Indian Plaza, Gallup, New Mexico, with "Indian" designs, some Katsina influenced, painted by Navajo Charlie Hafen. These "tepees" have been the subject of protest by Native Americans. Photograph by Zena Pearlstone, 1994.

Preservation Office, Leigh J. Kuwanwisiwma (Shaffer 1992). By the time the Hopi contacted Marvel and expressed their outrage and the publisher had agreed to do a recall, seventy-seven thousand copies had been distributed. At a meeting on February 27, 1992, Hopi officials discussed the harm that the comic had caused, but they also took some of the responsibility.[42] Kuwanwisiwma noted that all Hopi were guilty of producing and commercializing Katsina dolls, and then Hopi Chairman Vernon Masayesva pointed out that the Hopi actually teach others to carve through demonstrations. Chairman Masayesva reported at this meeting that Marvel Comics had apologized, expressed a willingness to meet with the Hopi to try to prevent this from happening again, and made an effort to recall the books. He also noted that the National Football League had extended an apology.[43] None of this was enough to curtail the damage. Some Hopis believe that the images used by Marvel were taken from sketches made at a ceremony. Religious leaders at First and Second Mesas, who had been closing some ceremonies to non-Indians for years, closed the remaining ones.

A few years after the comic book incident, the Hopi felt it necessary to intervene in the workings of "The Kachina Klub," an organization of 8,100 members, likely influenced by the "Smokis," and founded in Phoenix in 1974 as a branch of the Jesters, a Shriners group (see Spencer, this volume).[44] Ritual performances staged for members every year were based on the Hopi creation myth. Participants wore "elaborate replicas of kachina masks" and the purpose of the group according to their handbook is to "support mirth…and lend whatever support possible to assist the Hopi nation and other Southwestern native Americans." The business manager, Gerald Griffin, said the Kachina Klub made the decision to "drop use of Hopi religious rituals and names after receiving a protest from [the Hopi]."[45]

Applications of the Katsina name can be found, it seems, associated with anything "spiritual." In a particularly far-fetched example, Santa Fe acupuncturist Frederick Steinway compares "the seed spirit" of body orbs with Katsinam. The lung orb, he explains, as the realm of life, houses the "air kachinas…the kachinas of late autumn." This is probably

3.134 Collectible whiskey bottles representing "Katsinam" issued in the early 1970s by the Ezra Brooks Distilling Company, Frankfort, Kentucky. H: 35 cm. Ceramic. Private collection.

3.135 Installation photo from the exhibition *Arizona: Isamu Noguchi and Issey Miyake*, Genichiro Inokuma Museum of Contemporary Art, Marugame, Japan, 1997. Photograph courtesy Issey Miyake USA Corp.

3.136 Diana Mitchell, ornamental plate featuring "Katsina," circa 1995. Hand-thrown ceramic, fired, and hand-painted in Ecuador. Diam: 18.7 cm. Private collection

3.134

particularly surprising to the Hopi since Katsinam appear at all times of the year except autumn. Further surprises to the Hopi might be "the earth kachina" who "lives in the stomach and spleen's activities" and the "liver orb" that "shelters the hun or katsina of plan." "Acupuncture is a natural way to give the kachinas a treat. The filaments or needles are like prayer sticks" (1994, 5).

Katsina imagery, these days, is international. The French couture house Hermès unveiled a "Kachina" silk scarf designed by Waco, Texas, artist Kermit Oliver, who for three decades has been a postal worker by vocation and an acclaimed figural painter by avocation (see fig. 3.2). The scarf features a variety of Hopi Katsina-like figures as well as other Native American symbols.[46] In 1997 the Genichiro Inokuma Museum of Contemporary Art in Marugame, Japan,

presented an exhibition entitled *Arizona: Isamu Noguchi and Issey Miyake*. Mannequins dressed in clothes designed by Miyake were posed in front of a mural of a "Katsina" taken from a sketch by Genichiro Inokuma (fig. 3.135). Also displayed were Inokuma's "paintings and sketches, inspired by Kachinas, Hopi ritual folk dolls" (Grilli 1997, 35). Inokuma was introduced to the art of the Hopi by artist Isamu Noguchi and incorporated Hopi motifs into his paintings. These same designs "animated the clothing designs of Mr. Miyake" (Grilli 1997, 36).

In 1994 and 1995 the mail-order Pyramid Collection claimed "authenticity" for alabaster "kachina" figurines made in Italy (see fig. 3.5). The catalog entry states that "These legendary Pueblo Kachinas... reel with startling authenticity in handpainted, handcrafted Italian figurines of lifelike alabaster and

3.135

3.136

resin."[47] Ornamental plates featuring "Katsinam," which were sold through the Simply Southwest catalog, are designed by Diana Mitchell of Tucson. The plates are manufactured in Ecuador, hand thrown, fired, and then hand painted. Mitchell describes the plate borders as having "Inca designs" (fig. 3.136). Prior to this Mitchell designed "Katsina" and storyteller bread dough ornaments, which were conceived when a buyer from the Dillard stores asked for Southwest ornaments that were unusual. Mitchell researched Hopi Katsinam and designed the bread dough ornaments in 1990. The dough is laced with paint, and the ornaments are then manufactured by Ecuadorian Indians through assembly line production. The ornaments hang on Arizona and New Mexico Christmas trees, and the Goldwater family sent some to the White House. Mitchell says she has had only positive feedback from the Hopi and that she makes sure that the Ecuadorians making the items are well treated (personal communication, 1995).

Katsina imagery is so pervasive and so marketable that it is literally impossible to keep up with the production. Artists and designers, always vigilant, seem perpetually to have yet another manifestation to take to market. Hopis themselves would seem to have few options any more but to watch this happen, and in some, as yet rare, cases to participate.

Conclusion

> Authenticity can no longer be rooted in singularity.... That would be, in our culture of the copy, idiocy.
>
> Hillel Schwartz, *The Culture of the Copy*

James Clifford observes that the art of "ethnic" peoples differs from that of mainstream society because it is carried by its ethnicity. "Though specific artists have come to be known and prized, the aura of 'cultural' production attaches to ["ethnic" peoples] much more than, say, to Picasso, who is not in any essential way valued as a 'Spanish artist'"(1988, 225). It is this ethnicity, this Hopiness (or perceived Hopiness), in the form of Katsinam, that carries *tithu* and Katsina imagery on innumerable objects to an international audience. "Hopiness" is such a powerful marketing factor that, as noted above, the whole process today can proceed without the creator, seller, or buyer being Hopi.

Katsinam are among the most widely recognized Native American images. Feathered headdresses read "Plains," totem poles the "Northwest Coast," and Katsinam the "Southwest." I have found stunning the number of people who, no matter how far they live from the Southwest and no matter how little their lives and interests include Native peoples, know something about Katsinam. The meaningfulness and accuracy of what they know are quite different issues. People are drawn to Hopis and to Katsina imagery. Part of the attraction of these carvings to Euro-American buyers is that they provide an exotic, complex subject packaged increasingly in a familiar emotive, narrative style. Katsinam are Other, but they are also humanlike, and Westerners can think of them as akin to saints or dolls.

How members of the public buy into Hopiness depends upon their level of artistic sophistication, their finances, and perhaps their proximity to the Southwest. Collectors and connoisseurs may be attracted to "traditional" (carved) Katsina images because they are made by a Hopi artist, possibly a specific artist. Those sold through galleries can retail for hundreds or even tens of thousands of dollars. At the other extreme, tourists on a budget are drawn to inexpensive, mass-produced products bearing Katsina imagery. In almost all cases what cements the sale is the real or perceived Hopiness, the Southwestness. Objects with Katsina-like forms sell because they are, like the oriental carpets examined by Brian Spooner (1986, 200), "part commodity, part symbol" and because "[i]t is in the nature of a symbol to bear more than one meaning, even in a particular social context." The elastic range of meanings, authenticities, and traditions that become attached to Katsinam as symbols helps explain their phenomenal sales growth.

"Hopiness" carries with it the promise of authenticity, a concept that is culturally defined and can also be individually defined by members of a culture. The Hopi claim that the Katsinam that they themselves make are authentic, not because the objects simply exist, or because they are distinct from fakes, forgeries, or imitations, but because they exist as a result of Hopi culture, and no other. They would concur with Richard Handler (1986, 4), who describes "an authentic culture as one original to its possessors, one which exists only with them: in other words an independently existent entity, asserting itself... against all other cultures." It is thus the Hopiness that defines the authenticity—not the intent or style of the art. Under this definition, *tithu* made for ceremonial use are not distinguished from those made for sale, and "traditional" style is not a factor.

Authenticity for Hopis, regarding Hopi-made objects, is in no way tied to monetary value. Any number of Hopi artists make carvings both for village ceremonial use and for the tourist and collector trade; these are often of quite different design. Yet few, if any, Hopis would say that those destined for gifts are authentic but those made as commodities are not. Hopis thus exemplify Arjun Appadurai's (1986, 11) argument that there has been an "exaggeration and reification of the contrast between gift and commodity in anthropological writing." In the nineteenth century all *tithu* were made as gifts (Bol, this volume), but today, gifts can become commodities and under some circumstances commodities can be given as gifts. While some Hopis are beginning to question whether action figures can be considered *tithu*, I have never heard anyone question the authentic Hopiness of these carvings. Hopis emphasize, as is evident in the statements in this volume, that what distinguishes a work of art as Hopi is its spirituality (its Hopiness), a condition that trumps both quality and tradition. There are some Hopis, however, who see increased spirituality in older items and in their reinvention, the so-called "new old-style."

For most non-Pueblo buyers, the concepts of authenticity and tradition seem to mesh so greatly when applied to commodified Katsinam that it is usually not possible to separate them. With evidence of continuous *tihu* manufacture for at least the last 150 years, no one questions the practice as a Hopi tradition. No matter how intensely "traditional" (turn-of-the-twentieth-century) form has been manipulated throughout the twentieth century or how far manufacture by non-Hopis strays from the Hopi canons, any carving of a Katsina is seen by some buyers or consumers as authentic because its Hopi iconography speaks to its antiquity. The magic of the original—no matter how vaguely defined— that becomes merged with "tradition" is long lasting (see Taussig 1993; Benjamin 1969, 225).[48]

Hopiness, and thus authenticity, may be enhanced for purchasers by buying directly from the artist or enacting the sale at the Pueblo. The continuing success of Indian markets and gallery open houses speak to the power of these personal encounters. However, while manufacture by a Hopi may be utmost for some, others may care only that the object carry a nebulous Southwest authenticity. It was widely reported in the mid-1990s that former Arizona Governor Fife Symington kept a Navajo-carved Katsina-style figure in his office (Joseph 1996a; Shaffer and Donovan 1994). It is sometimes

difficult for those not well acquainted with Native American visual culture to distinguish Hopi-made from other Indian (particularly Navajo) items. Defining Katsina carvings as "simply" Indian made, and thus authentically Indian, has become a popular sales lure in mass marketing.

It is a source of great cultural pride to the Hopi people that their Katsinam and their *tithu* are unique and seen as Hopi intellectual and cultural property (see Spencer, this volume). There is no Western equivalent for the Katsina. But it is just this uniqueness that has allowed Katsina imitations to stray so far from those created by the Hopi and yet still speak strongly of Hopiness and tradition. People feel that they are buying into a unique tradition. Uniqueness of another sort can lead Hopi artists into a cultural tug-of-war. A number of Hopi *tihu* carvers move further and further from the older, static, geometric style to carvings that become more active, narrative, and idiosyncratic every year. Distinctive artists' styles are attractive to collectors, who seek novelty for artistic reasons as well as for market value (fig. 3.137). Hopi carvers, therefore, hang onto their cultural traditions with one hand just as they reach with the other into the Euro-American market of individualism. This is a balancing act that may be on the verge of teetering. A number of artists have moved so far from the *tithu* used in ceremonies that, as discussed above, some Hopi are asking whether these artworks—the action figures—even fall under the *tithu* category. The most elaborate of the action figures, unlike their less baroque counterparts, are hardly ever seen for sale at the Pueblo. They go directly to the upscale galleries in Santa Fe and Scottsdale and their sister shops around the country. While the artists often separate the Hopi world from that outside by creating more "traditional" carvings for ceremonies, at the same time, they attempt to bring these worlds together. Many innovative artists emphasize that they listen to, or sing, ceremonial music or think of ceremonies while they are working on carvings that today, at least, could find no part in a ceremony.

With the production of action figures, Hopi artists are moving, or may have already moved, from a non-Western Hopi aesthetic, where adherence to cultural norms is paramount, to a Western aesthetic where the uniqueness of the individual is central. These capable and sometimes worldly Hopi artists are developing a Western view of themselves, or at least a Western side. They are spurred to the novel not only through economic concerns—most could probably make a good living by continuing proven carving styles—but also by artistic pride in both what they produce and their recognition by the wider artistic community through remuneration, awards, museum presentations, and word-of-mouth. But it is no doubt also true, as Bennetta Jules-Rosette cautions, that even though the artists may "view themselves operating within the larger art world with an international audience [this] does not assure that their works are treated in a comparable manner by consumers" (1984, 207).

Dynamic and expensive Hopi-made carvings promoted by chichi galleries are an example of the changing "traffic in culture" (Marcus and Myers 1995). What was once anthropology has now become art. The art of the Other, which was previously evaluated in terms different from those used for Euro-American "high art" (see Price 1989; Hiller 1991), has now, in certain cases, been charged with equal status. This postmodernism speaks to an increasing difficulty with precise definition and is directly applicable to the case of Hopi Katsina carvings:

To invoke another culture now is to locate it in a time and space contemporaneous with our own, and thus to see it as part of our world, rather than as a mirror or alternative to ourselves, arising from a totally alien origin.... For what one might call an "ethnographic avant-garde," instead of "whole" cultures of extreme difference in the contemporary world, whose codes and structures might be subject to perfect translation and interpretation, anthropology is faced now with the interpenetration of cultures, borders, hybrids, fragments and the intractability of cultural difference to such authoritative interpretation. [Marcus and Myers 1995, 19–20]

Fred R. Myers notes that this shift from anthropology to art has further confounded some of the basic terminology pertinent to the present discussion of Katsina representation: "While anthropologists and [Native] painters have been inclined to emphasize the continuities between the paintings and

3.137 Herb Talahaftewa, Hopi Sweet-Cornmeal Tasting Mudhead Kooyemsi, 1990s. Wood, pigment, feathers, and thread. H (of tallest): 23 cm. Private collection.

indigenous [Native] traditions, emphasizing their authenticity as expressions of a particular worldview, these very terms—and their meanings—are among the most hotly contested in art critical circles" (1995, 73). Tradition and authenticity are likely to be interpreted differently by those assessing contemporary Hopi carvings as gallery or auction items than by buyers or Hopis themselves.[49] Despite the cultural equalization of some Hopi art, much still remains, as Wade described it in 1976, segregated from the comparable dominant-culture art and sold through Indian markets, separate galleries, and museum shows (18–19).

Much of the fine-art buying public may be largely unaware of the cultural struggles and schisms at Hopi, but it is involved in a conflict of its own. Many patrons today want artwork that is authentically Hopi but also modern and unique. If buyers are aware that their purchases differ from the carvings used at ceremonies, then they must be acquiring them as fine art; that is, they are buying carvings precisely because they diverge from past forms. Other buyers may be unaware of the aesthetic canons of Hopi. In these cases, the carvings would stylistically bridge the two worlds, and traditional subject matter and perhaps the cultural identity of the artist would be the lures.

The dynamic of the cultural and the modern becomes even more imprecise when Hopi artists represent Katsinam in nontraditional formats. Dan Namingha "safeguards the sanctity" of Katsinam by painting Katsina shapes or impressions, processed through the filters of medium and abstraction (Hightower 1994, 5; Deats 1998), but never produces actual representations. This view, however, would seem to be in contradistinction to that of Leigh Jenkins [Kuwanwisiwma] and Vernon Masayesva (in Wade 1995), who feel that any two-dimensional representation of Katsinam is acceptable as long as it is accurate. Namingha's art has journeyed from the "traditional" Katsina forms but in its reinvention probably creates a tradition of its own. His work may be removed from Hopi authenticity in the view of some Hopis, but it is certainly, in part, the Hopiness that sells the work.[50]

Much has been written on how outsiders have impinged on the sacred aspects of Hopi society. Peter M. Whiteley discusses how the Hopi have been violated with regard to religious rituals, sacred landscape, deity masks, and metaphysical beliefs (1993). Bursting files at the Hopi Cultural Preservation Office bear testimony to the number of such cases.

These acts are reprehensible, and it is as hard to imagine any Hopi who is indifferent to such behavior as it is easy to wonder how outsiders can be so insensitive. Katsina representation, however, falls into a grayer area. Hopis understand *tithu* to have "important spiritual meaning" (see Secakuku, this volume), but at the same time they commodify them, unlike other items used in religious rituals. In addition, Hopis present Katsina imagery on a variety of items (see pp. 62–83). Some Southwest scholars understand *tithu* not to be "truly sacred items" in the same sense as "masks and altar paraphernalia" (Jerrold Levy in Parezo 1983, xiv). Members of the non-Pueblo world who have cultural values different from Hopis are easily confused.

Hopis have become engulfed by and economically dependent upon cultures whose members often hold divergent beliefs. Major Western religions are open to all, and participants may learn as much about them as they choose. The use of images is not regulated. It is hard to imagine a Euro-American, Christian or not, who would consider checking with the Vatican, or his or her local church, about the appropriateness of Christian subject matter. Most non-Indians, undoubtedly, see images of Katsinam little differently than those of Christ in the sense that both are religious images in the public domain. Few Euro-Americans are educated to the fact that some religions wish to remain private.

The Southwest is for many people a magnet. Those who buy into Hopiness are a diverse group, and Hopiness is a significant aspect of the attraction of the Southwest. Tourism is a multilayered phenomenon and "the Southwest tourist" is not easily defined. Tourists may be those who come only once or a few times in a lifetime or those who make annual or more frequent pilgrimages. Serial tourists may have a specific goal, such as visits to the Santa Fe Indian Market every summer or to an annual festival. Some permanent residents can be seen as tourists if they tap into the Indian world only to buy or experience the unusual.

Visitors may seek the magical, spiritual qualities of the Southwest through vacations that have often been discussed as inversions of everyday life, "the sacred journey" spent in "the nonordinary/voluntary/ 'away from home' sacred state" (Graburn 1989, 25). This reversal is a condition that Alma Gottlieb sees as a necessity for Americans (1982). Travelers, who are drawn to ethnic tourism and find some satisfaction of their psychological needs in the Southwest (see Uzzell 1984), may imagine Hopis as the people of the area. One way "to get close to Nature's bosom is through her children, the people of Nature, once labeled Peasant and primitive peoples and considered creatures of instinct" (Graburn 1989, 31–32; see also MacCannell 1989).[51]

For symbols and proof of these sacred journeys, people buy souvenirs. What they buy reflects not only what speaks to sacredness for them but also what they can afford and how much they can carry. The Hopi Katsina, the primary visible Southwest vehicle for sacredness, has today been imitated and marketed so thoroughly that a representation can be found for every taste and every pocketbook. Consumers are not restricted to carvings—Hopi or other. If the traveler is drawn to a particular kind of object or a material, it can almost always be found in conjunction with Katsina imagery. There are Katsinam on pottery, baskets, spirit catchers, and jewelry, as well as on an enormous range of mundane objects—pens, notecards, refrigerator magnets, placemats, clothing, and even Christmas stockings. What has evolved is Edwin L. Wade's (1976) generic art market. As long as the object says "Southwest," or better, "made by a real Indian," it is salable and seen by some as conveying some kind of authenticity. Susan Stewart (1984, 132–51) speaks of the souvenir as a metonym, authenticating the experience for the purchaser. Through this tsunami of goods, culture becomes compressed, stereotyped. Objects get cut out of specific contexts (Clifford 1988, 220). Pueblo material and perhaps spiritual culture has been commandeered by non-Pueblo peoples and usurped by Euro-American culture. Dean MacCannell sees worldwide homogenization:

> Once all, or almost all, the groups on the face of the earth are drawn into a single network of associations based on the monetary and other systems of equivalences…the stage is set for an explosion of group-level interactions requiring greatly expanded production of "ethnicity" and a metalanguage for the global dialogue, an arbiter or referee which I have named "White Culture." [1992, 165]

"White Culture" for MacCannell ensures inequality because one group controls the wealth and the decision making. Hopi is part of this pattern as economic considerations become increasingly Euro-American. Some Hopi artists have become so successful that it could be argued that they have joined the ranks of the wealth controllers and decision makers.

The information available about those who produce *tithu* and Katsina imagery has allowed us in this publication to assess the marketplace from their perspective, but data about the vast body of consumers who buy this material is limited. While there is an increasing literature on what tourists do, there is less known about what they think, and it would be shortsighted to assume that all are learning or even observing the same things. Their needs differ from those of art critics, gallery owners, and Hopis. Imitation Katsinam, anathema to the Hopi, may convey to the tourists who purchase them the sacredness of their own journeys. Mary Douglas and Baron Isherwood in their study of 1979 on consumerism conclude that the transfer of goods is entangled with communications and identity but that finally what makes something "fit for consumption" is its being "fit to circulate as a marker for particular sets of social roles" (1996 [1979], xxiii). The key word for tourist purchases may be *sets*, the involvement of a number of social roles. These purchases encompass both interactions within the roles of buying and quite different relations called out by the roles of having. Segregation, Deirdre Evans-Pritchard argues, is the defining factor for any commercial transaction in the Southwest: "The respective roles of buyers and sellers keep tourists and Indians separate which is appropriate since the currency of cultural tourism is *difference*" (1989, 99). Even if tourists purchase items directly from Indians, there is a lack of connection between Southwest Natives and visitors:

> The exchange between tourists and Native Americans did not produce mutual communication. Mutual communication occurred back home between the tourist and his or her audience…. Removed from the site of the tourist encounter and taken home, souvenirs…became objects loaded with meaning, sources for narratives of the region. [Dilworth 1996b, 164]

The narrative though may ultimately tell us more about the possessor than about the object or its place of origin (Stewart 1984, 136–51).

Similarly, in researching African tourist art, Bennetta Jules-Rosette draws attention to the fact that objects attained from the Other can not be treated like objects from the buyer's home community.

> Because there are no conventional aesthetic standards for these works, the consumers are

hesitant about their quality and are persuaded by secondary explanations presented by middlemen, vendors, and experienced collectors. This point in the exchange system might be termed the crisis in quality for tourist art. This crisis in quality is magnified when the tourist consumer returns home with a piece for which there is no existing cultural and artistic context. Often such pieces are stored in attics and forgotten. Alternatively, great sentimental value is given to the piece as a gift or a souvenir of exotic lands or experiences. In this case, no objective standards of quality can approximate the emotional value of the piece. [Jules-Rosette 1984, 235–36]

Sociologist David Halle, has explored what happens to some of these objects "back home." His findings inform us of how little is really understood about the meanings that buyers attach to the items they purchase, and they should be a caution against assuming that all material collected from the Other and displayed back home is cloaked in sentimentality and emotionalism.

What is lacking is an understanding of art and cultural items in the audience's own terrain, namely the social life, architecture, and surroundings of the house and neighborhood.... I do suggest that many meanings emerge or crystallize in the context of the setting in which the audience views the work (house, neighborhood, and the family and social life woven therein) and that these meanings cannot be deduced from those of the artist, critics etc. These new meanings "have an impact on twentieth-century elite and popular-culture history via peoples 'demand' for certain kinds of art and cultural items that are suitable repositories of these meanings." [Halle 1993, 3, 11]

Halle studied ethnic art and objects in homes from a variety of neighborhoods in and around New York City. It is clear from his findings that the meanings that people attach to ethnic objects are diverse, frequently idiosyncratic, and often at odds with the creator's intent. A continuation of Halle's work should contribute to our understanding of the native/tourist dynamic and also the differences between the purchase of the unique "handmade" object as opposed to the mass-produced souvenir.[52]

Katsina imagery at the close of the twentieth century encompasses a myriad of messages sent and received, a multitude of forms shaped to the market, a continuum of perceived authenticities. It provides a window onto the real and the manufactured Southwest, an area that draws consumers of all social and economic classes. Virtually everyone who spends time in the Southwest is aware of Katsinam; some are aware of their Hopi significance. Hopis, at the center of this maelstrom of commodification, are buffeted by their own differences of opinion, a dynamic with a long history in the villages. While most are centered by the strength of a Pueblo-defined authenticity of Katsina representation, there are blurred issues at the boundaries. Questions are raised by individuals who have only part Hopi ancestry and Hopis who live away from the Pueblo and may have little contact. There are artists who have cut from the collective and perhaps see themselves as individuals first and Hopi second. "The point," to quote Sylvia Rodriguez, "is not that natives sold out to tourism but that individuals as well as groups respond to its inescapable advance in different, complex, and often contradictory ways" (1994, 118). Katsina art is a major economic index at Hopi, and each artist must define his or her artistic production against Hopi traditions. Hopis must continually reinvent themselves against the changing world, just as the Southwest is constantly reinvented by those who live there or visit and take away some aspect of the Katsina mystique. ●

Esther Jackson

Esther Jackson is a Hopi artist based in Sitsomovi, First Mesa, Hopi. The following are excerpts from an interview conducted by Zena Pearlstone at Sitsomovi, First Mesa, Hopi, July 25, 1997.

I am the middle daughter of five (the others are Mabel, Edna, Kayenta, and Roanna), and we all carve Katsinam. My two brothers, Roger and Skipton, also carve. My father, Clifford, became blind, and my mother, Otillie, learned how to carve from her neighbors, Heber and Ravena Andrews. When we finished high school, mother said, "You girls are old enough to carve because you don't know what is in the future." I started carving in 1973. Now I am teaching my daughters. My eldest daughter is sixteen and just started, and I will eventually teach my younger daughters.

Today we all sell our work from the top of First Mesa. Selling through the shops takes too much of the profit. But we have also sold through Wounded Knee, a store in Santa Monica. The carvings sell as fast as we make them. I also make pottery. If I have a lot of Katsinam, then I'll make some pottery.

I am the only one in the family carving one-piece figurines. I taught myself how to do the feathers and drapery and then taught my sisters. I carve to

support my family. A Katsina chief told one woman in my village not to carve, and she asked him if he was going to support her family. He said "No," and she replied, "Then you can't tell me what to do."

III.1 Hònkatsina (Bear Katsina), 2000. Wood. Shown in progress. Photograph by Zena Pearlstone.

III.2 Corn Maiden or Cloud Maiden, 2000. Wood and pigment. Photograph by Zena Pearlstone.

III.3 Angaktsina (Long-Hair Katsina) and Hahay'iwùuti (Happy Mother), 2000. Wood and pigment. Photograph by Zena Pearlstone.

III.4 Katsinmana (Unmarried Maiden), 2000. Wood and pigment. Photograph by Zena Pearlstone.

III.1

III.2

III.3

III.4

David Freeland

David Freeland is a Metis (French-Canadian Native) artist based in Arizona. The following are excerpts from a telephone interview conducted by Zena Pearlstone on January 19, 1998.

I draw my inspiration from the Indians of the Southwest. My interest in jewelry began when I was a young boy in Arizona where my parents traded with American Indians. I began producing my own gold and silver jewelry at the age of fourteen. I collected Hopi Katsinam for years and wanted to honor the Hopi. My way of doing this was by creating collectible silver sculptures modeled after the Hopi Katsinam. I began to do this in 1988. My small sculptures carry inlaid stones and shells, and each is unique. Recently I have begun to make these figures with removable parts. Masks, capes, and skirts can be detached from the figure and worn as pendants.

I do a number of different Katsinam—twenty-five to thirty—and add new ones all the time. I will create specific Katsina figures if asked by a customer. I make and sell hundreds of these small sculptures every year and can't keep up with the demand. They sell wholesale for between $450 to $1000 and retail for two or three times that amount.

IV.1 *Deer.* Silver, turquoise, and inlaid stones. Photograph courtesy of the artist.

IV.2 *Aholi.* Silver, turquoise, and inlaid stones. Photograph courtesy of the artist.

IV.3 *Screech Owl.* Silver, turquoise, and inlaid stones. Photograph courtesy of the artist.

IV.4 *Ahola.* Silver, turquoise, and inlaid stones. Photograph courtesy of the artist.

IV.1   IV.2   IV.3   IV.4

Ramson Lomatewama

Ramson Lomatewama is a Hopi artist based in Arizona. The following are excerpts from a telephone interview conducted by Zena Pearlstone on February 11, 1998.

I spent my early years at Hopi. When I was five or six we moved to Flagstaff. My family has always been involved with Hopi traditions, and I have been going back and forth to the Pueblo all my life. I started carving dolls when I was in my teens and continue to do this today. I learned from watching others. My father and my older brothers carve. When I was married, I learned Hopi traditional weaving, and I continue to weave.

I have a bachelor of arts degree from Goddard College in Vermont. When I graduated, I started writing poetry and have published three poetry collections. After college, I was offered a position teaching at a middle school at Hopi. Today I hold an adjunct teaching position with North Central College in Naperville, Illinois, and teach there every fall.

In New England I got interested in stained glass. I taught myself how to work with glass and started doing my own glasswork in 1987. In 1996 I began glass blowing. I occasionally represent Katsinam on my stained glass pieces, but mainly I do carved Katsinam.

v.1 Katsina-inspired figures, 1998. Etched glass. Photograph by Zena Pearlstone.

v.2 Pöqangwhoya (Warrior Twin, Older Brother), 2000. Wood, feather, straw, and pigment. Photograph by Zena Pearlstone.

v.3 Masawkatsina, 2000. Wood, feather, and pigment. Photograph by Zena Pearlstone.

v.4 Kwikwilyaqa (Imitator), 2000. Wood, straw, twine, and pigment. Photograph by Zena Pearlstone.

V.I

V.2

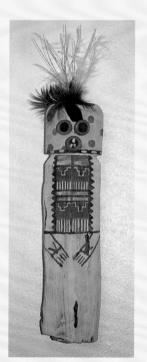

V.3

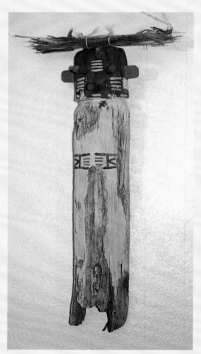

V.4

I believe that to make Katsinam, one must have the cultural prerequisites. Every culture has its own rules and procedures, and no traditional art form is art-for-art's-sake. Art has deeper significance, and the significance comes from religion. To engage in traditional arts a person should go through the process of initiation. This is a process of gaining knowledge, of learning what things mean. The ritual culmination, the closure to the process, is an endorsement that one receives. One has then earned the privilege to do certain things, one has the license to carve.

Two things are critical, the process leading to initiation and the person's intention to go through the process. When a non-Hopi represents Katsinam, the process is not there. There is no value in that creative process. Non-Hopis have no intent. They don't understand the meanings of Katsinam, they don't understand the significance of the colors and other details. It would be as if I wore a policeman's uniform without having gone through the academy. I may have the uniform on, but I am not sanctioned to carry out a policeman's responsibilities.

People need to understand why they are going through a process. For me it is so other people will benefit. I can transfer this benefit to nontraditional art forms such as Katsinam in stained glass. Making money is never my primary function. If I make art just for the money, then I am doing it for the wrong reason. My intention and my reward are to uplift someone's spirits. My art is in a sense a healing process. I have to keep that at the forefront of my art. I was brought up with the idea of sharing life and the belief that the things shared will come back to you.

The people who commission my dolls usually have a basic knowledge of Hopi life. If they don't have this knowledge, I direct them to Alph Secakuku's book (*Following the Sun and Moon*) to educate themselves. Art is more meaningful if people have the background. People must find their own way.

v.5

v.6

v.5 Suyang'ephoya (Left-Handed Katsina), 1999. Wood, feathers, and pigment. H: 25 cm. Private collection.

v.6 Sa'lakwmana platter, 1999. Etched glass. Photograph by Zena Pearlstone.

4 Early Euro-American Ethnographers and the Hopi Tihu

MARSHA C. BOL

Upon entering a Hopi house on March 31, 1852, Dr. P. G. S. Ten Broeck, an assistant surgeon in the United States Army, collected a *tihu* that is now in the United States National Museum. As he later recounted:

> Hanging by strings from the rafters I saw some curious and rather horrible little Aztec images, made of wood or clay, and decorated with paint and feathers, which the guide told me were "saints," but I have seen the children playing with them in the most irreverent manner. [Marcy 1866, 105]

This perceived dichotomy—"saint" versus "toy"—has remained a source of perplexity for Euro-Americans ever since.

From the moment that anthropologists arrived at the Hopi Mesas, they were fascinated by Katsina dolls. Early ethnographers found in the *tithu* ready-made miniature representations of the Katsina deities that they could purchase and take back to Euro-American institutions. Furthermore, the hospitable attitude of the Hopi allowed outsiders to view numerous ceremonies including Katsina performances. This stance was in marked opposition to the strict secrecy of the Rio Grande Pueblos where restrictions regarding these matters had been formulated under the repressive Spanish regime.

James Stevenson, traveling and collecting throughout the Southwest for the Bureau of American Ethnology in 1879, was the first to make a collection of Hopi *tithu*, although earlier Euro-American visitors had purchased a few examples (see fig. 4.2). Stevenson cataloged the twenty-four *tithu* that he gathered as follows:

> Statuettes. These objects vary in form, size and decoration, the largest being about thirty inches high, the smallest not more than five. They are objects of worship in one form or another. The illustrations in the woodcuts and colored plates will convey a better idea of them than could be given in a description. They are entirely composed of wood, with feathers and other small ornaments attached to them occasionally. [Stevenson 1881, 395]

Alexander M. Stephen's Observations of the Hopi Religious Cycle at Walpi

Scotsman Alexander M. Stephen was the first Euro-American ethnographer to spend considerable time among the Hopi, learning their language and recording their ceremonial life. He arrived in 1881, staying until his death in 1894. The majority of his time was spent studying the religious cycle at Walpi, a town on First Mesa, where he was allowed access to nearly all phases of Hopi ritual life and was even initiated as a full member into three ceremonial organizations (Dockstader 1954, 84). He began keeping a meticulous journal in 1891.

Fascinated by the *tihu*, Stephen recorded every instance of its usage that he encountered. He described *tithu* as playing a role in four ceremonial contexts: (1) Powamuy, (2) Nímaniw, (3) the kiva dance of the Barter Katsina (Hùuyankatsina), and (4) the rite of the eagle sacrifice. Although the Hopi Katsina ceremonial calendar begins in December with the Soyal, the *tithu* do not make an appearance until the Powamuy, or "Bean Dance" ceremony, in February. Stephen recorded that "[a]side from the usual occupations of weaving, etc. several in each kiva are carving figurines...these to be distributed by the kachina to the children on the *toto'kya* day, and the children are told that the kachina have made these figurines for them" (Stephen 1936, 194).

The carvers fashioned the figurines from the root of the cottonwood tree. Stephen observed of their tools that "pocket and hunting knives are used by all. They have also a hand saw and a small Mexican hand adze, one or two pieces of hoop iron with notched edges for use as saws, a wood rasp and numerous files of all sizes and numerous awls. Fragments of sand stone are used to obtain a finished surface on the figurines after carving" (Stephen 1936, 279).

As it was understood that the dolls must be fashioned with no children or women present to see them, Stephen was puzzled upon observing a small boy playing in the kiva during the carving process. When he inquired about this, he was told that "the figurines are now meaningless as none of them has yet the appropriate decoration. 'When we begin to decorate and attach meaning to the figurines, then I will leave the boy at home'" (Stephen 1936, 275).

Of the decorating process that followed carving, Stephen recorded: "All the figures are first coated over all with a white clay solution and, on drying, the colours are laid on, as usual with the yucca brush. Seeds of appropriate kinds are chewed for saliva to mix pigments.... The colours used are white, black, green, yellow, red" (Stephen 1936, 304–5). Another early ethnographer, J. Walter Fewkes (see below), corroborated this description: "A yucca stick with the end chewed into a brush, is used in painting lines. Plane surfaces of the doll are painted by squirting on the color from the mouth" (Fewkes 1894, 47).

On the final morning of the Powamuy, the Katsina personators, loaded with the tithu, bundles of bean plants, and other gifts, were instructed regarding their distribution to the children. The Katsinam then emerged from the kiva and passed out the presents. Again in July, at the culminating day of Nímaniw, or the "Going Home" ceremony, the Katsinam—now holding bundles of corn—distributed gifts to the children just prior to departing for their mountain home. In 1893 Stephen noted that "for weeks after this ceremony, the girls may be seen toddling around with the ti-hu on their backs, the head peeping from the upper edge of their mantles, just as a Hopi mother carries her infant" (1893, 84).

Tithu are reserved for girls (see fig. 3.10) with the exception of infant males who may receive them while still in the cradleboard and not yet separated from their mothers. On occasion they are given to women as well as young girls. When new brides who have married during the previous year are presented at Nímaniw, they each receive a tihu. Stephen also documented an instance where "[a] young Tewa woman was with child (her first) during the Powa'mu, and her husband gave her a present of a figurine, a Ko'kopeli ti'hu, and soon afterwards her child was born" (1936, 388)

Women also receive tithu during the Barter Katsina ceremony, held in a kiva on one of the nights of the Horned Water Serpent Dance during February or March. Stephen observed that

[i]n one of the Kiva(s) the members elect to be represented by the whimsical Katcina, called the Hu-hi-yan, or Barterer. As on other occasions, the ti-hu are secretly prepared, and on the night of the exhibition, women, both matron and maid, are permitted as spectators, and the spectators' portion of the Kiva is always crowded. These Katcina make no gifts, but with much rollicking fun, barter their ti'hu for fancy colored pi-ki, sweet parched meal, dried peaches, and other choice products of the women's culinary art. These ti'hu, obtained under very jocose conditions, are nevertheless held by the women, for a season, in a peculiar regard, as emblems of fertility. [Stephen 1893, 86]

The fourth annual occasion in which the tihu plays a role is in the eagle sacrifice. This event was recorded at Walpi by Stephen (1936, 569) and at Orayvi on Third Mesa by Reverend H. R. Voth (see below).

Every spring hunting expeditions set out to procure young eagles. These, when captured in their roosts, are usually tied to racks and carried to the villages where they are kept on the flat house tops, tied by one leg to some beam, rock or peg to prevent their escape. Here they are fed with rabbits, field mice, etc., til about July. [Voth 1912b, 107]

On the day following the Nímaniw ceremony, all of the eagles are ritually killed by choking so that their feathers can be used for ceremonial purposes in the coming year. Each carcass is buried in one of the graveyards especially devoted to eagles; the burial is accompanied by offerings—including a tihu made specifically for the purpose—and a prayer that "the eagles should not be angry but hatch young eagles again the next year" (Voth 1912b, 108).

While the young eagles are confined to the Hopi rooftops to mature, they receive toys, a miniature bow and arrow and a flat tihu, to keep them happy and to entertain them. When Stephen asked the purpose of the tihu given to the eagle, he received this reply: "These are said to be for the young boy and girl eagles, to play with, and become acquainted with the Hopi Katcina" (1893, 85–86).

J. Walter Fewkes equated the tithu with toys: "These images are commonly mentioned by American visitors to the Tusayan pueblos as idols, but there is abundant evidence to show that they are at present used simply as children's playthings which are made for that purpose and given to the girls with that thought in mind" (1894, 45). As a cultural artifact, however, the *tihu* has multiple layers of meaning, and Stephen hints at this when he states that "[t]he *ti-hu* is essentially a *pa-ho*...or prayer emblem, as much as if made specially for the altar; it is only another of their numerous forms of emblematic prayer" (1893, 86). As a prayer stick, the *tihu* may well be a prayer for the young girl not only to become a skilled good mother but to become fruitful and bear children, thus assuring the continuity of life for the Hopi people.[1]

If the various conditions where the *tihu* appears are examined together, it becomes apparent that the *tihu* is always linked with the female. Furthermore, *tithu* are always associated with increase and are given to young girls with the potential to bear children, to brides of child-bearing age, or to young eagles as a prayer incorporating a request that the deities send more of their species. When a Hopi woman exchanges some of her cooking for a *tihu* from the Barterer Katsina, she keeps this *tihu*, regarding it—as noted above—as an "emblem of fertility" (Stephen 1893, 86).

During the preparations for the Powamuy and Nímaniw ceremonies, the girl's father or maternal uncle acts as the Katsina's aide, making the gift in the image of the Katsina spirit and giving it through the Katsina dancer to the girl. The youngster is expected to toddle around with the *tihu* on her back, caring for her "baby" just as her mother carries her infant, and thereby pleasing the Katsina spirits who will reciprocate by granting her children of her own as she matures.[2] Although this aspect of playing with the *tihu* like a toy doll may seem incongruous to outsiders, it is important as a means of actuating reciprocity. The attachment of the bean sprouts to the *tihu* at Powamuy and corn bundles to them at Nímaniw furthers the association between the girls and fecundity (Stephen 1936, 574).

The *Tithu* in the Last Quarter of the Nineteenth Century

Stephen lived with Thomas Keam, an Indian trader who had established a trading post in 1875 at Keams Canyon. Keam, considered one of "the two most powerful Indian traders of the Southwest" (McNitt 1962, 142), amassed several important Hopi collections, including well over one thousand *tithu* (Dockstader 1954, 86), which are now variously

housed at the Museum für Völkerkunde in Berlin, the Peabody Museum of Archaeology and Ethnology at Harvard, and the University of Pennsylvania Museum of Archaeology and Anthropology. Although there is no recorded collection formed by Stephen himself, he did obtain *tithu*: "Ha'yi is carving a capital Owl kachina which I must try and get after the distribution" (Stephen 1936, 198). Any *tithu* that Stephen may have collected were probably left with Keam, who preserved Stephen's manuscripts after his death (Culin 1905, 172). Keam hosted practically every important ethnographic expedition to Hopi until he sold his trading post to Lorenzo Hubbell in 1902. During the summer of 1882 with the arrival of the first railroad in Holbrook—seventy miles to the south of the Hopi Mesas—the Hopi villages became a great deal more accessible to expeditions from the outside world.

The Hemenway Southwestern Expedition to Hopi was led by J. Walter Fewkes in the summers of 1891 and 1892. Fewkes returned repeatedly to Hopi throughout the next decade and collected close to five hundred *tithu* from Walpi (Dockstader 1954, 86). Writing of the *tithu* collected on the Hemenway Expedition, which are now housed in the Peabody Museum at Harvard, Fewkes noted:

> These carved wooden images are made in great numbers by the Tusayan Indians and present most instructive objects for the study of symbolic decoration. They are interesting as affording valuable information in regard to the *Hó.pi* conception of their mythological personages. [Fewkes 1894, 45]

Of note, all of the ethnographic studies mentioned thus far were conducted at Walpi on First Mesa, a town more accessible and thus better accustomed to outsiders than the more conservative Orayvi on Third Mesa. The latter was visited in 1892 by the Stanley McCormick Hopi Expedition directed by George A. Dorsey. The purpose of the expedition was to collect specimens for the World Columbian Exposition to be held in Chicago in 1893. These items were later placed in the Field Museum of Natural History in Chicago.

About this same time a Mennonite missionary, Reverend H. R. Voth, arrived at Orayvi, remaining from 1893 to 1902 (fig. 4.1). He established the first mission among the Hopi since they had driven Spanish missionaries out during the Pueblo Rebellion (1680–1692) and later at the Hopi village of Awot'ovi in 1700 (see Whiteley, this volume). Taking an interest in the traditional Hopi ceremonies and mastering the Hopi language, Voth set about documenting ceremonial traditions at Orayvi with numerous notes and photographs. The Katsinam particularly interested him, and he collected a vast number of *tithu*. A collaboration arose between Voth and Dorsey, the curator of anthropology at the Field Museum, which resulted in a number of joint publications and the museum's purchase of some two hundred *tithu* collected by Voth in 1898. Voth also prepared major collections for the Fred Harvey Company during the period when Dorsey was in its employ. Some of these collections were sold to large natural history museums, such as the Carnegie Museum of Natural History, Pittsburgh, in 1904. Voth also prepared a collection for the Harvey Company to display at the 1904 Louisiana Purchase Exposition in Saint Louis.

Embedded in the writings and systematic collections of these early ethnographers are visual and recorded documents concerning the Hopi *tihu* in the last quarter of the nineteenth century. Stephen provided information on the Hopi artists at work: "Nearly all of the kiva members, in all the kiva(s) prepare *ti-hu* in great variety, each man following his own fancy as to which katcina he will carve a likeness, some making two, three, or more of different katcina(s) for different children" (1893, 84). He pointed out that although all the men carve figures, some excelled at this skill.

These *ti-hu* effigies, or dolls, display all degrees of excellence or imperfection, according to the skill of the person making them, some with merely the crudest suggestion of feature, while in others, every detail of the Katcina

WOODEN FIGURINE REPRESENTING BUTTERFLY MAIDEN HOPI INDIANS

4.1 Sa'lakwmana (a Cloud Maiden) *tihu*, Orayvi, 1899 or earlier. Wood, pigment, and feathers. H: 48.3 cm. The Field Museum, Chicago, acc. no. 65726, neg. no. A68T. Photograph by Ron Testa. This *tihu* was collected by the Reverend H. R. Voth.

costume is reproduced with nicety. But in each, the prescribed colors and emblems of the Katcina, which it is intended to represent, are strictly conformed to, either in imitation or conventionally. [Stephen 1893, 83–84]

Stephen noted the various body shapes that the carvers produced: flat; flat with a half-round face; tubular with no appendages; or "effigy" carved in the round with appendages, assuming either a static or an action pose. At Walpi the Hopi had specific terminology differentiating these various figure types:

In Goat kiva, the flat figurine (*puchi' ti'hu*), devoid of relief carving; *puchi' ti'hu tai'owata*, the flat figurine with the face (*tai'owa*) or mask, in more or less relief carving; *wuko' ti'hu*, large figurine; *chako' ti'hu*, small figurine. The term *ti'hu* is applied to all figurines carved in more or less approach to an effigy. [Stephen 1936, 274]

James Stevenson discussing his collection of 1879, indicated that there was tremendous variation in size: "These objects vary in form, size and decoration, the largest being about thirty inches high, the smallest not more than five" (Stevenson 1881, 395).

Form, however, was not the characteristic that identified the particular Katsina spirit, nor was the figure transformed into a Katsina until it had been painted and detailed.[3]

About twenty-five to thirty of the flat figurines and thirty to thirty-five of the effigy figurines are under process of construction, among these latter are five or six animal forms, bird kachina, owl and eagle; but they say wait till they are painted, then we will know which they are intended to represent. Some of the special forms are of course specially carved, as the eagle and owl kachina, and the clown or other whimsical, but for the conventional figurine of kachina in mask and kilt the makers have

FIG. 520 (41963)

FIG. 572 (41969)

FIG. 571 (41951)

4.2 The central figure in this illustration is a late nineteenth-century *tihu* with a white kaolin-coated nude body decorated with vertical red stripes (Stevenson 1881, fig. 571).

4.3 Katsina *tihu* with a painted kilt, late 1890s–1905. Cottonwood, commercial and mineral paints, feathers, laundry blueing. H: 35 cm. Carnegie Museum of Natural History, 3165-147.

4.4 Nata'aska (Black Ogre Katsina) *tihu* representative of the cloth additive type, late 1890s–1905. Cottonwood, commercial cotton, tanned hide, cornhusk, feathers, horsehair, cotton, sinew, mineral paint, kaolin, adhesive. H: 40 cm. Carnegie Museum of Natural History, 3165-320.

4.2

4.3

not yet decided what kachina decoration they will paint on them. [Stephen 1936, 274].

Stephen reiterated throughout his journal that "the dolls have no significance until painted and decorated" (1936, 515). They do not become prayer sticks until this process is completed:

> The kachina is a *paho* (prayer messenger), so is the ti'hu, the figurine. Aside from the conventional significance of its details, the costume is also distinctly of a decorative intent, because the deities are naturally attracted by beautiful objects. When the deities see elaborate and brilliantly decorated kachina personators, they say, "Aha, what beautiful objects are those, they must be the admirable kachina of the Hopi!" [Stephen 1936, 216]

Three basic types of applied body decoration were used by the late nineteenth-century carvers based upon a tabulation of Stephen's findings and those of

4.3

other ethnologists: (1) body paint with no indicator of clothing, as in figure 4.2; (2) carved and painted kilt, as in figure 4.3; and (3) cloth and other additives, as in figure 4.4. Stephen described the first type when discussing an example of Ma'lo Katsina:

> This style of *ti-hu* being easily made, is very common, and there is no attempt to reproduce the kilt, girdles, mantle, nor ought of the costume, except the mask, by which it is identified. The body is that of the personator, decorated in the prescribed colors before he assumes his costume. He first smears himself completely with white clay—so was this *ti-hu*—then...he lays the yellow pigment. [Stephen 1893, 87]

As Stephen indicated, the *tihu* covered only with body paint was very common due to ease of manufacture. The majority of *tithu* collected by Stevenson in 1879 display a white kaolin-coated nude body with vertical red stripes. So prevalent is this type of body decoration among early examples that it is surprising that no one has noted its significance. Stevenson explains it thus, "Garters are represented at the knees.... The body is decorated to represent fancifully colored clothing" (Stevenson 1881, 396). It is quite apparent from the attributes, however, that the figures are unclothed. Hence perhaps this is another instance similar to that of Ma'lo Katsina where the *tihu* is decorated with the body paint used by the Katsina personator before he assumed his costume. A *tihu* illustrated by Dockstader shows the upper body painted in red and white stripes and the lower body covered with a kilt (1954, 100, fig. 22). Stephen illustrated two examples of the second type of body decoration, the carved and painted kilt (1936, 196, 218). These figures tended to be blocky and static in their pose. The third variant with cloth additives used as body decoration was not mentioned by Stephen, but Stevenson specified that one of his specimens had a skirt of real cloth (1879, 396). This type does not seem to have been common in the Walpi collections of the time.

In the collection formed by Fewkes with the Hemenway Expedition in 1891 and 1892, all of the body types and decorative modes are represented. Fewkes purchased most of his specimens, the majority of which were "modern," directly from the owners (Fewkes 1894, 45). He indicated, however, that *tithu* could be ordered, "It is of course possible to have the *ti-hus* of different *ka-tci-nas* manufactured to order and certain men have a reputation as being clever workmen in this line" (Fewkes 1894, 59).

Fewkes accurately observed that "[t]he representation of the body is subordinate to that of the head" (1894, 46). He failed to recognize, however, that the power of the personator resides within his mask, and that this is reflected in the priority given to the representation of the *tihu's* face. Fewkes clearly demonstrated a bias for the action figure, a form that Euro-American buyers came to prefer: "I have a good *ti-hu* of *Na-tac-ka*.... The doll is a large one and is slightly stooping in posture. It is exceptional in that the arms and head are separate from the body and admit motion" (Fewkes 1894, 60).

The earliest collection amassed by Voth in the 1890s and sold to the Field Museum in 1898 allows an opportunity to compare and contrast the *tithu* from Orayvi with those of Walpi collected at the same period. According to the descriptions given by Voth (1901), the uses of the *tihu* at Orayvi were essentially the same as at Walpi, although regional differences between Orayvi and other Hopi villages have been noted in other respects (Wright 1979, xiii).

According to Dorsey, Voth's method of acquiring *tithu* differed from that employed by the collectors at Walpi.

In his studies of the complex questions of the Hopi *katcinas*, Mr. Voth soon discovered that many of the common *tihus* made by the Hopi are manufactured with little regard for accuracy, at least so far as the details of symbolism are concerned; hence many of the *tihus* were made to order in accordance with the true symbolic details of the personages which they are designed to represent. They are thus more accurate miniature reproductions of the *katcinas* than are those generally manufactured by the Hopi for sale. [Dorsey 1899, 349]

Dorsey did tend to exaggerate to enhance sales potential and significance, but, as noted above, he did work closely with Voth for many years to form a number of collections that were distributed through the Fred Harvey Company.[4] It may also be that Third Mesa (Orayvi) carvers purposefully deleted details on their commercial *tithu* to offset their discomfort in making them available to outsiders.

Voth's collection of Orayvi *tithu* made in the 1890s shows significant differences from those collected at Walpi. The Orayvi carving style is much cruder and less finished, and Orayvi *tithu* are elaborated with a multitude of additives such as clothing, fur, feathers, and hair—all giving the appearance of dolls that have been dressed.

Voth's desire was to obtain all of the *tihu* representations "so far as they are known" (Dorsey 1899, 394). This created some conflict when he commissioned certain representations. "As this katcina (Chowilawu) never appears in public it was very difficult to get a *tihu* of the katcina made, and the maker has been severely censured for it by the priests" (Voth 1901, pl. L). Today it is readily recognized that no one can collect *tithu* of all the Katsinam since the Hopi continually add, subtract, and temporarily retire certain deities (see David 1993). Despite the intervention in the carvers' usual mode of working, Voth's collection, as well as those of the other early ethnographers, supplies the only catalog of the types of Katsina representations that existed during the last quarter of the nineteenth century. A tabulation of the *tihu* collected by Stevenson (1881) in 1879, Fewkes (1894) in 1891–1892, (1901) prior to 1898, Voth ([1912a] 1967) prior to 1912, and Stephen (1936) in 1891–1894 yields the following results: Out of 162 examples, there were 97 different representations with 25 representations listed by two or more ethnographers. Such variety in a small sample probably indicates that the Katsina pantheon was large at that time.

Although many of these collectors were striving for diversity in their collections rather than a representative sample of those *tithu* most favored by the Hopi themselves, a few representations appear with greater frequency than the rest:

fifteen Sa'lako—nine Sa'lakwmana, six
    Si'osa'lako
five Hemiskatsina—two Hemiskatsina, three
    Si'ohemiskatsina
four Hahay'iwùuti—made for eagles (Voth
    [1912a] 1967, 9)
four Tasapkatsina (Navajo)
four Taatangaya (Hornet Katsina)
three Angwusnasomtaqa (Crow Mother Katsina)

The overwhelming popularity of Sa'lako was confirmed by Fewkes who stated: "Dolls of *Sa-li-ko-ma-na* are among the most numerous which the children have. They are found of all degree of complication from simple decorated flat slabs to elaborately clothed dolls with complicated *nak-tci*" (Fewkes 1894, 67)

The majority of the dolls represent Sa'lakwmana, the female member of the Hopi male-female pair (fig. 4.5). The tall Si'osa'lako, on the other hand, was borrowed from Zuni perhaps in the 1860s when many Hopi fled to Zuni for refuge during a severe drought. Although often creating confusion, the Hopi and the Zuni-derived Sa'lako are different beings. Fewkes noted that "[t]he Hopi, however, have a Calako of their own. They distinguish it from the Siocalako, which they not only recognize as of Zuni origin, but are also able to designate the family which brought it up from the Zunians" (Fewkes 1897, 308).

Although nineteenth-century carvers made many Hopi Sa'lakwmana *tithu*, none of the ethnographers was able to record a single instance in which the Hopi male-female pair appeared in a dance. Nor was the Si'osa'lako performed with any frequency. In 1893

Stephen observed that "[i]t is between thirty and forty years ago since last the Hopi rendered an exhibition of the Sio Sha'lako" (Stephen 1936, 441).

He also recorded a story in 1884 about the Hopi Sa'lako during a time when the Hopi were perishing from hunger. One brave Hopi boy appealed to Sa'lako and his two Hopi wives.

> The boy said he had seen the Salyko, but could not tell how Salyko looked, his wives were very beautiful and elegantly painted. They wore great headdresses displaying all the kinds of corn they were to give to the Hopitu—white, yellow, red, black, blue, blue and white speckled, red and yellow speckled,

4.5 Sa'lakwmana (a Cloud Maiden) *tihu*, late 1890s–1905. Cottonwood, unidentified wood, commercial and mineral paints, laundry blueings, wild turkey feathers, large owl semiplumes, feathers, steel, resin, commercial dye. H: (Katsina) 37 cm; (*tablita*) 35 cm. Carnegie Museum of Natural History, 3165-168 (Katsina), 3165-302 (*tablita*).

sweet corn, *chico* (a small sweet corn), *kwapi* (a seeded grass), and all these bunches of corn were wreathed around with clouds. [Stephen 1929, 58]

The Sa'lakwmana wears an ear of corn on her forehead and an elaborate headdress of stepped-triangle clouds. Her headdress tells the story of Hopi survival and the continuity of life. "To Hopi people, corn is life. It has sustained the Hopi people throughout their history. It is the first solid food fed to infants at their clan naming ceremony. It is also prepared for the deceased, to sustain their essences as they journey into the spirit world" (Lomawaima 1996, 253). The assurance of that life is secured by adequate rainfall to germinate the seeds and sustain the corn crop, hence the clouds on Sa'lakwmana's headdress.

Corn is repeatedly linked with Hopi females—both are fruitful and bear children, thus assuring the continuity of the generations. "The rain will come, that the corn maidens may grow high…the little corn-plants are corn maidens. When the corn is no longer little but grown…then come the corn ears and these are the children of the corn. We call the corn 'mother.' It nourishes us, it gives us life,—is it not our mother?" explained an unidentified Hopi man (Curtis 1907, 481). These Sa'lakwmana dolls with their connection to corn were especially potent prayer sticks when presented to young females upon whom the regeneration of the family, the clan, and the people depended and still depends.[5]

After 1900

By the first decade of the twentieth century, the era of ethnographic expeditions was drawing to a close at Hopi. The railroad made it possible for the public to travel through the American Southwest, lured by exotic destinations such as the Grand Canyon. Recognizing the potential tourist market, the Fred Harvey Company, food services concessionaire in partnership with the Santa Fe Railway, entered into the retail sale of American Indian arts. The Harvey

Company began as a curio business in 1899 and bought Navajo and Pueblo silver jewelry, Navajo rugs, and Hopi Katsina dolls for resale. It established its Indian Department and Museum in 1902, headquartered in the Alvarado Hotel near the railroad tracks in Albuquerque. In preparation, the company set about purchasing large quantities of Southwest Indian art including Hopi Katsina dolls. Regional traders, who operated trading posts near native villages and communities, supplied the Harvey Company with stock.

It was at this time that evidence of the commercialization of the *tihu* began to appear.

Entries in these [Fred Harvey Company] ledgers begin in July 1903 with a purchase of 14 Hopi kachina dolls, some of the earliest of several thousand bought from 1900 to the present. Temptation to sell sacred articles had been having its effect on the Hopi, for later in the same month eleven masks were purchased. Even kachina dolls were not originally supposed to be sold, but the large collections of

4.6 A *tihu* collected by Voltz, late 1890s–1905. Cottonwood, feathers, leather (?), wool, horsehair, dye, cotton, paint, clay, sinew(?). H: 33 cm. Carnegie Museum of Natural History, 3165-192.

Thomas Keam and J. Walter Fewkes of the Smithsonian in the 1880's and 1890's furnished ample precedent. [Harvey 1963, 38]

By 1913 there is documented evidence of an effort on the part of Euro-American patrons to stimulate manufacture of *tithu* specifically for commercial purposes, although attempts at such may have occurred prior to this. Charles L. Owen of the Field Museum in Chicago

encouraged the Hopi to make items for resale. In a 1913 letter to Herman Schweizer [of the Fred Harvey Company] regarding shipments he states: "Boxes 8 and 10 are chiefly commercial tihus…. Examine the tihus and give me an opinion as to their salability, etc. Two men have promised to rush the making of more. [Harvey 1963, 39]

Frederick Voltz who had a trading post at Canyon Diablo, Arizona furnished nearly four hundred *tithu* to the Harvey Company in 1901 (Harvey 1976, 3). This large group of *tithu* share some remarkable similarities in carving and decoration (fig. 4.6). The bodies are elongated and thin with long narrow arms that hang loose from the torso; the arms are often carved separately and then attached to the body. The figures are clothed in miniature outfits fashioned from real cloth and other additives. Embroidered sashes; cloth neck rings; yarn garters; twig bows, arrows, and rattles; feathers; and even jewelry adorn them. On close inspection, many of the accoutrements were obviously made by the

same seamstress. These dolls were probably carved and adorned in an assembly line workshop by the same individuals (Erickson 1977, 25–27; Brody 1994, 149–50).[6] Zena Pearlstone suggests that these Hopi carvers may have intentionally patterned their figurines after the Zuni type to avoid censure for disregarding tribal prohibitions against making *tithu* for commercial purposes (Pearlstone, personal communication, 1998).

The tastes and desires of Euro-American patrons began to exert influence on the Hopi carvers (see Wright, this volume). Patrons utilized the volume of drawings of Hopi Katsinam that had been executed by Hopi artists and commissioned by Fewkes in 1903, much like a Sears and Roebuck catalog. In the 1930s when Dorothy Maxwell began her *tithu* collection (now in the Maxwell Museum of Anthropology at the University of New Mexico, she would indicate which illustration from the Fewkes book that she wished the Hopi carver to reproduce (J. J. Brody, personal communication, 1980).

Hopi *tithu* continue to have dual roles. Carvers make the figurines both for traditional ceremonial use during the Hopi Katsina season and as objects in great demand by non-Hopi patrons. In his autobiography Hopi artist Fred Kabotie expressed his dismay at this dual audience: "Hundreds of them are sold each year in gift shops all over the Southwest. We sell them at the craft guild [at the Pueblo]…. I wish kachina dolls weren't such big business. When Hattie, our daughter, was little I made dolls for the kachinas to give her…. Hattie still has every one of her kachina dolls. That's the way it should be" (Kabotie 1977, 128). ●

Michael Horse

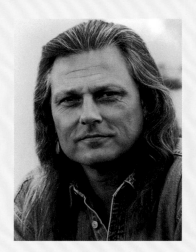

Michael Horse is an artist of Zuni, Apache, Yaqui, Latino, and Euro-American ancestry based in California. The following are excerpts from an interview conducted in Los Angeles by Zena Pearlstone on May 21, 1994.

I'm half Native American, a quarter Latino, and a quarter Swedish. I grew up in Pascua on the Yaqui Reservation. But I go home to Zuni; I go home to Mescalero. I began making Katsina jewelry in 1973. I studied with the Navajo Philip Long and his family and with members of my family at Zuni who are silversmiths. Working with Katsinam gives me balance. They are images of power and balance, and I try to understand and respect them.

I like the clowns because I like humor. That's pretty much the way I survive in Los Angeles. I do Mudheads, one of the bears, and eagles, but there are certain ones that I'm told that I can't do. I try and have deep respect, and if a very traditional elder says, "I don't ever want to see you do that again," I won't do it. It's not just a commercial enterprise, it's an image that I know. I once asked one of the elders, "Can I use these to do a contemporary version of one?" and he said, "Oh yes because these are universal images, these are healing images." Sometimes I do contemporary versions, but they are not any particular Katsina.

At some point representing Katsinam became an art form. Some people ask me why I don't stick to traditional Indian art. If I'm working in steel and plastic and chrome, it's still traditional art. I will always look at things from that point of view—even when I walk around the city—because that's the way I was raised.

I do see a lot of disrespect for my culture. I see prostitution of the images of these sacred deities and that makes me very angry. Liquor bottles, for example, made in the 1970s by the Jim Beam and Ezra Brooks companies represent Katsinam (see Pearlstone, this volume) and also Sitting Bull and Crazy Horse.

I see a difference between making Katsina dolls and representing Katsinam in other ways. I object to people marketing dolls as Hopi when they are not. Jewelry seems to me different. People are not as offended by Katsina jewelry or Katsinam in paintings as they are by the making of dolls. Katsinam are religious deities. The carvings seem to me to have more life and are more than just images. There may be no difference. Some say these images belong to

the people, and they're not to be sold, so I may be wrong. I never had any spiritual person tell me that they found these offensive, but it may be. I would never carve Katsinam.

VI.1

VI.1 Hehey'akatsina bolo tie, 2000. Silver, turquoise, and leather. H: 4.65 cm.

VI.2 Taawakatsina (Sun Katsina) ring, circa 1997. Silver, turquoise, and inlaid stones. H: 5.5 cm. Private collection.

VI.3 Pàngwkatsina (Mountain Sheep Katsina) ring. Silver and turquoise.

VI.4 Hònkatsina (Bear Katsina) bolo tie. Silver, turquoise, and leather. Photograph by Zena Pearlstone.

VI.5 Kooyemsi necklace. Gold and diamonds. Photograph by Zena Pearlstone.

VI.2

VI.3

VI.4

VI.5

VII.I *Shalak'mana,*
1995. Acrylic on canvas.
61 x 50.8 cm. Photograph
courtesy of the artist.

VII.I

John Farnsworth

*John Farnsworth is a Euro-American artist based
in New Mexico. His statement given below is dated
summer 1997.*

I paint Katsinam because:
they are there;
they are beautiful;
they are a part of me;
they are timeless and enduring;
they are intriguing and mysterious;
they are powerful and evocative and alive;
they are carved and textured and painted and aged;
they are feathered and masked and costumed
     or unclothed;
they are primordial and sophisticated and speak
     of other worlds;
they are carriers of messages and of prayers and
     bringers of rain and life;
they are subtle and complex, terrifying and
     comforting, animal, man, spirit, cloud;
they are hope and fear, promise and admonition,
     deliverance and instruction, comfort and song;
they are of the earth and of the sky and of the air
     and of the water that flows through everything.

I was born in Williams, Arizona, and grew up in
towns along the railroad and in the logging camps
of Northern Arizona. When I was nine years old, I
visited Taos, my mother's birthplace. In the galleries
of Taos, I realized that I would be an artist. When
I returned to Flagstaff in 1962 after four years in
the military, I was aware of how much I had missed
the Navajo and Hopi influence in my life. I was
fortunate to find people to finance my work so that
I could spend the next years drawing and painting.
In 1968 I began to visit ceremonials where I sketched
and watched.

   I painted, mostly Indians or Indian-related subjects
and camped and traveled among the Navajo and
Pueblos until 1973. In 1977 I quit painting Indian
subjects. I was feeling burned out, as though I'd been
"run over" by the immense popularity of Indian
subject matter. I also stopped attending Katsina
dances because of the crowding and rude, thought-
less behavior of so many non-Indians. I painted
other things, but unable to completely sever my
connection to Indian topics, I also did a few large
Katsina faces. Until 1994 I successfully painted
cattle and horses, showing at the Suzanne Brown

Gallery and getting commissions from large corporations like IBM and Texas Instruments and from the ARCO collection. I was commissioned to do the twenty-by-thirty-foot mural for Wells Fargo Bank that now hangs in Phoenix's Sky Harbor Airport. In 1994 I began to paint large Katsina images once again.

The Katsina dolls from which my paintings are usually derived are in the collections of the Southwest Museum, Los Angeles; the Heard Museum, Phoenix; the Museum of International Folk Art, Santa Fe; and the Millicent Rogers Museum, Taos. Some are from private collections. I have occasionally been asked whether the Hopi and Zuni people are offended by my painting the Katsinam. I have never known them to be. I am not trying to replicate or imitate the spiritual beings of the Hopi. Like the many non-Indians who have written about them, I am merely *reporting* on them and on their visual beauty, which has so moved me.

VII.3

VII.2 *Hoote*, 1995. Acrylic on canvas. 61 x 61 cm. Photograph courtesy of the artist.

VII.3 *Holi VI*, 1995. Acrylic on canvas. 61 x 76.2 cm. Photograph courtesy of the artist.

VII.4 *Calak'mana*, 1995. Acrylic on canvas. 91.4 x 122 cm. Photograph courtesy of the artist.

VII.5 *Shalako Blue*, 1993. Acrylic on canvas. 64.1 x 61 cm. Photograph courtesy of the artist.

VII.4

VII.2

VII.5

5 The Drift from Tradition

BARTON WRIGHT

Change has come to the Hopi at ever-increasing speed, transforming them in less than 150 years from farming people to active participants in the dominant technological culture. Many factors have effected these changes in their lifeways, far too many to address in a short essay. Nevertheless, it is possible to isolate a single element of Hopi culture that documents this passage over the quicksands of acculturation. The slow drift by some from traditional beliefs and actions and the efforts to compensate by these practical people can be documented by following a single thread: the changes in the role of the *tihu*, or Katsina doll, in Hopi culture.

Before the middle of the nineteenth century the *tihu* was solely a religious icon, a manifestation of a centuries-old tradition that was probably derived from more than one ancient population. Hints of its presence can be found in paintings on pottery, a few small wooden and stone images, petroglyphs, and drawings on cliff faces, as well as its discovery in the houses and *kivas* of the Pueblo people by horrified Spanish priests.[1] Its role in the native religion was well established, its function and purpose explicit. It was and is a visual prayer from Hopi men to unmarried girls, one designed to form an alliance between the young women and the Katsina spirits to enhance the well-being of the former.

Ideally, the doll as a prayer was given to the girls by a male relative in the guise of a Katsina. *Tithu* were given to boys only when they were babes in arms and considered to still be a part of the mother. The figurine represented any one of a multitude of Katsinam, whose identity was established by symbolic features on the head, details of the body being negligible to nonexistent. Among the Hopi the choice of material from which to make a *tihu* was always the cottonwood, a tree whose roots are lightweight and easy to carve with simple tools, and which have the added symbolic advantage of seeking water as did the Hopi farmers themselves. Girls played with the dolls if they wished but were taught that it was better to respect them by hanging them

on the walls of their homes. It was there that the dolls were first discovered by Euro-Americans.

The arrival of an outside market occurred in 1857 when Dr. Edward Palmer, a surgeon with the United States Army brought back a *tihu*.[2] Unfortunately this Sa'lakwmana was destroyed by a fire in the Smithsonian National Museum.[3] Nine other *tithu* were collected by the Hayden Survey in 1870 and the Wheeler Survey in 1871, but little information was gathered on the dolls (Hayden 1870; Wheeler 1871).[4] Among the first comments was that of Lieutenant John Gregory Bourke in 1881, whose information, while uncomplimentary, sheds light on the perceptions of the time when a non-Hopi market first began. He purchased several dolls saying:

> In Tegua [Tewa] I bought several flat wooden gods or doll-babies. They are both. After doing duty as a god, the wooden image, upon giving signs of wear and tear, is handed over to the children to complete the work of destruction. These gods are nothing but coarse monstrosities, painted in high colours, generally green. [Bourke 1884, 131, 144]

Dr. Herman F. C. Ten Kate Jr. visiting in 1882 and 1883, had much the same impression of the dolls but also gave their value, as he wrote:

> Not rarely we found gaily painted wooden dolls with monster-like faces and strange head gear. Sometimes a row of these dolls is put on a cord which is hung above the chimney or elsewhere in the room. Sometimes, also, some of them lie on the floor, and one of my companions made the remark that the Moquis do not handle their house-gods very respectfully by treating them this way. He erred in this as did Oscar Loew, and many others as well. The supposed house gods are nothing but models of persons from the Corn Dance, and children's toys. The Moqui name for

these dolls is *dicha*. [It is presumed that he means *tihu* as no other meaning is apparent.] The fact that a Moqui is always perfectly willing to give you one or more of these *dichas* for a quarter is proof enough that this opinion is in error. [Ten Kate 1885, 246–47]

The dolls of this era have simple proportions. The head takes up one third of the body; little attention is given to hands or feet; the arms are generally clasped against the midsection (generating the term "stomachache dolls"); in a great many, male and female genitalia are shown; and the pigments used are almost entirely of native origin (see fig. 3.7).

The 1880s were marked by a surge of interest in collecting when Frank Hamilton Cushing and Colonel James E. Stevenson added enormous numbers of acquisitions to the Smithsonian National Museum.[5] Between 1880 and 1883 twenty-four dolls were bought, but in the next two years, when Matilda Coxe Stevenson continued her deceased husband's efforts, a total of eighty-two more were purchased. It was during this period that the salability of the doll became firmly established in the minds of the Hopi, although there was at the same time a strong resistance to selling them. This reluctance to sell was sometimes outweighed by the desirability of the merchandise, coffee, sugar, and so forth, that was open through trade or for the newly available cash. A factor not often considered in the acquisition of dolls is the fact that the *tihu* is a symbol of a prayer offered, and it is believed that it should be respected.

The urge to collect increased through the 1890s and into the first decade of this century with Thomas Keam, Frederick Volz, and Reverend H. R. Voth buying great numbers of dolls for resale to museums that were filling out their collections and to the traveling public as curios (fig. 5.1).[6] It was a period when amassing numbers of artifacts was of prime importance, a time when most museums in the eastern United States and a number of those in Europe acquired their collections. The prices paid for the dolls are either unknown or inextricably mixed with purchases of other items.

There are two other factors that affected the production of dolls at this time. One is the question of what the Hopi were buying with the money received for the dolls. Did this include tools, paints, and other items that could affect the appearance of the *tihu*? Certainly during this period native paints

5.1 A. C. Vroman, *"Collection of Curios Belonging to Captain Thomas Keam," Keam's Canyon, 1900.* Seaver Center for Western History Research, Los Angeles County Museum of Natural History, V-1011. On the left a wall is filled with the *tihu* of the time.

disappeared and poster paints made their appearance. There was also a burgeoning experimentation with oil house paints and dyes, such as red ink and bluing, and almost certainly tools were affected as well.

The second factor, one that sets a pattern for the future, is the impact of non-Indian approval or dis-approval of the appearance of the *tihu*. It is during this interval that dolls with male genitalia ceased to be made. It is also the time when the Sa'lakwmana and other dolls change from a nude form to a fully clothed one. If there had been more interest in gar-nering information rather than numbers of artifacts during this critical period, we would have more answers to various questions. Suffice it to say that while the salable nature of the dolls was established in the 1880s, the 1890s saw the recognition of outside demands with the beginning of efforts to satisfy a non-Hopi market, and the period of 1900 to 1910 brought an increased sophistication in tools and supplies. The first evidence of the separation of economic art from ceremonial art begins during this time span.

The dolls made from 1910 until after World War II were carved primarily for internal use with little attention given to the vagaries of the non-Hopi buyers. Interest in the dolls on the part of outsiders varied widely as the touring public's curio buying changed with the economic conditions of the country. The crash of 1929 and the resulting Great Depression cut drastically into the buying ability of the public.

There were a few carvers who could be termed commercial during this period, individuals who led different lifestyles through exposure to outside mar-kets or who used the dolls as a form of currency. The Hopi chief of Old Orayvi, Tawakwaptiwa, used his idiosyncratic dolls[7] to repay political debts (fig. 5.2). Orin Poley in Winslow made pseudo-dolls as curios for travelers on Highway 66. Others like Porter Timeche at the Grand Canyon or Jimmie Kewanwytewa at the Museum of Northern Arizona were individuals whose dolls were bought as remembrances of the personalities of their makers (fig. 5.3). At the urging of Mary Russell Ferrell

5.2

5.3

Colton of the Museum of Northern Arizona, Jimmie became the first Hopi to sign his dolls, using his initials, and was roundly castigated by other Hopis for this break in tradition, as children believe the dolls are made by the Katsinam.

The dolls made during the interval from 1910 to 1945 retained many of the characteristics of the earliest dolls: they were still hung from the walls, they were rigid in stance, and attention was still focused primarily on the head although it had diminished in size (fig. 5.4 and see fig. 3.21B). The strongest evidence of change was the total supplanting of native pigments with poster paints and indications that technology had improved to allow more precise work. The dolls, although still static in posture, were carved with more freedom of movement as the arms loosened and moved away from the body. There was more separate carving of arms, legs, and accoutrements and an increasing use of pegs and glue to attach them and of plastic wood to cover joints or flaws. During this period there was no difference between the dolls made for home use and those that were sold. The difficulty of selling any craftwork during the Depression years inspired Mary Russell Ferrell Colton to help the Hopi by establishing an exhibition to display their work. The data from the Hopi Show gives both the quantity and price of Katsina dolls in the interval from 1930 to 1941. Admittedly this information is a limited sample, but the results are interesting. The average price per doll was just under two dollars with a range from fifty cents to six dollars. The number of dolls from each village over this eleven-year period was as follows:

Walpi -2
Sitsomovi - 14
Tewa - 13
Musangnuvi -2
Supawlavi - 2
Songoopavi -22

Lower Orayvi (Kiqötsmovi) - 52
Old Orayvi - 40
Paaqavi - 46
Hotvela - 20
Munqapi - 11

Two hundred and twenty-four dolls were offered for sale in eleven years.

World War II caused enormous changes in Hopi culture for it broke the control of the priests and elders over the young men returning from service with a broader awareness of the world. The changes in Katsina doll carving were small with little visible impact in the final years of the 1940s. But the next decade brought the "action" doll. Departing from the earlier static stance of the doll, the knees began

5.2 Wilson Tawakwaptiwa, composite-figure "Katsina" *tihu*, early twentieth century. Wood, pigment, string. H: 33 cm. Private collection.

5.3 Jimmie Kewanwytema, Qötsa Tsuku Wimkya Katsina (White Clown Katsina) *tihu*, 1940s. Wood, pigment, feathers, and cord. H: 31 cm. Private collection.

5.4 Tseeveyo (a type of Black Ogre Katsina) *tihu*, 1930s. Wood, pigment, and string. H: 25 cm. Private collection.

5.4

to bend, and the arms were extended, growing slowly more exaggerated until the doll began to show the movement of the Katsina dancer (fig. 5.5). The appearance of these "action" dolls caused some commotion in popular Indian shows like the Inter-Tribal Indian Ceremonial in Gallup, New Mexico, as it was believed that they were not truly *tithu*, and for a while they occupied a separate category in competitions.

At this time there was still not much of a market for the dolls, but the cost had risen to a dollar an inch. The people who bought them, however, did not want to hang them on their walls; they wanted them to stand on mantels, tables, dressers, coffee tables, and the like. Most of the older dolls stood flat-footed, and rigidly vertical. When they teetered, it was no trouble to correct this with a piece of cardboard or a thumbtack in the feet to keep them upright. But the action dolls did not stand easily,

as they stood on one foot and could be thrown off balance by their extended arms, etc. Since the Hopi hung their dolls, they paid little attention to this, but the non-Hopi wanted them to stand. Some Hopi who carved for the non-Hopi market began to try and overcome the problem.

Their first efforts were to make the feet bigger, which produces some very strange looking extremities. Sankey George, for example, made feet longer from heel to toe than the legs were from heel to knee. Then came experiments with bases. Sometimes these were of cardboard, plywood, or planks of various dimensions, but few were aesthetically pleasing until some unknown soul cut a slice off a cottonwood root and attached it as a base. It is not known whether this individual was Indian or Euro-American; it happened in the early 1960s.

At Sitsomovi on First Mesa in the 1950s Otillie Jackson's husband had gone blind, and in desperate

5.5

5.6

need for money to keep the family fed, she learned how to carve and paint Katsina dolls. Her work was good, and it marked the first example known of a Hopi woman carving Katsina dolls. This does not seem such a radical departure to outsiders, but it was a major break with tradition for the Hopi. Females receive dolls as gifts from males, and for a female to make dolls is a change in the traditional social order. Some Hopi priests feel that women should not carve even if they are only selling in a commerical market. In the course of time, every one of Otillie's five daughters took up the craft of carving dolls for sale, as did an increasing number of other women.

The 1960s were characterized by often amateurish experimentation, and changes appeared with increasing rapidity. Earlier neck ruffs had always been made of small evergreen branches, which, of course, dried and fell off, an acceptable occurrence for the Hopi but not for the developing outside market. Dolls began showing up with carved, round wooden ruffs, then artificial plastic greenery or green yarn, followed in the mid-1960s by English seaweed, the shrubbery used in architectural models (figs. 5.6). The use of Popsicle sticks for feathers in Eagle Katsinam, or using complete bird wings, jewelry made of sewing supplies, and small exotic shells—all make their appearance at this time (fig. 5.7). Peter Shelton, artist and silver designer, introduced acrylic paints, which did not powder and flake off as had the earlier tempera paints, although these dolls had a tendency to look shiny and plastic. It produced comments that his dolls "looked like a Disney product" (fig. 5.8). All of those innovations catered to the outside market and were efforts to satisfy or capture the attention of buyers even though there was still a muted resistance to selling. None of these innovations were ever completely abandoned, and they slowly appeared on *tithu* given during ceremonies, long after they had lost favor in the expanding commercial market. The rate of change in the dolls given in ceremonies was

a slow seepage of innovations marked more by new accoutrements than body styles.

This decade was also marked by the fad of gigantism. There is some evidence that large dolls and even action dolls were made on occasion fairly early, as shown in the photograph taken in Sitsomovi in 1902 by A. C. Vroman (Webb and Weinstein 1973, 64, pl. 32). But it is only in this period that a more widespread increase in size slowly manifested itself, possibly driven by the practice of buying dolls by the inch (fig. 5.9). Bigger meant a higher price, and when one thirty-inch doll sold for about five hundred dollars, there was an immediate rush to make even larger dolls. Unfortunately, the very size of the dolls reduced the possible number of purchasers as most houses do not easily accommodate a number of two- to three-foot dolls. The big dolls faded slowly with the marked reduction in buyers, but this produced a swing in the opposite direction as miniature dolls became the rage in the early 1970s. The largest "dolls" exceeded five feet in height, while the smallest were less than one-quarter of an inch in height. Neither of these extreme forms of carving can properly be called *tithu*, and they were not given during traditional ceremonies. On the

5.5 Paatangkatsina (Squash Katsina) early action *tihu*, 1960s. Wood, pigment, feather, yarn, cord. H: 45 cm. Private collection.

5.6 L. Lewis, Poliikatsintaqa (male butterfly) *tihu*, 1960s–1970s. Wood, pigment, yarn, leather, sequins, and feathers. H: 28.5 cm. Private collection.

5.7 Navankatsina (Velvet Shirt Katsina) *tihu*, 1950–1960. Feathers, Cotton, velvet, cottonwood, and plastic. H: 32.5 cm. Maxwell Museum of Anthropology, The University of New Mexico, 64.61.205.

5.7

mesas there was still resistance to the sale of Katsina dolls regardless of economic gain, as it was equated with selling your sister or daughter.

It was in the 1960s that Theodore Puhuyesva, a Hopi commercial carver, made the first removable mask on a Katsina doll for a friend and incurred the wrath of most traditional Hopi. Obviously this form of doll could never be given to a child in ceremonial circumstances as children are taught to believe that the Katsinam visit the mesas. The aberrations of gigantism, miniatures, and removable masks mark the first complete separation of dolls, those made explicitly for an external market from those made for a ceremony.

In the late 1960s or early 1970s, following an article in a nationally known newspaper on the increase in value of some Indian products in the last fifty years, a rush to buy any object made by a Southwestern tribe was precipitated. This demand was focused on jewelry, but it affected other crafts as well and increased steadily until 1974 when it crested. The later years of the 1970s were marked by a decided downturn in interest by collectors and other buyers of Indian arts and crafts. The production of Katsina dolls for the market leveled off until the early 1980s. However, it was in this interval that prices rose dramatically for all crafts.

The late 1960s and early 1970s were marked by dolls carved with ever-increasing realism, most of the inspiration coming from the work of Alvin James Makya of Hotvela. This artist's pieces, primarily of secular figures such as the White Buffalo, were aimed solely at the outside buyer. Attention was concentrated on correct proportions of limbs and heads with

5.8

5.9

muscles, veins, and fingernails accurately portrayed, the exact antithesis of a *tihu*. Within a matter of months after the sale of Makya's White Buffalo Dancer for nine hundred dollars, dozens of other Katsina carvers were attempting similar carvings, but of Katsinam rather than social figures, undoubtedly spurred by thoughts of elevated prices. The drive toward complete realism that had its beginnings with the action doll was now the dominant trend in doll making.

A brief flurry of metal castings of Katsina dolls began at this time when Clay Lockett, a dealer, had Henry Shelton's Snake Dancer cast in bronze. This process completely destroys the wooden original and leaves a product that is a diminution of the original rather than an enhancement. It was not too successful an effort although a number of master carvers had bronze castings made of their work. However, it also sparked a number of Katsina reproductions done in silver or bronze by non-Hopi that were sold in jewelry stores, as well as a few attempts at producing ceramic Hopi dolls.

The year 1974 brought the enactment of a federal law to protect migratory birds that had an immense impact on doll carving. This law restricted the use of feathers or any other part of a listed bird and was so comprehensive that only five types of birds were legal. These were pheasants, pigeons, chickens, guinea hens, and domestic turkeys. Up until this time the Hopi had used a wide variety of specific bird feathers, those traditionally required for particular purposes. After the passage of the "feather law," none of these could be used, and dolls with feathers on them could not be bought or sold, although the same feathers could be legally used to stuff pillows or tie flies for fishing. Because tradition did not dictate the use of feathers from any of the five legal birds, they were used indiscriminately on the dolls regardless of appearance (fig. 5.10). The result was so unsatisfactory that many carvers began to experiment with carving wooden

feathers and painting them correctly. Although this has produced a new type of doll, efforts to stay within the law have destroyed countless legitimate specimens that predated this ruling. Dealers have ripped off the correct plumage and replaced it with chicken feathers or nothing. The rights of religious freedom allowed the carvers to continue to use the necessary feathers on the dolls used in ceremonies, but these could not be sold unless they were stripped.

On the mesas the carving proceeded in a more or less traditional style. Men and boys with varying artistic skills carve and paint dolls to be given in ceremonies. Some may be sold later for a reasonable price, others are kept as valuable and cherished gifts. In some instances where the need is great and time is short, a man may buy a doll from someone who does good work for use in a ceremony.

5.8 Peter Shelton, Wakas Mana (Cow Woman) *tihu*, 1950s. Wood, pigment, feathers, plant fiber, and string. H: 36.2 cm. Private collection.

5.9 Claude Sikyayesva, Tuhavi (Paralyzed Katsina and Kooyemsi) *tihu*, 1960s. Wood, pigment, leather, velvet, feathers, yarn. H: 56 cm. Private collection.

5.10 Kowaakokatsina (Rooster or Chicken Katsina), 1970s. Wood, pigment, animal hide, yarn, feathers, and beads. H: 24 cm. Private collection.

5.10

The last two years of the 1970s continuing into the mid-1980s were a period of massive change in doll carving. It was a time of many gifted craftsmen, of work being signed, of new tools and paints, of new forms, and of Navajo carvers copying Hopi dolls. It was an era of experimentation when carving ceased to be a cottage craft and became an art form rooted in tradition but displayed and sold in art galleries. Carvers became known by name and were patronized, publicized, and paid accordingly. In the Hopi villages the quality of the dolls presented in the traditional way was now roughly equivalent to the better Katsinam of the 1960s that were sold on the commercial market.

The commercial artisans of this era represent a final step in what amounts to the secularization of some Katsina doll carving. The dolls produced for art galleries are too delicate and too valuable to be given in ceremonies. They are artworks by master craftsmen designed to be sold to collectors. Because of their value they have been copied by all manner of individuals: some trying to realize a profit, others carving their own to avoid the costs of collecting, and still others who simply like to carve. Dolls are made by school teachers, dentists, doctors, and lawyers, by Norwegians, Dutch, Latinos, English, Germans, and others, but, contrary to general belief, not by the Japanese. Navajo, who have no

5.12 Brian Honyouti, Qötsa Tsuku Piptuqa (White Clown Katsina) and Tsuku Wimkya (a human clown from Third Mesa). Collection of Scott Simpson.

5.11 Von Monongya, Katsinmana. Wood and pigment. Photograph courtesy of the artist.

5.13 Wilmer Kaye, "Kau-A-Kachi Mana" Katsina, 1980s. Wood and pigment. H: 32 cm. Collection of Tom and Nancy Juda.

tradition of Katsinam in their culture, produce the largest number of copies.

A few of the new artisans are known for their contributions and inspiration to other carvers. Von Monongya of Old Orayvi, who carved superbly realistic dolls after the manner of his uncle Alvin James Makya, was either the first or among the first to use burning tools to produce black, textured cloth, flowing hair, and other adornments. However, it was his care in sanding his dolls to a satiny finish that inspired many (fig. 5.11). In Hotvela it was the Honyouti family that either emphasized or introduced many changes. Clyde, whose penchant was for carving in one piece so that he did not have to carry many small pieces, taught his sons Brian and Ronald the same method, although other carvers as well worked with a single piece of wood (fig. 5.12). It was Ronald Honyuti whose Butterfly Girl, made from a single piece of wood, had the first carved decorations on her costume. He also initiated the elaborate carving of bases. Brian was one of the first to use stains to color his creations. Among women carvers, it was Muriel Navasie who was noted for her miniatures and for the occasional spark of humor that showed in her work. Her husband, Cecil Calnimptewa, belongs to the group of master carvers, like Lowell Talashoma, Loren Phillips, Jonathan Day, Ros George, Jonathan Cordero Sr., Arthur Holmes, Dennis Tewa, and others too numerous to mention whose works are avidly sought by art galleries.

In meeting this increasing demand, a number of innovations appeared. Wilmer Kaye added a new dimension to the carving of dolls when he began his sculptural pieces, shifting the emphasis to tall graceful figures often dressed in long flowing robes or grouping them into units of two or three figures (fig. 5.13). By the late 1990s some of the carvings may contain as many as twenty individual Katsinam. These sculptural or conceptual figures have appealed to many other carvers. Neil David Sr. is credited with being either the first or among the first to produce dolls that were not entirely painted, leaving the bare wood to represent the white of textiles. However he was not the first to make a bare wood doll as Henry Shelton produced the first one known in 1957. Along with the idea of bare wood, there has been an interest in using other woods that might be more beautiful or easier to work, and consequently there have been efforts to use tamarisk, oak, aspen, mahogany, ironwood, basswood, cocobolo, and tulipwood. Both Shelton and David have also experimented with carving only the heads of Katsinam.

In this they were surpassed by Delbridge Honanie whose works have left Katsina dolls almost completely to become symbolic art done in wood.

Carvings aimed at art galleries now fall into several different categories. The most important are the realistic interpretations of the Katsina dancers as they appear in the plazas of the villages. The second is sculptural carvings with their long graceful figures or the clustering of numerous figures into one unit. There is also a group that is composed of beautifully carved but unpainted dolls and another where the identity of the Katsina is carried almost entirely by symbols. A recent trend that has many followers was begun by Manfred Susunkewa and is

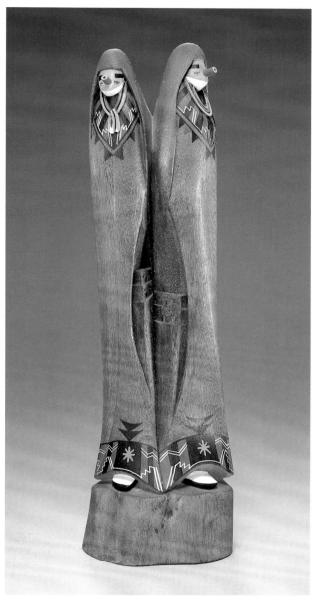

5.13

an attempt to return to a simple old-style big-headed doll decorated with native paints. Lastly there are the *puchtihu*, or flat "cradle" dolls. These are made of small, flat pieces of wood with the head painted on one end and a symbolic pattern on the body. Originally cradle dolls were intended for Hopi babies, and they continue to be given to them, but in the outside market they have been commercialized. They make an excellent collectible because the cost is low and yet they look like Katsinam and make nice presents. The result has been a wild proliferation of Katsinam adapted to this form.

While none of the elaborate art gallery dolls are given on the mesas during ceremonies, there has been so much change that the ceremonial gifts are often as good as the commercial dolls of the 1960s and 1970s, enough so that they sometimes inspire a spirit of one-upmanship among the girls receiving them. Despite this, there is a definite difference between the two types of carving.

The Hopi have always enjoyed carving and have never felt constrained to carve only the sacred (fig. 5.14). The result has been a wide variety of figures that are not Katsinam, although often believed to be such by non-Hopi. Among these are clowns, Butterfly or Buffalo Girls, Snake Dancers, mythical figures, and, of course, whatever may be sought after by the non-Hopi market. Before 1900 an unknown Hopi carved a train crew, complete with brakeman,

engineer, fireman, and conductor. Another carver during that period produced the entire cortege of Snake priests and Antelope priests. Through the years this penchant for carving has produced some unusual figures: a lone farmer squatting with hoe in hand, Mickey Mouse, a "Black African" inspired by a film on Africa, a Ninja Turtle, a local auto salesman, Hopi brides, and so forth, but not one of these could be called a Katsina. There have been countless numbers of Polimana, the Butterfly Girl, and Koyaala, the Hano Clown carved—none being Katsinam although often confused with them. One of the most commonly seen figures mistaken for a Katsina is Homichi, the Warrior Mouse. This figure is derived from a story told to children by their grandparents that was given visual form by Fred Kabotie in the 1940s. In the same time period Jimmie Kewanwytewa carved two bare wood sets of a Hopi man and woman. In the 1960s Henry Shelton carved a Hopi bride in bare wood that was the inspiration for Alvin James Makya's nude *Princess*. After seeing a European jumping jack toy, Ben Seeni from First Mesa produced a Koyaala with jointed arms and legs threaded with crossed strings, which when pulled on caused the doll to perform acrobatics. This eventually led to pornographic Kookopölö (Kokopelli) jumping jacks that had their nether parts covered with feathers until they were flipped about on the strings. There are a

5.14 Theodore Puhuyesva, Set of Four Cradle Dolls, 1980s. (A): Santa Claus. Wood, pigment, and synthetic. H: 15.2 cm. (B): Pumpkin figure. Wood, pigment, yarn, and plant stem. H: 19.9 cm. (C): Witch. Wood, pigment, and yarn. H: 21.5 cm. (D): Rabbit. Wood, pigment, monofilament, and yarn. H: 18 cm. Private collection.

number of carvers—Fletcher Healing, Marlin Pinto, and Neil David Sr. among others—who specialize in the production of clowns that are not Katsinam. Their efforts are humorous and avidly collected.

Hopi carvers will on occasion honor a request from a non-Hopi for a "Katsina" that fits some preconceived notion or purpose. From these circumstances come carvings of an astronaut, a watermelon, or a Haley's Comet "Katsina," but the Hopi themselves are also prone to producing exotic or humorous figures. Both Jim Fred and Muriel Navasie have made carvings that were political comments on conditions on the Reservation. The trial of a Navajo Tribal Chairman, the Joint Land Use dispute, and the eccentric dress of a buyer have all been rendered as carvings.

In surveying Katsina dolls over the last hundred years, it is clear that the tradition of sacred carvings has remained relatively stable, but a split slowly developed between these and the dolls made specifically for a commercial market. In addition there has been a tradition of secular carvings from the earliest known period, and these images fall into the commercial category as there is no reluctance to sell them. Sale of the sacred carvings was ineffectively resisted for over fifty years before collapsing in the face of economic gain. It can be argued that the commercial market began with the first changes that accommodated the desires of the non-Hopi. This would have occurred when the Sa'lakwmana ceased to be nude in deference to Victorian standards. Over time, powered by an increasingly strong economic prod, the demands and desires of the non-Hopi first produced a cottage industry reflecting various fads and then finally a class of artists whose works are inspired by Katsina dolls but whose efforts do not conform to the social demands that gave rise to them. The commercial Katsina dolls are not *tithu* when they depart from traditional requirements. This aspect brings about economic competition between the product of the Hopi commercial carver and the carvings produced by the Navajo who copy Hopi dolls. Often these copies are so well done that tribal identification of the maker is difficult. As a consequence most Katsina dolls made for sale are now identified by the name of the artist and the outlet where they are sold.

Traditional dolls, however, remain relatively unchanged from their age-old role. They remain an integral part of the Katsina Cult that is still being carved by male relatives and given to girls during the appropriate ceremonies, accompanied as always by a prayer that the Hopi continue to flourish through the well-being of their women. ●

Gerry Quotskuyva

Gerry Quotskuyva is a Hopi artist based in Arizona.
His statement given below is dated January 1998.

I grew up in the country just outside of Flagstaff, Arizona. Our home was located between the Hopi Reservation and Flagstaff. We had many relatives stopping by for a "pit stop" and, if they timed it right, a hot meal—so dinnertime could be quite informative on occasion. Generally, the conversations were random, but the one recurrent theme centered around the ceremonies of the Katsinam. All I really could understand back then was that there were all these frightening creatures running around the place my relatives called home. This was further reinforced by my great-grandfather who seemed to save the scariest stories for me! It wasn't until much later in life that I recognized the wealth of knowledge one could gain from these very same stories.

I started carving Katsina dolls in 1995. My thoughts focused around the desire to produce an artistic piece that would be recognized as my work. Sculpture was the most appealing to me because it allowed more artistic freedom. After studying the works of other carvers, I found the pieces made by Delbridge Honanie gave me the freedom to be an artist without limitations. As a result, several of my designs aren't exactly Katsinam, but rather an interpretation of them. The carvings produced by Wilmer Kaye appealed to me also. The techniques he used for the finished work present a clean and refined piece of art.

My first pieces were kind of rough, yet the concept I was seeking seemed to be there. It wasn't until I began experimenting with woodburning that my style really began to develop. I could create textures with woodburning, and more of the natural wood could be left exposed. This really appealed to me since it gave the piece more depth, and carving suddenly became a passion. I started carving full-time, and the quality of my work improved. Recently I pulled one of my first pieces out of storage and just laughed. Every possible mistake seemed to exist in this doll! At least now, I know that I am heading in the right direction. In the last two years I have won several ribbons from competitions throughout the Southwest.

As a hobby I started experimenting with painting and was lucky enough to win a couple of ribbons in this medium also. It wasn't until my eleventh

VIII.1

VIII.2

VIII.3

painting, however, when I won a poster contest for an annual Hopi show, the Hopi Tutootsvolla, that I began to take painting a little more seriously. My paintings reflect the Hopi way in general, however, the Katsina in a modern fashion still seems to be present.

I have thought a lot about the difference in styles between the artists who live on the Hopi Reservation and those who don't. There doesn't appear to be any formal training program, yet most of the art from Hopi has a common style. This "commonality" seems to come from living the culture with its everyday exposures, and those of us who grow up away from Hopi just have a different perspective. Both viewpoints are good. They carry the same message. The important thing, however, is that there is room for growth that ensures the continuation of Hopi.

VIII.1 *A Homage to World Hunger*, 2000. Acrylic on canvas. 122 x 182.9 cm. Photograph courtesy of the artist.

VIII.2 *Crow*, 1999. Wood and pigment. H: 58.4 cm. Photograph courtesy of the artist.

VIII.3 *Warrior Woman*, 1999. Wood and pigment. H: 48.3 cm. Photograph courtesy of the artist.

VIII.4 *Whirlwinds*, 2000. Wood and pigment. H: 143.5 cm. Photograph courtesy of the artist.

VIII.5 *Doorway of Light*, 1999. Acrylic on canvas. 152.4 x 106.7 cm. Photograph courtesy of the artist.

VIII.4

VIII.5

Christopher Pardell

Christopher Pardell is a Euro-American artist based in California. His statement given below is dated January 10, 1998.

I have been sculpting all my life—well at least since I was four years old. All through my teens, I was absolutely certain that I would be a sculptor. After two years of art college, I left for the opportunity to learn and earn my living as an apprentice sculptor at a Chicago statuary. It was an "Old World" education in art.

It was while working in Chicago that I was asked to create some pieces portraying Native Americans, and being a stickler for detail and accuracy, I dove into researching the subject. The histories and ethnographies of these diverse peoples were absorbing and inspiring. All the lessons of human weakness and nobility that I knew from Western classical mythology were played out in the tragic fates of the various tribes; this was, of course, made more poignant by virtue of the fact that these events had happened to real people. Furthermore, the rich and complex aesthetics of Native Americans were visually compelling. I was hooked. I felt that the culture and perspective of these peoples and their conflict with the technological West evoked timeless truths that all people could learn from, could draw strength from.

My feeling for the subject must have found expression in my sculpture, for I soon realized that, of all my creations, my Native American work was the best received and the most successful. This has been so much the case that these subjects now constitute the bulk of my artistic output. Over the years, I have received letters from the descendants of Sitting Bull, Quanah Parker, and American Horse, all very complimentary of my treatment of their famous relations in particular and of their people in general. This feedback has been the best validation that a predominantly White artist could ask for.

My work has focused principally on the Plains tribes and their more noted leaders. Eventually, I was asked to create something for the Southwest tribes. I suggested a series of small pieces based upon a representative sample of Katsina dolls. Sensitive to the beliefs of the Hopi and Zuni, I hold that only they can make true Katsinam, and in any event, certainly not in metal. I wanted to create figures depicting, not the Katsinam themselves, but Native Americans physically personating the

IX.I

Katsinam as they do in ceremonials. For this reason the sculptures were called "Kachina Dancers" and featured Native American people wearing the costumes of the Katsinam.

Of the hundreds of Katsinam that have appeared on the mesas over the years I selected twelve personations that were representative of the various basic styles, such as the ogres, clowns, and animal spirits. Some were of the more frequently appearing Katsinam. I, however, wanted to avoid merely marketing Katsinam that were popular with tourists and instead to offer the public a broad overview by selecting others that may be more obscure, yet vital to gaining any real insight into the complexity of Pueblo culture and worldview. As an artist, I endeavor to explore the humanity within the things we, as human beings, do, create, and believe. Doing so reveals that the beauty we put into what we become is the beauty that resides in us all.

IX.1 Left: *Hilili*, 1992. Bronze and pewter. H: 23.5 cm. Right: *Koyemsi*, 1992. Bronze and pewter. H: 25.4 cm. Photograph courtesy of Legends.

IX.2 Left: *Tawa*, 1992. Bronze and pewter. H: 23.5 cm. Right: *Kwahu*, 1992. Bronze and pewter. H: 23.5 cm. Photograph courtesy of Legends.

IX.2

6 Authentic Hopi Katsina Dolls

ALPH SECAKUKU

Introduction

The Katsina tradition is unique to the Pueblo tribes and does not appear in the religious systems of any other American Indians. Nineteen Pueblo tribes are located in New Mexico; Hopi is the only one in Arizona. Each Pueblo tribe is an independent cultural entity with ties to a common ancestry, a common way of dress, common customs and traditions, and a common language. The Hopi people, for example, have always shared a deep connection to Mother Earth and have long felt a clan responsibility for stewardship of this Fourth World we live in. Sharing life experiences and established tribal values, the Hopi people look at the world in the same way, regarding the same things as important. Hopi values are integral to our culture and make it unique. Our historical experiences and, more importantly, our values cause us to act and make decisions that "outsiders" sometimes cannot understand.

Hopi culture is very old and complex. We do not have a written tribal language, and no one knows exactly how long the Hopi people have been living in northern Arizona. We do know we were here before recorded history. I base this on the Hopi creation story, which is integral to our religion and to our ceremonial calendar. Our tribal migration stories and legends are recounted through illustrations and symbols painted on rock walls in archaeological sites throughout the Southwest. Also in evidence are the ruins of Pueblo-type dwellings, traces of Hopi terrace gardens, crude tools, domestic pots, pottery sherds, and ceremonial chambers with religious objects

Overview of Hopi

As noted above, the Hopi creation story is the foundation of our religion, which is our greatest bond (see also Whiteley, this volume). It has given us strength and unity since time immemorial. Our religion teaches that "life" originally existed in the underworld, which was happy and peaceful. People fulfilled their responsibilities and respected each other. Eventually, however, greed and jealousy began

to set in, and life became disorderly. Corruption occurred, eventually making things unbearable. It became necessary for "life" to have a new beginning. The people had often heard the thump of footsteps from above and knew there was life up there. The few leaders of the priesthood, clan wisemen, and medicine people who had not become corrupt performed rituals to "step" life up to a new place. The prayers and meditations of these men were honored, and life was spiritually guided to come to this, the Fourth World of the Hopi. The emergence of life took place at Sipaapuni, which is located in the Grand Canyon. Shortly after their arrival in the Fourth World, the Hopi were met by Maasawu, the earth god or the supreme deity on this earth. The Hopi leaders and wisemen made sacred vows to Maasawu, and he in turn entrusted them with the responsibility of caring for *tuuwaqatsi* (earth), the Hopi *tutskwa* (land). The Hopi lands are barren and dry, experiencing an annual rainfall of between five and seven inches.

To help the Hopi with their responsibility and to sustain the wholeness of all things in great balance, Maasawu and his priests guided them in the development of a complex and multifaceted religion. Our religious beliefs are based on the philosophy that all things, living or not, are melded into a great wholeness. The clan system, the annual ceremonial calendar, the unique relationship we have with the land and with plant and animal life, our prayers for rain and snow and for the sustenance of all life forms are integral parts of Hopi religion.

The religious mission of the Hopi is to promote and achieve the wholeness of the earth and the unity of everything in the universe, because everything has its rightful place. The Hopi also strive for world peace, because they believe life is very precious and should be lived to its fullness. In order to maintain the harmony and pleasantness of this Fourth World and to ensure a long healthful existence for all life forms, the Hopi use positive concepts and processes to secure a meditative relationship with the Katsinam, benevolent spirit beings who live among them for about a six-month period each year.

The Hopi Ceremonial Calendar

We follow an annual ceremonial calendar that begins sometime in November. (I use the months of the Gregorian calendar because most readers will be familiar with this system.) Individual ceremonies begin either at sunrise or sunset, depending on the time of year, and are further confirmed by lunar observation. November and December ceremonies are reserved for men's religious societies, while the ceremonies of women's religious societies are carried out during the months of September and October.

Within the larger ceremonial calendar, Katsina season formally begins in February (Powamuya) with the Bean Dance. Before that, however, the chief Katsinam arrive during the winter solstice (Kyaa'muya) to open the kiva (ceremonial chambers) and other "homes" so that other Katsinam can appear in greater numbers during Bean Dance season. Social dances are performed in January prior to the Bean Dance. After the Bean Dance ceremony is completed, an Ogre Katsinam family appears to discipline the people for all of the unacceptable life practices that are going on in the village. Symbolically, this represents a purification of the entire world with a driving out of all the "wrongs." The Katsina night dances begin, and these are held in all the village kivas. The Katsina day dances then follow in the village plaza. Other Katsina-related ceremonies are also held during this season, such as the appearance of the Racer Katsinam, and so forth, beginning around April and continuing until the Home Dance (Niman) ceremony in July, which marks the end of the Katsina season.

Children ten to fifteen years of age are initiated into the Katsina tradition during the Bean Dance season. A special ceremony is held in honor of the initiates. A godfather is chosen for the male children and a godmother for the females. These godparents are responsible for taking the children through the Katsina initiation ceremony and will provide them with religious and spiritual guidance for the remainder of their lives. Part of this guidance is aimed at establishing a "personal" relationship between the initiate and the Katsinam. Later the initiates may be initiated into other religious societies. Thus, my godfather initiated me into Katsina tradition at age twelve and into the male priesthood religious society of the Two-Horn when I became an adult. Even to this day, he provides me with spiritual guidance, which I in turn pass on to my own fourteen godchildren.

Authentic Hopi Katsina Doll Carving

Katsina dolls are personifications of the Katsina spirits and were originally created by the Katsinam as their physical embodiments. They are presented by the Katsina spirits to females as personalized gifts to award virtuous behavior and to publicly recognize special persons, such as brides, who are presented at the Niman ceremony. Because of the manner in which the Katsina dolls were initially created, and the tradition of carving passed on to the men who have received special Katsina initiation rituals and guidance in Katsina tradition, we are firm in our belief that there is a special sacred spiritual connection to Katsina dolls that have been carved by one who is initiated in the Katsina tradition. Accordingly, we do not perceive Katsina dolls as simply carved figurines or brightly decorated objects. They have important spiritual meaning to us, the Hopi people. The first Katsina doll for an infant, regardless of sex, is a flat doll, a cradle doll. The doll is a Hahay'iwùuti, sometimes referred to by non-Hopi as the "Happy Mother" because she has a smiling face. Spiritually, this particular doll possesses all the attributes of good motherhood, which are symbolically passed on to the child to carry him or her throughout life.

One way of teaching and establishing a "personal" relationship between male children and the Katsinam is through the carving of Katsina dolls. The godfather is the teacher of the male child, making sure all the "correct" information is taught. Initially, carving of Katsina dolls begins in the godfather's kiva, which is also the godson's kiva. Only male children are taught Katsina doll carving. The kiva, however, is where all the religious and spiritual guidance is provided for both men and women. Women receive their religious and spiritual guidance during the women's religious ceremonies, which, as noted earlier, are held during the months of September and October.

Comprehensive religious guidance is essential for male children because only the men have the responsibility for carrying out all of the religious functions. Women take on a supporting role for their male clan relatives, such as their uncles and children. This supporting role is equally important because of the sacredness of the clan and the clan house, where all of the clan religious paraphernalia is kept. Sacred food is also prepared in the clan houses by women.

We have a maternal extended family system, clan membership being traced through the mother. Clan members are the guardians of their respective ritual knowledge and share clan contributions, responsibilities, and duties in the overall Hopi religious practices. Clan responsibilities are taught in the clan houses to both men and women. The matriarch of the clan and uncles provide the guidance to the clan's children. As you can see, Hopi religious and spiritual training begins early in life, and there is a strict division of labor that is well respected: men are responsible for all the religious functions, and women play a very important supporting role. All religious guidance is provided in the kiva by godparents, and clan responsibilities and functions are taught in the home by clan relatives.

Hopi tradition emphasizes that Hopi women are not allowed to carve Katsina dolls. Carving of Katsina dolls is a religious function reserved strictly for men. Hopi religion is very serious business. Those who knowingly violate Hopi religious principles will suffer penalties. Religious philosophy teaches that women who violate these principles will suffer difficulty in childbearing. This is believed to take the form of bearing an unhealthy child, specifically one who is incapable of speech. This may seem archaic or sound very primitive to some, but the world is filled with many mysterious happenings. I would assume that those Hopi women who carve Katsina dolls have limited knowledge of the Hopi religion. If they are fully trained in the Hopi religion but still choose to willfully disrespect it, I can only think that this is done out of economic desperation.

Types of Katsina Dolls
Although I cannot claim to represent the views of all Hopi, based on my own observations and experience, I would say that there are basically four types of Katsina dolls made by the Hopi people today. It should be noted that all Hopi Katsina dolls are carved from the root of the cottonwood tree.

1. *Old-style Katsina dolls*—These dolls are very simply carved, painted in earth tones, and dressed with nonmigratory bird feathers, cloth, plants, leather, seashells, strings, fur, and hair. The dolls appear somewhat "stiff"; they resemble the Katsinam but are not lifelike. They are carved and dressed in a manner resembling as closely as possible the earliest Katsina dolls. The carvers of these dolls try to use "traditional" clay- and plant-based pigments. The colors used for body paint are not bright, and the style of dress closely resembles Hopi ceremonial wear.

2. *Traditional Katsina dolls*—When finer tools became available to the Hopi, the carving of dolls improved and their appearance changed. Traditional dolls are more refined than old-style dolls, although they are still not "lifelike." The limbs and other parts of the body are separately carved and fastened together with commercial glue. This assembling gives the doll a feeling of more action, specifically suggestive of dancing. Water-based commercial paints are used, so the dolls are more brightly painted. The methods and items used to dress the old-style dolls are used for traditional dolls as well.

3. *One-piece Katsina dolls*—This type of Katsina doll is fully carved from one piece of wood. Sometimes an artist will add very small accessories, such as feathers, bows and arrows, or rattles. These require larger pieces of cotton wood root and more careful planning throughout the carving process. One-piece carvings developed as a result of federal laws prohibiting the possession and sale of the feathers of migratory birds. These dolls are especially challenging and require the talents of a master carver. They are decorated with oil- or water-based paints. In most cases, one-piece dolls are carved on the base, which is also fully carved and painted.

4. *Sculptures*—Sculptures are not Katsina dolls. The Katsina figures, including the head and ceremonial wear, are carved into the wood with other Hopi designs and scenes to present a story. This type of carving has now been on the market for about twenty-five years. Katsina sculptures are very colorful pieces of art, but they are simply not Katsina dolls, and they are not usually used in the Hopi Katsina ceremonies.

Fake Hopi-Style Katsina Dolls
Any commercial success will be copied. Thus fake "Katsina-type" dolls are being carved by non-Hopi who know very well the spiritual and aesthetic importance of Katsina dolls to the Hopi. As a Hopi and as a citizen of the United States, I vehemently object to the intrusion, sale, and owning of these fake "Katsina-type" dolls. They are produced for motives of pure greed. As far as we, the Hopi people are concerned, these counterfeits have no spiritual, aesthetic, or monetary value.

Hopi religion is certainly as old as the European religions. Hopi people are United States citizens and should be protected under the Constitution. Katsina tradition is unique to the Pueblo Indians, and only qualified people of Pueblo Indian descent should be permitted to carve and benefit from the sale of authentic Katsina dolls. Any person who lacks these credentials should not be allowed to misrepresent the Katsina dolls.

Indian arts and crafts have been protected against misrepresentation since 1935 with the passage of a federal law creating the Indian Arts and Crafts Board, as an independent agency under the United States Department of the Interior. This law established criminal penalties for misrepresentation, for purposes of sale, of Indian-produced goods and products. Although the law has been in effect for many years, very little has been done to enforce its provisions.

Travelers from all over the world come to Hopi and other parts of Arizona to visit the Indian reservations. I envision tourism on Hopi as a rare opportunity for visitors to experience the culture of a people who have maintained their traditions and lifeways for thousands of years. The Hopi people welcome visitors who are interested in learning about our culture and are willing to share our heritage in a meaningful way while providing financial well-being for Hopi tribal members.

It was very difficult for me to write this chapter. All too often, the Hopi Katsina tradition and information about it has been purposely distorted, ignoring spiritual context and religious significance in favor of highly dramatic or picturesque portrayals. Accurate, as well as inaccurate, published accounts have been misused as public guides for the replication of the Hopi ceremonies and ceremonial objects for profit—among them fake "Katsina-type" dolls. These practices are unacceptable acts of intrusion on the Hopi way of life. I represent about fifty families who are involved in Hopi artwork, and I firmly believe there is an urgent need to safeguard the authenticity of Hopi-made products. As Hopi people, we are also very serious about protecting the tourist-consumer from fraud, misrepresentation, and deceptive business practices. ●

Clark Tenakhongva

Clark Tenakhongva is a Hopi artist based in Polacca, First Mesa, Hopi. The following are excerpts from an interview conducted at Polacca by Zena Pearlstone, July 21, 1997.

In the 1980s when I returned from the military, I gave up the contemporary one-piece figurines that I had been carving in the 1970s, which looked like everyone else's, and I started carving what people call "old-style dolls." I got smart. Why should I be in competition with everybody else? Why shouldn't I do something that was originally ours? So I went back to this style, carving the dolls the way they were, because they are of ceremonial significance. My daughter was born in 1984; probably that's when I started going back to this style. I use only natural pigments, feathers, pieces of leather, hair, and plant dyes. I use no commercial paints or acrylics.

I saw Manfred Susunkewa's work about fifteen years ago and was impressed with it. The first time I saw his carvings, I thought they were really old, perhaps from a museum collection. I too started going back to the traditional style, but our styles are different. Manfred's style is cruder. His goes back to late 1800s, mine is probably early 1900s. I didn't sell these traditional style dolls until about 1992 when Joe Day came and said, "Where did you get all these old dolls?" He thought my dad maybe made them. He said, "Why don't you ever sell me these kinds of dolls?" I told him that I thought

nobody wanted to buy them. Now I have my own name, buyers, collectors, and market.

My preference is to call this style "traditional." People who are not knowledgeable say "old-style," but those who are, know that there never has been an old-style doll. They were made like that in the 1800s and 1900s, and they didn't change. Will dolls made today be referred to as old-style in ten years? I don't make a distinction. I refer to them as traditional because that's the way they were made. I always try to do my own dolls for my daughters unless I have no time, and then I'll buy one. I feel differently about the ones I do for my children. The certain things I do to them personally stay with me. There is no such thing as a Katsina carving. The proper word is *tihu*, which means a doll and means a child. They are replicas of the Katsinam.

X.1

X.2

X.3

X.4

If you are an initiated Hopi then anything you carve is *tihu*. Anyone else carving is an outsider who has nothing in here of what I've got in terms of the education that began when I was born and raised. But even if one is initiated and looks solely at the dollar value of *tithu*, then that person is not looking at significance. Until you are educated within your own culture, you do not know about significance. Anyone can make a carving if he or she wants to put mind and skill to it. But you can't become a Hopi by carving. You are always going to be what you were born.

The action dolls, the contemporary dolls of the 1980s and 1990s, I refer to as the "Michelangelo dolls." They are still *tithu*. How else can I identify them with a Hopi word? What can I say they are? I can call them modern, stylized, contemporary carvings, detailed to the max and all painted with oil-based paints or acrylics or linseed oil. My grandfather said, "These are spiritual beings. Why would you want to contaminate another one's body—making them drink a quart of oil?" They're all living beings, and they're all in the spirit world. That's the reason I use plain old whitewash. *Tithu* were made early as crude dolls, not the detailed dolls with fine line carving that they do nowadays. That's why I call

those "Michelangelo dolls." I have my own taste and my own identity. There's a reason why dolls were carved the way I carve them. It is educational for the children.

A *tihu* is educational to the young child who receives it. She takes it like any child. Any child with a Cabbage Patch doll learns the fundamentals of what a person is. Katsinam have eyes, mouths, sometimes ears—all the parts. They have all the body parts that you and I have, and that is what a child two years old starts learning. If a child licked the natural colors off one of my *tihu* or the old ones, she would not get sick. This bonding gives them the advantage of learning our language. Children don't learn our language any more because Katsina dolls are all painted in modern acrylic paints. The colors don't rub off, they don't rub off into the skin, they don't rub off into the body. If you can't taste the mineral paints, you can't speak the language. A relationship develops because of the bonding of the doll with the person. Katsinam have a lot of good songs—harmony. There is language within the songs, there is the beauty of it. That's what's supposed to run off onto you. So where does that leave us losing our traditions and customs? First of all it makes us lose our language.

x.1 Hiilili, 2000. Wood, feathers, hair, and pigment. Photograph by Zena Pearlstone.

x.2 Qöqlö, 2000. Wood, feathers, and pigment. Photograph by Zena Pearlstone.

x.3 Wakaskatsina (Cow Katsina), 2000. Wood, feathers, and pigment. Photograph by Zena Pearlstone.

x.4 Sólàawitsi (Zuni Fire God), 2000. Wood, feathers, and pigment. Photograph by Zena Pearlstone.

x.5 Patro (a shore bird), 2000. Wood, feathers, and pigment. Private collection.

x.6 Old-style Palhikwmana (Moisture Drink Maiden). Wood, feathers, and pigment. Photograph © Jerry Jacka.

x.5

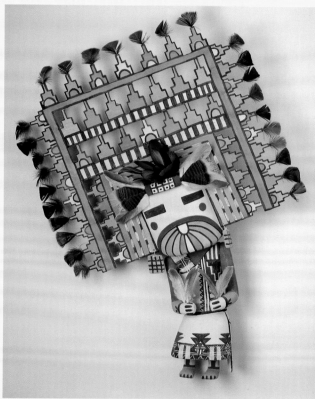

x.6

Poteet Victory

Poteet Victory is an artist of Cherokee and Choctaw ancestry based in New Mexico. The following are excerpts from a telephone interview conducted by Zena Pearlstone, July 23, 1998.

I was born in 1947 in Idabel, Oklahoma, the heart of Choctaw country. I was raised by my full-blood Choctaw and Cherokee paternal grandmother, Willie Victory. "Poteet" comes from my father's side of the family and was originally my last name. I grew up around Indian imagery and started painting and drawing when I was a kid.

I didn't know what to do with my abilities until I met Harold Stevenson, a painter and friend of Andy Warhol, who was from Oklahoma and came back in the summers to paint there. The summer that I was sixteen, he asked me to model for a series of paintings that he was doing of Alexander the Great. For the first time, I got to see how a professional artist worked.

I attended the University of Oklahoma, Norman, from 1971 to 1972. Harold Stevenson had suggested that I study at the Art Student's League in New

XI.1 *Icons of Faith II*, circa 1998. Oil and sand on canvas. 152.4 x 111.7 cm. Photograph by James Hart Photography.

XI.2 *Eclipse*, circa 1999. Oil on canvas. 101.6 x 76.2 cm. Photograph courtesy of the artist.

XI.3 *Spirit People*, circa 1996. Oil and sand on canvas. 152.4 x 101.6 cm. Photograph by James Hart Photography.

XI.4 *Whispers That Carried Their Prayers*, circa 1997. Oil and sand on canvas. 127 x 152.4 cm. Photograph courtesy of the artist.

XI.1

XI.2

York, and I went there after college in Oklahoma. I spent most of my time in New York doing classical works. When I grew up, being Indian wasn't "cool," and I wasn't interested in Indian art. I struggled to make a living painting in New York but finally came back to Oklahoma and worked in the oil fields. I also enrolled at Central State University, Edmond, where I received a bachelor of fine arts degree in 1986. Before I graduated, I took a trip to Hawaii where I was attracted to their native art. In 1988 I decided to move to Santa Fe, and it was there that my art blossomed. There was Indian art everywhere and for the first time I saw good Indian art. This art inspired my own. I see my life as a spiritual journey, and the Katsinam that I first saw in Santa Fe meshed with my own spiritual feelings. I knew nothing of Katsinam before this time, and these images were so strong. They reminded me that mankind has never been able to worship spirits without a form.

I never try to reproduce specific Katsinam, and I usually don't draw on any one in particular. Sometimes I will start with one that attracts me, but I never replicate it. I create my own, and some are very abstract. The forms and colors are adapted to my own spiritual feelings. My paintings are always my own interpretation. I will sometimes draw on other religious patterns, like Gothic or Italian church forms. My work has changed a good deal over the ten years that I have been in Santa Fe. My early works were detailed, but now they have become quite abstract. My colors are brighter. I feel that the spiritual message is stronger today than it was.

My work now is about 80 percent Katsina imagery. The remainder is abstract, landscapes, and figurative works. I am, at the moment, working with the Oklahoma Arts Council on a large (twenty-four by fourteen foot) painting of the Trail of Tears.

XI.3

XI.4

7 Intellectual and Cultural Property Rights and Appropriation of Hopi Culture

VICTORIA SPENCER

> The very cultural heritage that gives indigenous peoples their identity, now far more than in the past, is under real or potential assault from those who would gather it up, strip away its honored meanings, convert it to a product, and sell it. Each time that happens the heritage itself dies a little, and with it its people.
>
> Tom Greaves[1]

The basis of traditional Hopi life is religion. The Hopi have developed a complex ritual structure and an attendant ceremonial cycle, which serves as the nexus for all other sociocultural institutions and manifests itself most obviously in highly stylized "dances" in the plazas of the Hopi villages. The principal figures in these ceremonies are the Katsinam, personators of supernatural beings who form a company of deities regularly and ritually employed to assist with the agricultural endeavor and to promote general well-being and harmony. Attention to the round of ceremonials is considered crucial if crops are to grow, animals and man are to propagate, and the seasons to continue in their proper succession. Without competent and timely enactment of the prescribed rituals, there is *koyaanisqatsi*, or chaos, and all life falls out of balance. This relationship of reciprocity between the Hopi and the Katsinam is the very cornerstone of Hopi culture. The Katsinam are not simply figures manifested by Katsina "dancers" in ceremonies; they represent a complex belief system that pervades the everyday experience of most Hopi people.

Tithu—small wooden representations of Katsinam—are physical extensions of the spirit beings and integral elements of Katsina ceremonies. They are presented as gifts, or blessings, to female children and occasionally to women by the Katsina dancers during the plaza ceremonies. As the child's collection grows, so does her knowledge and understanding of the figures in the vast Hopi pantheon. These *tithu* are encoded with Hopi culture and are essential to the child's education about "the Hopi way." They also serve as tangible reminders of the central role of the Katsinam in Hopi society. They are both crucibles for and perpetrators of culture and, as expressed by Hopi Alph Secakuku, are not simply "carved figurines or brightly decorated objects. They have important meaning for us, the Hopi people: We believe they are personification of the katsina spirits, originally created by the katsinam in their physical embodiment" (Secakuku 1995, 3–4).

Tithu, or Katsina dolls, created for ceremonial use are imbued with sacredness for the Hopi and have intrinsic religious value. Katsina dolls and the Katsina image in all of its manifestations are symbols of Hopi religion and are thus to be treated with respect. Yet crude representations of them are produced by non-Hopi, and these adorn coffee mugs, beer steins, T-shirts, key chains, coloring books, and other memorabilia in cafes, gas stations, and gift shops throughout the Southwest and beyond (see Pearlstone, this volume).[2] Three-dimensional Katsina figures, ranging from nicely crafted sculptures made by neighboring tribes to pathetic "knockoffs" imported from the Philippines, line store shelves, and they are often displayed for sale on car hoods in parking lots. Books are available that provide instructions for making your own Katsina shrine, kiva altar, or Katsina costume. In the view of Hopi Tribal officials, these are all clear instances of appropriation and exploitation of Hopi religion. Hopi religion is a source of great cultural pride to the Hopi people and, as a symbol of that religion, Katsina imagery is considered by many to be the domain solely of the Hopi and other Pueblo peoples.

Officials of the Hopi Tribe have expressed concern—and even outrage—with appropriation and exploitation of what they consider to be the exclusive "intellectual and cultural property" of the Hopi people, and Katsina imagery or other elements of Hopi religion are usually at the center of the controversy. Tribal officials are regularly engaged in both formal and informal battles against violations of

Hopi intellectual and cultural property rights and in developing strategies to restrict or reduce continued appropriation.

This chapter examines the general issue of intellectual and cultural property rights of indigenous people, and how those rights have been violated through time by appropriation of elements of Hopi culture. The focus here is on images and practices associated with Hopi religion and spirituality—referred to as Katsina throughout this chapter. Cultural appropriation will be viewed in its historical context and both global and specifically Hopi responses to violations of intellectual and cultural property rights will be examined.

Intellectual and Cultural Property Rights

"Intellectual property rights" (IPR) is a topic that has captured worldwide attention and has generated a range of speculation, proclamation, policy, and legislation since the 1970s. In its broadest sense IPR refers to the legal rights of ownership that individuals and corporations have over the products of individual creativity and inventiveness. IPR battles rage in boardrooms over industrial secrets, in the literary agent's office over authorship, and in courtrooms over software designs. Increasingly, however, IPR has become identified and concerned with the rights f indigenous people to have control over their traditional cultural knowledge and property.

The emerging literature concerned with "intellectual" and/or "cultural" property rights reveals a tangled mass of distinctions between the two, which are complicated by definitions and interpretations that have been created mainly by Euro-Americans with little input from the very people whose property is being considered. Definitions vary widely and there is not always agreement about what constitutes "intellectual property" and how that differs from "cultural property."[3] Very generally, "intellectual property rights" tend to deal with indigenous knowledge bases in areas such as medicinal plants, environmental management, and agricultural bio-diversity—knowledge that is viewed by many to have universal value and therefore to be part of a global heritage. "Cultural property rights" (CPR), on the other hand, focus on "enabling indigenous peoples to preserve and control the use of their relics, archaeological sites, textiles, skeletal remains, rituals, songs, legends, and other materials."[4] Using this model, we are concerned in this study primarily with cultural property—with Katsina religious practices, Katsina "dolls," and the Katsina

image in its myriad variations and adaptations. For this study, "cultural property" will be defined as "any collectively-held heritage, material or non-material, not created for sale or for purposeful dissemination, that can be traced to a specific cultural and historical origin" (Clemmer 1995, 282); it will be understood to include cultural knowledge.

The primary issue in intellectual and cultural property rights is *ownership*—ownership of knowledge and of things—and, by extension, control of the use or disposition of the knowledge or things. There are several issues surrounding property rights and the Hopi that must be clarified before proceeding further. Both IPR and CPR deal with concepts that are culturally constructed, and they have been constructed in this case by Euro-Americans, not the Hopi. The concepts of *property, ownership, rights,* and *knowledge*, for example, have widely divergent meanings in these two groups, and these differences are often at the root of what may be perceived to be or not be violations of IPR or CPR.

The Hopi view *property* (be it land, a story or song, or ritual paraphernalia) as a resource, something to be used, not owned—something for which there is a sense of stewardship rather than ownership. Further, stewardship responsibilities almost always reside in a very particular collective—such as a household, clan, village, religious society, or "tribe"—rather than an individual. Stewardship is considered by the Hopi to be a privilege and responsibility, not a right in the Western sense of the term.

It is in the area of *knowledge* that we see two particularly divergent cultural paradigms. Euro-Americans highly value shared knowledge—freedom of the press, free speech, and academic freedom—so there is very little "classified" or "private" information in American society outside of that deemed necessary for "national security." For the Hopi, however, knowledge is consistently and purposely segmented, compartmentalized, and shared on a "need-to-know" rather than "right-to-know" basis. Hopi society is by nature noninquisitive and the idea of restricted information is deeply embedded in traditional oral histories as well as in contemporary Hopi life. In Hopi accounts of their clan migrations and subsequent settlement in their current place, for example, each group brought as their admission to the village a special knowledge or skill or a ceremony—known only to their bounded membership—to contribute to the benefit of the whole (see Whiteley, this volume). Each group fiercely guards its knowledge from outsiders—including other Hopi whose nonmembership in a particular group excludes them from access to the knowledge. Yet, each group willingly contributes its unique part to the whole, through prescribed ceremonies or rituals, for the survival of the Hopi people and to maintain harmony and balance in the universe. Here, the whole is far greater than the sum of its parts. Knowledge, particularly ritual knowledge, is a privilege that is gained through a series of highly ritualized initiations and instruction by elders through oral accounts specific to a particular group. Knowledge, in Pueblo society, carries with it the burden of responsibility to keep it private, to protect it; there are "ethical obligations of reciprocity and responsibility when one receives cultural knowledge" (Pinel and Evans 1994, 53).

Segmentation of knowledge is described in a statement issued by the Hopi Cultural Preservation Office under the heading "Respect for Hopi Knowledge," which emphasizes the difference between Hopi and the dominant Anglo culture reading of *knowledge*.

> Certain activities are considered the private domain of specific clans, societies, or individuals. Therefore, Hopi individuals typically will not inquire about specific sacred matters concerning certain ceremonies and practices from other tribal members. This helps guard the integrity of specific cultural knowledge for those members who are privileged to that knowledge. Asking questions about such things is not a common practice.... Protection of Hopi wisdom over the centuries has helped it to survive as a wellspring of social and spiritual nourishment for our own future generations and the world at large.[5]

Leigh J. Kuwanwisiwma, the director of the Hopi Cultural Preservation Office, elaborated on the issue as part of a panel discussion on cultural property rights: "You profane [traditional Hopi laws] when you begin to divulge information, when you, for academic or commercial reasons, place this information into public domain" (Greer 1995, 79).

Illustrated here are some of the profound cultural differences between two peoples with the Hopi operating under rules that are utterly foreign, perhaps even incomprehensible, to those who value and practice free exchange of knowledge. One begins to see some of the complex issues involved in intellectual and cultural property rights and how violations of these rights may sometimes occur without any awareness on the part of the offender. Violations of property rights occur on many levels and assume many forms, as we will see in the following sections.

Cultural Appropriation

Underlying any consideration of intellectual and cultural property rights is the more basic issue of power relations between two peoples. IPR/CPR cannot be discussed apart from the issue of "cultural appropriation," for it was recognition of acts of appropriation that resulted in legislation that acknowledges and supports the need for protection of intellectual and cultural property. Simply stated, appropriation is the taking of something that belongs to one individual or group and making it into the property of another individual or group. That something can be tangible or intangible property, but most frequently it is some element of material culture—pottery, ceremonial paraphernalia, or a Katsina image, for example.

IPR as a conceptual and legal issue became formally problematized and publicly discussed in the 1960s, but the problem of cultural appropriation and the commodification of religious and other indigenous cultural objects was widespread a century earlier in this country. Beginning in the 1860s, when the United States government began to deal with "the Indian problem" and instituted a policy of "assimilation or annihilation" of all Native Americans, several agencies and institutions dispatched investigators and collectors to "Indian country" to capture for posterity images and artifacts of these vanishing people and their culture. The intent, ironically, was to capture "culture" and preserve it, while destroying the creators and bearers of that culture. This betrayed in the collectors a sense of longing for the very thing they were helping to destroy.

These organized investigations were increasingly dominated by the belief that Native Americans were disappearing, leading to a frenzied acquisition period in which large-scale collections of material culture, human remains, and antiquities were amassed. These collections of material goods were supplemented by related oral history as well as linguistic and other cultural information often compiled by anthropologists and others in what we now term "salvage ethnographies." By the early twentieth century, Native American material culture filled the storerooms and showcases of American museums, and a substantial body of related literature filled our libraries and archives.

Native Americans, as we know, did not disappear either physically or culturally; however, because of the massive appropriation of their cultural and intellectual property begun in the 1860s and continuing in new forms today, their culture and vitality have been, in many ways, seriously compromised. This early collecting, which included massive looting and pillaging of ancestral sites and burials, led to discord between Native groups and the scholarly community—a discord and distrust that lingers to a great extent today.

Early Appropriation of Hopi Culture

Hopi provided a fruitful field for private collectors and organized museum expeditions at the end of the nineteenth century. Great quantities of Hopi artifacts found their ways to vaults, storerooms, and showcases in some of this country's most venerated museums, including the Smithsonian in Washington, D.C., Harvard's Peabody Museum in Cambridge, Chicago's Field Museum, the Museum of the American Indian in New York, and the Southwest Museum in Los Angeles. The collecting was highly competitive and often frantic.

Appropriation of Hopi culture in the form of collection and documentation was accomplished both by institutions and individuals, and by professionals and lay people—missionaries, explorers, tourists, and others. One man in particular, H. R. Voth, a Mennonite missionary who lived in the Hopi village of Orayvi from 1898 to 1902, represents for the Hopi one of the most intrusive and offensive individuals engaged in turn-of-the-century cultural appropriation and violations of IPR. During his residence at Hopi, Voth systematically documented rituals, prayers, songs, and stories—providing detailed drawings of both sacred and secular objects and revealing the most intimate and sacred details of Hopi religious ritual.

Voth's collection, or appropriation, of intellectual and cultural property was published by the Field Museum in the form of numerous articles and books, now part of the public domain.[6] While these publications (together with the monumental journals of Alexander M. Stephen)[7] form the backbone of anthropological knowledge about the Hopi during this time, they have caused profound problems for the Hopi people. Many of the details provided by Voth breached the Hopi compact of segmented knowledge described earlier, particularly ritual knowledge. A Hopi could readily find in Voth's publications clan or other ritual secrets intended for a

select group and protected by that group for several hundred years. In an article in *Hopi Tutuveni* regarding respect for Hopi privacy, Voth is remembered as committing "the most egregious…of intrusions and infringement of Hopi intellectual and cultural resources." The article further notes that "The Hopi stories which are carried down orally through the generations document that the Hopi people strongly objected to Voth's strong arm techniques [for gaining access to information and artifacts]."[8]

In addition to his collection of nonmaterial cultural property, Voth amassed an enormous collection of artifacts for the Chicago Field Museum in his role as "collector" with the museum's Stanley McCormick Hopi Expedition. The artifacts he secured for the Field Museum "form one of the most valuable Hopi collections possessed by any museum" (James 1990, 158). The McCormick Expedition was only one of many to visit the Hopi region and carry away vast quantities of material culture, creating a number of "valuable Hopi collections" for museums.

During this same turn-of-the-century period, in addition to being a destination for a stream of Anglo ethnologists, archaeologists, collectors, traders, and missionaries, the Hopi Reservation became a tourist destination, and curious and adventurous Americans seeking encounters with "the Other" began to have a presence in the Hopi villages. Entrepreneur Fred Harvey and the Santa Fe Railway joined forces and played a pivotal role in moving the Hopi into public visibility and accessibility; they created places and circumstances where tourists could not only view these "exotic" people and rituals, but could also purchase mementos of the encounter.

In 1905 the Harvey Company opened Hopi House on the south rim of the Grand Canyon— a structure designed by Mary Jane Colter with architectural features replicating those of Hopi dwellings at Orayvi, a village noted as the oldest continuously inhabited town in the United States. Hopi House became a living museum with artists and dancers from the Hopi villages (over one hundred miles distant) frequently in residence. Travelers to Hopi could now see ceremonies and purchase "authentic" Hopi wares directly from their creators. For the Hopi, this marked the beginning of new kinds of economic and creative opportunities. Now, any Hopi people who chose to could participate in the commodification of Hopi objects from their homes, not just those who were willing and able to make the arduous journey to the Grand Canyon or to Anglo towns along the railroad line. Tourist art of the region began to flourish as the Harvey Company brought the Southwest and the Hopi into a prominent place in American popular culture. Appropriation of Hopi cultural and intellectual property by outsiders would assume new forms and meanings.

Global and National Responses to Cultural Appropriation

In the 1960s, cultural appropriation became an international issue as a worldwide marketplace for Native artifacts grew and commodification of cultural property of indigenous peoples reached new heights. Once again, the Hopi mesas and the surrounding remnants of ancestral villages proved to be fruitful fields for traffickers in Native goods. There was a new wave of massive looting of archaeological sites, and professional "pot hunters" erased for all time enormous swaths of indigenous architectural and cultural history in their quest for saleable artifacts. Cultural material garnered through this on-site looting and in widespread museum thefts found a ready market, both locally and through organized international piracy rings. All of this conjoined to engender new levels of awareness—among the Hopi and others—about the nature and significance of cultural property and the critical need to develop strategies to protect it.

Violation of intellectual and cultural property rights became an issue of increasing national and international concern through the 1960s. The protests and sense of global collective outrage over looting and other illicit cultural activities eventually led to formal policy: the 1970 United Nations Educational, Scientific and Cultural Organization (UNESCO) Convention created an initiative concerned with ethics of acquisition and identified archival materials for protection as patrimony. "Cultural property" was defined by UNESCO as "property which, on religious or secular grounds, is specifically designated by each State as being of importance to archaeology, prehistory, history, literature, art or science." States were asked to quell illicit trade in cultural property, to return artifacts acquired illegally, to educate the public about the significance of cultural heritage, and to require museums to develop new acquisitions and other procedures regarding cultural properties. Cultural appropriation issues became front page news.

The UNESCO Convention served as a catalyst for other important cultural policy developments that would have significant impact on the Hopi. In 1978, with the passage of the American Indian Religious Freedom Act (AIRFA), Native Americans were given

the freedom to worship where and as they wished, "including but not limited to access to sites, use and possession of sacred objects." Museums shuddered: AIRFA required them to provide tribal access to the massive store of "sacred objects" in their collections. Throughout the 1980s, there were continued calls for changes in museum relationships with Native American communities, spurred in large part by the "Suggested Guidelines for Museums for Dealing with Requests for Return of Native American Materials" issued by the North American Indian Museums Association (NAIMA) in 1981. These guidelines presaged the sweeping changes in areas of sovereignty and intellectual and cultural property rights that would be legislated a decade later.

The Native American Graves Protection and Repatriation Act (PL 101-601) was enacted by Congress in 1990 and was celebrated as a watershed event in United States-Native American relations and in the relationship of American museums to Native American communities. The Act (known as NAGPRA) has four primary components: it (1) established legal protections for Native American burials; (2) makes it illegal to deal in Native American remains and designated cultural items, such as sacred objects, in the marketplace; (3) requires museums and federal agencies to summarize their cultural property holdings, inventory human remains, and provide open access to Native Americans; and (4) requires museums and federal agencies to actively seek consultation with tribes and repatriate human remains and relevant cultural materials. NAGPRA shattered the status quo for museums and federal agencies as well as for Native American communities. The traditional relationship between museums and Indian communities suddenly shifted with regard to stewardship of cultural artifacts.

Contemporary Appropriation of Hopi Culture

The problem of cultural appropriation persists today, despite the formal efforts described above to eliminate or control such activity. Violations of intellectual and cultural property rights take many forms, ranging from outright theft and illegal purchase or sale of cultural artifacts, to more subtle, less well-defined (certainly in terms of the law) acts of cultural appropriation—those involving symbols, practices, and knowledge.

I have chosen three cases to illustrate various kinds and dimensions of property rights issues facing the Hopi recently. The most frequent and offensive instances of appropriation of Hopi culture from the Hopi view are those associated with some element of Katsina religion; the examples cited here are representative of the range.

Case One

In 1988, Thomas E. Mails, retired Lutheran minister and author of New Age and self-help books, published *Secret Native American Pathways: A Guide to Inner Peace*, in which he shares with the general public spiritual "secrets" of four tribal groups, one being the Hopi. Like H. R. Voth (although the two draw from very different motivational wells), Mails provides detailed drawings of ritual paraphernalia and descriptions of previously secret ritual activities, and he does this with the full knowledge that he is exposing privileged information. He writes, "In every Hopi pueblo the populace is organized into a number of secret societies, each of which is responsible for a single ceremony. A particular clan has charge of each society and of its associated ritual and paraphernalia" (Mails 1988, 89). Later, with blatant disregard for the acknowledged secrecy, Mails reports details of a particular "secret" Katsina ritual, complete with drawings of kiva altars and other elements of the ritual, and provides instructions for constructing mock Katsina masks and a facsimile of an altar that can be used "for personal purposes" (Mails 1988, 82–108, 176–81).

Tribal leaders have expressed strong disapproval of what they consider appropriation by Mails of Hopi spiritual and ritual practices—their intellectual and cultural property—and his misrepresentation of sacred Hopi rituals for his personal economic gain. Mails has trivialized and desecrated Hopi religion by decontextualizing it from its inherent spiritual and cultural underpinnings, and even more troubling, he has torn the veil of secrecy that has protected Hopi ritual knowledge for centuries. In an article in the *Arizona Daily Star*, Fred Lomayesva, a Hopi, comments, "These are very old issues. They raise some problems regarding the right to publish and the right to free speech versus the right of Hopis to be left alone. And there are no good solutions under federal law or state law." The article continues, "The problem is particularly severe for tribes such as the Hopi, where villagers initiated into religious societies generally respect a duty not to disclose what occurs in their kivas."[9] Despite both private and public protests from the Hopi Cultural Preservation Office and others, Mails has since published two more books about the Hopi that Tribal officials find equally insensitive and destructive.

Case Two

While Mails has used Hopi religious ritual for personal economic gain, the transgressions of Hopi cultural property rights by others stem from less easily discerned and more complicated motives. In December 1995, a full-page article in *Hopi Tutuveni* lamented the existence and activities of the "Kachina Klub," a national corporation which, according to the article, was formed in 1973 near Phoenix, Arizona. The Klub was founded as a branch of the Jesters, a Shriner's group, evidently dedicated to fun making. In 1995–1996, membership in the Klub required an initiation fee of two hundred dollars, annual dues, and purchase of a bolo tie with the Klub logo—not surprisingly, a Katsina—and the Klub boasted about eight thousand members nationwide. Executive Committee and Ritual Committee members were given titles of Hopi leaders or supernatural and mythological figures—*kikmongwi* (village chief), Bear Chief, Eototo, Crow Mother, and Spider Woman, for example. Ritual performances enacting the Hopi creation myth were held "using a written script and authentic Hopi costumes and scenery in a setting which depicts a Hopi Kiva," according to the article.[10]

The main purpose of the Klub as stated in its handbook, "Kachina Klub, Member Listing 1995," is to "lend whatever support to assist the Hopi Nation and other Southwestern Native Americans in the preservation of their native villages and their ancient culture and customs." Such a mission statement presumes collaboration with Hopi Tribal officials, but the *Tutuveni* article states that the "Cultural Preservation Office has no record of any request to use Hopi cultural resources in this way."[11] Tribal officers enlisted the support of all Hopi and the general public to press the issue and seek abolishment of these sacrilegious practices. The Kachina Klub, it was later reported in the *Indian Trader*, elected to "drop use of Hopi religious rituals and names after receiving a protest from [the Hopi]."[12]

It seems reasonable to believe that the Kachina Klub had its roots in a group called "The Billingsley Hopis." In the 1920s, a "Colonel Billingsley" enlisted a group of Hopis to perform a Snake Ceremony at "Phoenix' El Zaribah Shrine temple in order to convince the public of the religious and harmless nature of the Snake Dance" (Clemmer 1995, 138–39). Anthropologist Richard Clemmer notes that Hopis "condemned his [Billingsley's] commercialization of Hopi ceremonies," yet the tours continued until 1935, and an "authentic" kiva was constructed for him at his home in Phoenix, Arizona (Clemmer 1995, nn. 53, 54). Although I have found no reference to support my assumption that "The Billingsley Hopis" had been transformed into the "Kachina Klub," there are too many coincidences—Shriner-based, Phoenix, kiva reconstructions, dramatizations of Hopi ceremonies—to discount it totally. This being the case, it is unlikely that the recent protest from Hopi officials about the Kachina Klub will have ended this group's long-term appropriation of Hopi culture. Similar groups, notably the Smokis of Prescott, Arizona, persisted for several decades despite protests from Hopi leaders about desecration of religious rituals and violation of cultural property rights.

Case Three

The last example concerns a case that, although resolved in legal terms, has had serious effects on the Hopi people. Rodney Tidwell, an Anglo, was convicted in federal court in December 1997 on assorted felony counts under the Native American Graves Protection and Repatriation Act (NAGPRA). *Hopi Tutuveni* reported that "beginning in 1995 Tidwell illegally obtained and sold 11 Hopi cultural items associated with various Hopi kachina ceremonies."[13] Traditional leaders from the three First Mesa Villages (where the stolen items resided) testified that "each of the eleven items…has an ongoing traditional, historical and cultural importance."[14]

There are several serious issues here. NAGPRA, the Tidwell Case reveals, has become a double-edged sword. The act was designed to protect the intellectual rights and property of Native Americans and has been highly instrumental in raising public awareness about the issues associated with cultural property and IPR. On the other hand, as mentioned earlier, both the definition of the problem and the "solutions" are constructs of Western culture and, in this instance, the solution has had unintended negative consequences impossible to foresee by those crafting the legislation. The Tidwell case represents the first time that a NAGPRA trial became a full jury trial. While this may appear to be a victory for Native Americans, in fact Hopi religious leaders who were subpoenaed to testify on behalf of the Tribe found themselves immersed in a system of Western law at odds with traditional Hopi beliefs and customs. The trial required them to share privileged information in a public arena in order to support charges against Tidwell. A reporter for the *Navajo-Hopi Observer* commented that "The blatant exploitation of Hopi religious objects has led to an emotional division between Hopis and non-Hopis as thousand-year-old religious secrets have been compromised in federal court, causing outrage across the [Hopi] mesas."[15]

The Tidwell case raises another sensitive issue that has caused profound internal strife for the Hopi people—the need to deal with a member of their own group who sold the items to Tidwell. Maxine Namoki, a spokeswoman for the Hopi Tribe, explains, "These items do not belong to an individual. Sacred items belong to [all Hopi]."[16] Namoki says that the breach of trust manifested by the sale of sacred items by a Hopi to an outsider has caused the Hopi to examine their relationships with one another, as individuals, as clan members, as members of a particular village, as members of religious societies, and as a Hopi generally. The ramifications of this case have extended to embrace the total sphere of Hopi cultural and social institutions, and of Hopi-Anglo relations.

• • • • •

The three cases cited here are believed very strongly by the Hopi to be clear instances of violation of intellectual and cultural property rights. Mails, they contend, is guilty of prostituting Hopi Katsina religion for personal economic gain. The Katsina Klub has decontextualized and therefore desecrated Hopi religion. Both play into the "wanna-be" phenomenon of European and Euro-American "yearners" who seek spiritual adventure or personal fulfillment by attempting to adopt Native American religious systems or reconfiguring them into new mock-Native forms. Despite Hopi protestations and allegations of wrongdoing, however, neither Mails nor the Kachina Klub has committed an unlawful act.

The Tidwell case is both more simple and more complicated. On one side, this is a proven case of illegal appropriation of ritual objects by Tidwell (the purchaser and, later, a seller) and a Hopi man (the initial seller): Tidwell was sentenced to thirty-three months in jail and a ten thousand dollar fine.[17] On the other, the case created reverberations that penetrate to the very core of Hopi social relations, religious practices, and cultural identity.

The issue of complicity of Hopi individuals with outsiders seeking to purchase religious items has become a common topic of discussion and area of concern for the Hopi. Economic needs and interests too often outweigh the responsibility to protect one's cultural heritage, and Hopi Tribal officials are making it clear that offenders will be prosecuted. In May 1998, for example, nine Hopi Tribal members were arrested on federal charges of illegal trafficking in Hopi cultural items. The *Navajo-Hopi Observer* reported that "the charges arise out of the theft of religious items from kachina ceremonies and sale to an undercover Bureau of Indian Affairs agent," and those charged face sentences of up to a year in jail and a fine of five thousand dollars if convicted.[18]

Concluding Remarks

Violations of intellectual and cultural property rights, as we have seen, have a range of manifestations and ramifications. There is a strong feeling among Hopi Tribal officials and many Hopi individuals that the Katsina image—in whatever format—is the exclusive (cultural) property of the Hopi. Many hold that, because Katsina imagery belongs traditionally within the realm of Hopi religious ritual, any representation outside of that context is disrespectful and sacrilegious. Others, taking a more liberal stance, believe that it is permissible for Hopi (and other Pueblo) artists to create and sell Katsina imagery, but for a non-Hopi to do so constitutes a violation of cultural property rights.

The range of opinions on the subject is well represented by other authors in this volume and will not be repeated here. A common theme, however, is the requirement for *respect*—respect for the Katsina as a sacred symbol, because, for the Hopi, there is no bifurcation of sacred and secular. Katsinam are inextricably intertwined with all other elements of Hopi culture. It is the centerpiece of Hopi social structure and a cultural conception that is critical to Hopi identity.

This chapter began with a description of the reciprocal relationship shared by the Hopi people and the Katsinam, the covenant for mutual obligation forged at the beginning of time to maintain life and balance in the universe. To not understand and respect this arrangement, most Hopi believe, may threaten the covenant, and life itself. When Katsina dolls and other forms of Katsina imagery in the public domain are viewed from this position, Hopi outrage at appropriation of these sacred symbols becomes easier to understand. Protection of the Katsina image goes well beyond cultural pride or Hopi nationalism; the Hopi must protect the Katsinam from exploitation in order to protect the ancient trust. This is the Hopi legacy. The Hopi have become increasingly interested in educating others about the sanctity of the Katsina image to the Hopi people, particularly with the explosion of popularity of Katsina dolls. In recent years, several museums have mounted exhibitions of Hopi cultural items with the cooperation and collaboration of Hopi Tribal officials and with participation of Hopi individuals. Increasingly, Katsina exhibitions focus on the importance and religious significance of Katsinam to the Hopi and aim to educate viewers about the covenant for reciprocity. The goal is to have non-Hopi see the Katsina "dolls" not as toys or decorations or simply colorful, whimsical figurines, but as cultural property of the Hopi people.

What, in the final analysis, is the significance of cultural property? What is the role of intellectual and cultural property in Hopi society today, and to what end should it be protected and preserved? Cultural property is one of the most basic elements of a people's identity; material objects often epitomize collective identity—for example, a clan, village, religious society, kiva group, or "tribe." A group's cultural heritage is their legacy for future generations, their cultural immortality. Preserving this cultural heritage is what will prevent the Hopi from becoming simply another "ethnic group," subsumed in the dominant Euro-American culture. ●

Verma Nequatewa

Verma Nequatewa is a Hopi artist based in Hotvela, Third Mesa, Hopi. Her statement given below is dated February 9, 1997.

As Hopi, our introduction to Katsinam begins before birth. Katsinam came to Hopi centuries ago and became Badger/Butterfly clan, so they are a part of me. The presence of Katsinam is with us every day at Hopi. We look out at the mesas and feel beauty all around us.

In jewelry, I use elements from Katsinam. My Uncle, Charles Loloma, called it "Katsina themes" and taught me to see how the face of a Katsina could become the focus of a bracelet, bolo, or buckle. The beautiful coloring of Katsinam can be captured in any piece. My uncle taught me that the Katsinam are beautiful, handsome spirits who understand design to the highest. Through understanding of Katsinam, I could discover the strength, simplicity, and beauty of design itself.

My work comes from the spirit of Katsinam, not so much their appearance in ceremonies. The happy feeling from observing Katsinam is present as I create. I try to show their deeper elements rather than the

detail. I would rarely try to depict a specific Katsina so it could be recognized. Rather, their strength, beauty, and presence should come through in a piece.

XII.I Assorted Katsina-inspired jewelry. Photograph © Jerry Jacka.

XII.2 Assorted Katsina-inspired jewelry. Photograph © Jerry Jacka.

XII.I

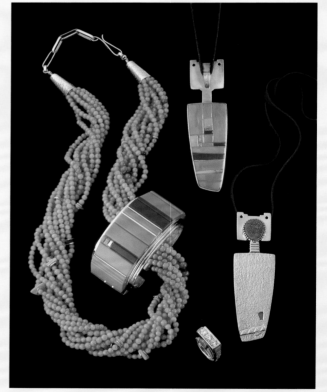

XII.2

Jean Healey

Jean Healey was a Euro-American artist based in New Mexico. Her statement given below was dated April 1, 1997. Ms. Healey passed away on August 5, 2000.

Forty-five years ago, when I was pregnant with my first child, I taught myself to crochet. The first bonnet was a disgrace, large enough for my grandmother, who asked for it, cherished it, and wore it. After my children were grown and I "retired" to New Mexico, I made and sold stuffed animals and toys. Then for several years, I made and sold Pueblo and Navajo style dolls to Tiovivo, a toy store in Taos, New Mexico. A number of people asked me to do Katsinam, but I didn't at the time because I knew that some members of the Hopi Nation objected to anyone, including their own people, selling Katsina representations, and I didn't want to offend anyone.

After two years I bought Barton Wright's *Hopi Kachinas: The Complete Guide to Collecting Kachina Dolls* and made six dolls. Two days after receiving them, the toy store owner called and told me, "You have a winner, Jean. I just sold the last one." In 1989 I bought Wright's more comprehensive book, *Kachinas: A Hopi Artist's Documentary* with original paintings by Cliff Bahnimptewa. I have made and sold over two thousand Katsinam, using the Bahnimptewa illustrations for reference. To date, I have had no complaints. I do eighty-one different Katsinam. The most popular are Tsih (Chile Pepper), Hano (clown with watermelon), Patung (Squash), and Tawa (Sun).

A few years ago the folks at Tiovivo asked me if I could do storytellers, which I did. They have been a huge success. I make them with seven little people because that is the number of children I had myself. Sometimes when we attempt to put an experience into words, we diminish it. I would simply like to say that I make Katsinam because I love them.

XIII.1

XIII.1 Left: Paatangkatsina (Squash Katsina), 1995–1999. Yarn and cotton. H: 34.5 cm. Center: Mong.wùuti (Owl Woman Katsina), 1995–1999. Yarn, feathers, and cotton. H: 33.5 cm. Right: Taawakatsina (Sun Katsina), 1995–1999. Yarn, feathers, and cotton. H: 35 cm. Private collection.

XIII.2 Left: Kawàykatsina (Horse Katsina), 1995–1999. Yarn, feathers, and cotton. H: 40.5 cm. Private collection. Center: Angwusnasomtaqa (Crow Mother Katsina), 1995–1999. Yarn, feathers, and cotton. H: 37.7 cm. Right: Mongwu (Great Horned Owl Katsina), 1995–1999. Yarn, feathers, and cotton. H: 35 cm. Private collection.

XIII.2

Wallace Youvella Sr.

This statement has been reprinted from Dialogue with the Hopi: Cultural Copyright and Research Ethics *(Hotvela: Paaqavi Inc., 1995). It was originally presented at a conference hosted by the Hopi Cultural Preservation Office at the Heard Museum, Phoenix, 1995.*

Before I speak on the subject of the closure of the kacina ceremonies at First Mesa I want to deliver a message from my uncle, who is now the kacina priest at First Mesa. He hopes that there can be some kind of respect among the anglo and Hopi. Respect for what he feels is his responsibilty to carry forth irregardless of what is happening today. As you are aware, the Hopi ceremonial cycle, the kacina ceremonies are both winter and summer ceremonies so the kacina clan has two ceremonies it is responsible to carry out throughout the year. There have been kacina ceremonies that have generated a lot of interest through publications, prompting visitation from foreign countries. There is great interest in kacinas especially now with the carving of kacina dolls and what they represent.

There was talk about closure of Walpi village at an earlier point in time while another uncle of mine, who is now deceased was beginning to have some concerns. He felt that eventually, something would have to be done. How can you close the ceremonies without offending anyone, hurting anyone, because this is a responsibilty that he had carried for them. It was a hard decision to make. But yet, he felt that it needed to be done. Those of you who have been to Hopi are aware that we have a lot of prayers. When you come to Hopi there are a lot of questions of those who are Hopi whether they are members of the clan or the society itself. Many of you get whatever interpretation a person wants to give you about kacinas so there is a lot of interpretations about kacinas and what it represents.

This kind of information, misinformation was beginning to have impact. It was dividing the people adversely about who owned kacinas. Who do the kacinas belong to. For some reason every Hopi on the Hopi Reservation that is initiated into the kacina society feels that it is his right to give information on kacinam, which is improper. The property, as a term, belongs to the kacina clan just as the snake dance belongs to the Snake clan. Every female, every male upon reaching a certain age has the opportunity to become initiated into the kacina

society and so the interpretation among Hopis is that I am a Hopi so, therefore, I have a right to it. Which is not true. They have a privilege. As they learn about what kacinas are they are not to discuss that with anyone. We don't have that right to speak about certain things.

So, it was with this thought and the incident that broke the camel's back was the publishing by Marvel comic books of Nataaska in the March, 1991 issue which saddened my uncle. He was in great distress and was very hurt. His interpretation of this was that now the masses were initiated. If you read the comic book you would understand what I am talking about. If you know him as a Hopi, you would understand what I am talking about. He was very hurt by this. It was, do I continue this from this day forth because my responsibility [has] already been done. What is my responsibility has already been completed. Therefore, should I continue with my responsibilities. We talked about this as he was sad-dened and hurt by this. I felt this was done in the name of exploitation and perhaps someone as a child out there did not know what responsibility was, what respect was. So, I felt that he need not worry about it that he had a responsibility to carry out regardless of what happened. This kind of activity should not put an end to something that has been going on from time immemorial. So with the help of the Hopi Cultural Preservation Office we contacted Marvel comic books. They apologized for what they did and the price of the comic book, March issue of 1991 went up in value.

With this incident came the proclamation that all of the dances in First Mesa over which my uncle had responsibility was closed to non-Indians. This then started another controversy. We have friends from the outside. Many Hopi who are artisans and have friends so this obviously had a big impact. There was now dissention among Hopis at First Mesa and also talk about the kacina chief wanting to close the dances at First Mesa. This type of exploitation has been ongoing so what was the big deal about the comic book. It has been going on forever and perhaps it will continue forever. My uncle felt he had a responsibility. It was his right and he did close off the kacina ceremonies to the non-Hopi public.

So it continues up to today. Those of you who have been to First Mesa know that it is not a very wide piece of property. It is very narrow so it can only hold X number of people. We have a lot of visitors and it gets very crowded so there is the safety factor to consider and the prohibition against videotaping of the village. There had to be some control but the Marvel Comic incident was the last straw and this is how it came about. So, it continues today. It is not that you are not invited. You are all invited in spirit and to be in harmony with what goes on in Hopi. We do not want to complicate what the ceremonies represent, we do want you to understand it. It is difficult for a non-Hopi to understand it and I don't know how I can explain it to you. I have had many discussions with my anglo friends, we have gone many hours debating the issue and our understanding of it. It is very difficult to find the words to express our feelings. Somehow we can come to a mutual agreement that is based on respect. That we can respect one another and understand what is happening. You can only understand the surface part of it. The meaning part I am afraid you will not be able to get to. The surface is there, understand it. Then you will be able to relate to Hopi. Beyond that, it would be very difficult. Perhaps at some point in time when we become one, truly one. We will only have that when we have respect for one another.

It has had an adverse impact on the kacina clan. We are very small in number. Yet, we can have a very large impact, universally. Look around you. You see it everywhere. *Kacina* Boulevard, *Kacina* Shopping Center. Where do we stop this exploitation of the word kacina. Many of you understand what the word actually means. Life, simple—*kaci*. Look inside yourselves and at least understand that much about it. I want to thank you for being here today to listen. There are a few of you here but everything starts with something small and moves on and I am sure that will happen.

Appendix: The Gourd Rattles of Edmund Nequatewa

The following is a partial catalog of the Edmund Nequatewa gourd rattles in the collection of the UCLA Fowler Museum of Cultural History. Captions for the rattles may be found on page 186. The presence of an asterisk in the caption to a rattle indicates that it does not represent a Katsina.

A.1

A.2

A.3

A.4

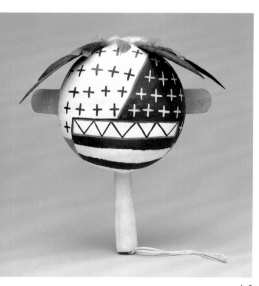

A.5

A.6

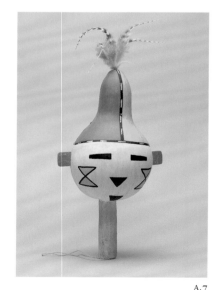

A.7

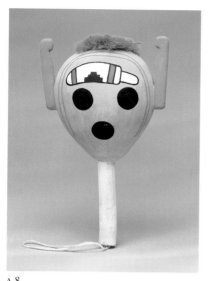

A.8

A.9

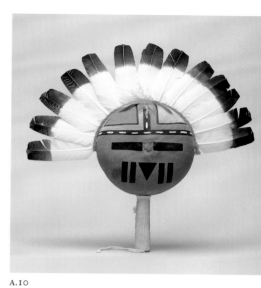

A.10

A.11

A.12

A.13

A.14

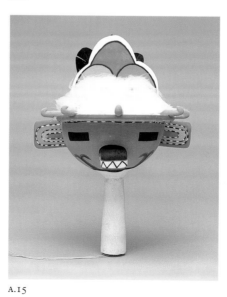

A.15

A.16

A.17

A.18

A.19

A.20

A.21

A.22

A.23

A.24

A.25

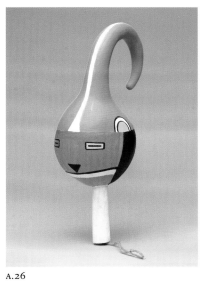

A.26

A.27

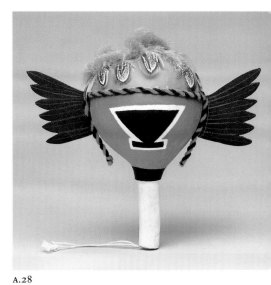

A.28

A.29

A.30

A.31

A.32

A.33

A.34

Appendix Captions

A1. Masawkatsina (Earth God Katsina). Gourd, cottonwood, feathers, and paint. H: 25.4 cm. FMCH X90.674.

A2. Wuyaqqötö (Broadface Katsina). Gourd, cottonwood, feathers, paint, and yarn. H: 35.5 cm. FMCH X87.44.

A3. *Homiytsi (Field Mouse). Gourd, cottonwood, feathers, and paint. H: 27.5 cm. FMCH X87.35.

A4. Qa'omana (Corn Maiden). Gourd, cottonwood, feathers, and paint. H: 36 cm. FMCH X87.38.

A5. Eewiro (Warrior Katsina). Gourd, cottonwood, feathers, and paint. H: 22.8 cm. FMCH X90.688.

A6. Paatangkatsina (Squash Katsina). Gourd, cottonwood, feathers, and paint. H: 22.8 cm. FMCH X90.687.

A7. Sootukwnangw (Star Katsina). Gourd, cottonwood, feathers, and paint. H: 42 cm. FMCH X87.42.

A8. Putskòovmoktaqa (Rabbit Stick Cricket Katsina). Gourd, Cottonwood, paint, and yarn. H: 25.4 cm. FMCH X90.683.

A9. *Poliiy'wu (Butterfly). Gourd, cottonwood, feathers, and paint. H: 40 cm. FMCH X87.39.

A10. Taawakatsina (Sun Katsina). Gourd, cottonwood, feathers, paint, and yarn. H: 39 cm. FMCH X87.140.

A11. Koyaala. Gourd, cottonwood, feathers, and paint. H: 36 cm. FMCH X87.139.

A12. Ahöla (Chief Katsina). Gourd, cottonwood, feathers, and paint. H: 22.8 cm. FMCH X90.675.

A13. Nata'aska (Black Ogre Katsina). Gourd, cottonwood, feathers, and paint. H: 24.1 cm. FMCH X90.679.

A14. Masawkatsina (Earth God Katsina). Gourd, cottonwood, feathers, and paint. H: 31 cm. FMCH X87.52.

A15. Tumo'alkatsina (Devil's Claw Katsina). Gourd, cottonwood, feathers, and paint. H: 30.5 cm. FMCH X90.690.

A16. Soyah-taqa (Laguna Corn Dancer, "Gambler" Katsina). Gourd, cottonwood, feathers, paint, and yarn. H: 34.5 cm. FMCH X87.37.

A17. Hoote Katsina with Hooked Side Horns. Gourd, cottonwood, feathers, paint, and yarn. H: 27 cm. FMCH X87.51.

A18. Sivu'ikwiwtaqa (Vessel Carrier Katsina). Gourd, cottonwood, feathers, and paint. H: 22.8. FMCH X90.676.

A19. Pöqàngwkatsina (Warrior Katsina). Gourd, cottonwood, feathers, and paint. H: 38.5 cm. FMCH X87.36.

A20. Nangöysohu (Chasing Star Katsina). Gourd, cottonwood, feathers, paint, and yarn. H: 33 cm. FMCH X87.48.

A21. Wakaskatsina (Cow Katsina). Gourd, cottonwood, feathers, and paint. H: 27.9 cm. FMCH X90.681.

A22. Toson Kooyemsi. Gourd, cottonwood, feathers, and paint. H: 31.5 cm. FMCH X87.41.

A23. Taawakatsina (Sun Katsina). Gourd, cottonwood, feathers, paint, and yarn. H: 30 cm. FMCH X87.46.

A24. Kooyemsi. Gourd, cottonwood, feathers, and paint. H: 27.9 cm. FMCH X90.689.

A25. Payuk'ala (Three-Horn Katsina). Gourd, cottonwood, feathers, paint, and yarn. H: 36.8 cm. FMCH X90.673.

A26. Muy'ingwkatsina (Germination God Katsina). Gourd, cottonwood, and paint. H: 31.7 cm. FMCH X90.692.

A27. Kooyemsi. Gourd, cottonwood, feathers, and paint. H: 24 cm. FMCH X90.672.

A28. Angwusnasomtaqa (Crow Mother Katsina). Gourd, cottonwood, feathers, paint, and yarn. H: 22.8 cm. FMCH X90.671.

A29. Koyaala. Gourd, cottonwood, and paint. H: 22 cm. FMCH X90.670.

A30. Nangöysohu (Chasing Star Katsina). Gourd, cottonwood, feathers, paint, and yarn. H: 25.4 cm. FMCH X90.684.

A31. Angwuskatsina (Crow Katsina). Gourd, cottonwood, feathers, and paint. H: 20.3 cm. FMCH X90.680.

A32. *Rain Cloud Rattle. Gourd, cottonwood, feathers, and paint. H: 31.7 cm. FMCH X90.686.

A33. Hiilili (a Whipper Katsina). Gourd, cottonwood, feathers, and paint. H: 31 cm. FMCH X87.47.

A34. Wuyaqqötö (Broadface Katsina). Gourd, cottonwood, feathers, paint, and yarn. H: 20.3 cm. FMCH X90.678.

Endnotes

Chapter 2 (Whiteley)

1. The Hopi language is a distinct branch of the Uto-Aztecan family, which includes, among others, Shoshone and Nahuatl, the language of the Aztecs. Despite major cultural similarities among the Pueblos, a striking factor is linguistic diversity. There are six separate languages (not dialects, full-fledged languages) in four language groups. The Tanoan languages include Tiwa, Tewa, and Towa: Tiwa is divided into northern (spoken at Taos and Picuris) and southern dialects (spoken at Sandia and Isleta). Tewa is spoken at San Juan, Santa Clara, Nambe, Pojoaque, San Ildefonso, and Tesuque. Nowadays, Towa is only spoken at Jemez, although Pecos Pueblo (inhabited into the 1830s) was also Towa. South of the Tewa villages along the Rio Grande or its eastern tributaries are several Keresan-speaking villages: Santo Domingo, Cochiti, San Felipe, Santa Ana, and Zia. Farther west, Laguna and Acoma both speak more distant dialects of Keresan. Keresan is a language isolate (i.e., it has not been convincingly linked to any other languages to form a "family"), as is Zuni, the language of Zuni Pueblo.

2. See, for example: Voth 1901; Parsons 1933; Parsons 1939; Stephen 1936; Earle and Kennard 1938; Titiev 1944; F. Eggan 1950; Dockstader 1954; B. Wright 1973; Whiteley 1988; E. C. Adams 1991; Schaafsma 1994; B. Wright 1994. And for additional sources, see Laird 1977.

3. The Hostiles eventually included Lewis Tewanima, winner of a silver medal at the 1912 Olympic Games, and Fred Kabotie, one of the most important Hopi painters of the twentieth century.

4. The current Hopi population is about 10,900.

Chapter 3 (Pearlstone)

1. The *Hopi Dictionary* (1998) defines a *Koyaala* as a Northeastern Pueblo type clown that is now present on all the Hopi Mesas.

2. Bendheim 1982; M. Wilson 1982; *Southwest Art* (July 1992): 25; Kuwanwisiwma, this volume; Robert Breunig, personal communication, 1997.

3. Since the late 1970s visitor intrusion (Rivera 1990, 152–56) or incidents such as the Marvel comic book (see pp. 119–20) have led Hopi villages to close some ceremonies to non-Indians. This is always done at the village level, and the decisions need not be permanent. At closed ceremonies, non-Indian friends of Hopis may be permitted entrance. Around 1916 visual and auditory reproductions of ceremonies were banned, and photographing villages without permission was prohibited (Clemmer 1995, 295).

4. Peter Whiteley (personal communication, 1998) speculates that it is possible that George C. Yount, who visited Hopi in 1828, or some of the educated explorers, such as the governor of New Mexico Don Juan Bautista de Anza, even earlier, could conceivably have acquired *tithu*.

5. Indications of Katsina religion date back to at least the late 1200s as evidenced by masks and masked figures in kiva murals, rock art, and ceramics in several areas including the Hopi Mesas (E. C. Adams 1991; P. Schaafsma 1994; Hays 1994; Lekson and Cameron 1995). When Parsons (1930) proposed that Katsina religion was introduced by the Spanish, Southwest scholars at the time refuted the idea (C. Schaafsma 1994, 124–25). The discovery of murals with Katsina-style figures at Kuaua, a fifteenth-century pueblo now in Bernalillo, north of Albuquerque, and at Awat'ovi and Kawaika-a, fourteenth- to sixteenth-century pueblos at Hopi, indicate that Katsinam were present during that period.

6. See Fewkes 1892, 1897, 1901; Frigout 1979; Hieb 1979; Loftin 1991; Ortiz 1972; Parsons 1939; E. Sekaquaptewa 1976; Stephen 1936; Tedlock 1994; Titiev 1944, 1972; Voth 1901, [1912a] 1967. See also the Hopi autobiographies of Edmund Nequatewa (Seaman 1993), Helen Sekaquaptewa (1969), Don Taleyesva (Sun Chief; Simmons 1942), and Albert Yava (1978).

7. The *Hopi Dictionary* gives the primary meaning of *tithu* as children, daughters, sons, or offspring. It is used here in its alternate meaning as a Katsina carving (1998, 591). The carvings, however, can be considered as the offspring of Katsinam because they were created by them in their images (see A. Secakuku 1995, 4).

The earliest wooden carvings known are those recovered from the Walpi project, which date to the eighteenth century (J. Adams 1980). According to E. Charles Adams (1991, 83), to date, no pre-contact examples of Katsina figurines are known, but a "possible fourteenth century flat katsina doll, possibly the Hemis Katsina, was reported by Haury (1945, 198–200) from Double Butte Cave near Tempe, Arizona...however [this] is more likely a nonkatsina ritual effigy, similar to ones still used by Hopi and other Pueblo groups, usually on altars (Stephen 1936, figs. 22, 62, 484). A set of six 'statuettes' excavated in 1959 near the Puerco River in eastern Arizona were given to the Museum of Northern Arizona (Danson 1966)...they also do not resemble masked katsinas." Precontact *tithu*, if made of wood, may not have been preserved, or it is possible that Katsina figurines were developed after contact (E. C. Adams 1991, 83). E. Charles Adams (1994, 39) suggests that "carved stone figures associated with twelfth-century pueblos in the upper drainages of the Little Colorado River.... could be precursors to a katsina doll form that evolved a century or two later; however, there is no archaeological evidence of this development" (P. Schaafsma 1994, pl. 1; Brody 1991, fig. 36). In recent years scholars have investigated the relationship between early *tithu* and *santos*. "Pre-hispanic images of katsinas recall many santos in their formal presentation and tutelary function.... There can be no doubt that the two forms of representation converged, mutually influenced by one another" (Farago 1998).

8. The objects discussed in this section have often been subsumed under "tourist" arts. The term "tourist art," however, has been used in various ways. It has been narrowly defined and equated with "airport" art, a demeaning term that Graburn (1976, 6) defines as art produced "when the profit motive or the economic competition of poverty override aesthetic standards." Or it has been broadly defined as any art made by a native group to be bought by outsiders (Jules-Rosette 1984, 9). The latter definition is used in this study, but the term applied to Hopi material is inadequate. Tourists, whether discerning or unsophisticated, are

only one component of the buying market. The outsiders buying the material can be collectors, dealers, museum personnel, or interested persons not easily designated as tourists, any of whom may be situated near the villages, across the country, or across an ocean. Hopi commodified art is bought directly from artists at or away from Hopi, indirectly from artists through a gallery, from a wholesaler, a retailer, or an intermediary. One place where it is unlikely to be found is at an airport. Airports, rather, carry works by non-Hopis that imitate those of Hopis or items that appropriate Hopi symbols. Clifford's division of commodified items into fine art, folk art/craft, and tourist art may fit the material better, although "folk art/craft" has a belittling connotation (1988, 223–26). As Wade notes, there is no consensus for any of these terms (1976, 268 n. 1). It is presumptuous for outsiders to decide what is art for another culture, particularly when that culture's language has no comparable term. Further, as is clear from the artists' profiles in this volume, they themselves do not agree as to whether their work should or should not be dubbed art. Finally, it is not uncommon for one artist to produce objects so different that outsiders might consider some of these to be "art" and others to be "craft."

9. In the early 1970s, Manfred Susunkewa, feeling a spiritual emptiness in his work and voicing concerns that Katsina carvings, specifically the action figures, were losing their connection to Hopi religion and culture, went back to what he called "the old style" (Walsh 1993). Susunkewa remembers early lessons about Katsinam. "When I was a child.... We could draw anything, and some of us drew the kachina figures [this would have been in the 1940s]. I remember the elders saying that we should not be drawing these things—if we did, an ogre would visit us and discipline us. This was their way of telling us that the kachina was only for certain purposes and was to be respected. So we stopped drawing them. I've always remembered that" (Wallis 1992, 46). Susunkewa expresses concern about communication with the spiritual world for Hopis and feels that this communication can only be realized if "natural resources, not man-made chemical materials" are used. For non-Pueblo people the carvings are just merchandise, but for him "it is an issue of respect and of honesty for the kachina" because "its tradition and my identity both come from the Hopi belief system." Susunkewa insists on control. He will not deal with galleries and only occasionally deals with museums but notes that he must also earn a living for his family (Wallis 1992, 48–49). Today, the "old-style" has become a movement within katsina carving (Walsh 1993; Tenakhongva, this volume; Day 2000).

10. On the selling and collecting of Katsinam see, for example: Brody 1971, 1979, 1980, 1994; Bromberg 1986; Dockstader 1985; Erickson 1977; Goldwater 1969; Kenagy 1986; Stevenson 1879, 1881; Voth 1912b; Wade 1976, 1985; B. Wright 1975, 1977.

11. Parezo documents the parallel case of Navajo artists who have adapted religious dry paintings for commercialization. She devotes a chapter to the forms of rationalization used by the artists involved in this enterprise (Parezo 1983, ch. 4). These include changing details, omitting certain symbols, saying prayers at the conception and completion of each project, selecting neutral beings, creating new beings, or depicting subject matter (including Katsina imagery) that would never be seen in a sacred dry painting. She notes that these rationalizations were in place by the 1930s and still existed in the 1980s when she was doing her research (Parezo 1983, 4).

12. A discussion of twentieth-century social and economic transitions at Hopi is beyond the scope of this study, but many factors have contributed to changing conditions and thus to changing art production and the art market. The reader is referred to Clemmer 1995; Rivera 1990; and Rushforth and Upham 1992 for detailed examinations.

13. Native American artist and activist Jimmie Durham has spoken to the larger issue of conforming, even if inadvertently, to government stereotypes: "If your job, when you are colonised and you have no power, is to make souvenirs of your culture for commercial use, you are doing what the government says Indians do.... If you do things that are 'Indian' to sell commercially I think you are necessarily destroying your community because you are destroying the identity by doing it as though it was the identity and then doing and selling it. Every time someone buys it, it is reinforced that that is your identity. That's the trap that artists also have" (Papastergiadis and Turney 1996, 36).

14. Barton Wright (personal communication, 1998) has called my attention to an articulated carving depicted in an A. C. Vroman photograph of 1902 (Webb and Weinstein 1973, 33, 64, fig. 32). Wright notes that this makes it clear that action figures were possible at the beginning of the twentieth century, but that they were labor intensive until the technology changed. The other *tithu* in this photograph (taken in the the house of the then-governor of Sitsomovi) and in another taken by Vroman at this time (Webb and Weinstein 1973, 74, fig. 45) are in the more usual geometric style of the period. See also Bol, this volume.

15. Dunn (1968, 195) notes crayon drawings of Katsinam done in 1908 by Hopi students at the Sherman Institute in Riverside that were sent to Fewkes at the Smithsonian Institution. Katsina paintings on pottery by some Hopi-Tewa were done between about 1905 and 1915 (Brody 1980, 89). At the turn of the twentieth century, Katsina representations on tiles were instigated by Thomas Keam (Barton Wright, personal communication, 1998).

16. Eddie was ill when I began to investigate these rattles and died December 14, 1987. I met him briefly in February of 1987, but he was in the hospital at Keams Canyon and not able to reminisce about Katsina rattles. The information relayed here comes from his wife, Annabelle, his son Merrill, and Richard and Margo Mehagian. His family does not remember the circumstances in which the earliest Katsina rattles were created.

17. This privacy does not mean that Katsina religion is less well developed in Rio Grande communities. The Eastern Pueblos, to protect their religion, closed ceremonies to outsiders. See C. Schaafsma (1994) and Tedlock (1994).

18. Alex Seowtowa is best known for his paintings of Katsinam on the walls of Zuni's Our Lady of Guadalupe Church. The church was built in 1629, abandoned in 1820, and restored in the 1960s. Between two paintings of the Virgin Mary, and above pictures of the Stations of the Cross, are now murals of more than two-dozen life-size Katsinam, who seem to dance across the walls toward the altar. Seowtowa, who began this project in 1970, describes himself as "a Catholic who is also a 'cultural practioner' of Zuni traditions" (Niebuhr 1995). The original walls were decorated with Zuni Ogre Katsinam as a reminder to encourage parishoners to live according to the teachings of the church and Zunis (Seowtewa 1992, 12). Seowtewa decided to paint more benign figures, Katsinam that would not only preserve Zuni tradition but also "describe the similarities between Catholicism and Zuni spirituality" (Seowtewa 1992, 14). The winter solstice, including the Katsinam of Sha'lak'o, are now seen on the north wall because of the association of the north with the

cold. The south wall is decorated with Katsinam associated with summer, spring, and fall events, including summer rain dancers. Above the altar, a twenty-two-inch figure of Jesus, dressed in Zuni blankets and turquoise jewelry, hovers on a stylized rain cloud above the church. Seowtewa is being assisted by his sons Kenneth and Edwin.

19. This study does not consider mainstream, twentieth-century European and American artists such as Emil Nolde, Marsden Hartley, and Max Ernst who have been influenced by *tithu* (see Rhodes 1994, 179; W. Rubin 1984, 381, 458–59, 561–66).

20. Letter to the author, April 4, 1997. See also Poteet Victory, this volume.

21. Katsina-like images that have removable masks are deeply disturbing to most Hopi because they preempt aspects of Hopi ritual (see pp. 119–20). It was, however, Hopis who initiated these representations. According to Wright (this volume), the first was made in the 1960s by Theodore Puhuyesva, a Hopi commercial carver. Similarly, Alvin James Sr. made a figure with a removable mask (Wade 1976, 136). James told Bassman (1991, 90) some decades later that he had been told "never to make a kachina doll with a mask that can be removed."

22. *Southwest Art* (August 1997): 120; *Yippy Yi Yea* (winter 1998): 16.

23. *American Indian Art Magazine* 19, no. 3 (1994): 108.

24. "The Booming Kachina Business," *Indian Trader* (August 1980) and "Imitation Kachinas Are Becoming a Large Part of the Market," *Indian Trader* (September 1980).

25. "Hopis Issue Brochure to Warn Consumers about Fakes," *Indian Trader* 27, no. 4 (1996): 20. See also "Hopis Attack False Kachinas," *High Country News* (April 18, 1994): 3; Link 1994; Hall 1996; Shaffer and Donovan 1994; Walsh 1994.

26. Hopi Cultural Preservation Office, Minutes of Meeting, February 27, 1992.

27. Some Hopi traditionalists take cultural conservatism further. Marilyn Masayesva, when an attorney for the Hopi Cultural Preservation Office, stated that "[t]raditionally in the Hopi way of thinking…we know we have to respect the ways and cultures of each Hopi village…that is why Third Mesa doesn't make pottery, Second Mesa doesn't make wicker baskets and, First Mesa doesn't make coil baskets, because we respect the cultural rights to these things" (Joseph 1995).

28. Around the same time, in the mid-1990s, and perhaps coincidentally, "The society of Navajo healers called for the removal of the ceremonial masked figure of the Ye'ii Bicheii…from public art, including murals in tribal buildings and a commemorative poster for the Shiprock, N.M. fair" (Norrell 1994a, 17; also Norrell 1994b). Parezo (1983) and Wade (1976, 141–46) discuss the commercialization of Yeibichai figures and images, parallel in many ways to that of Katsina imagery

29. "Imitation Kachinas Are Becoming a Large Part of the Market," *Indian Trader*, September 1980.

30. This law would have gone beyond the Indian Arts and Craft Act of 1990 (Title 1 of Public Law 101-664), which states that it is unlawful to offer or display for sale any goods, with or without

a government trademark "represented to be authentic Indian arts and crafts unless the products are in fact authentic Indian arts and crafts." Further, the law states that it is illegal to "sell or offer to sell nonauthentic Indian arts and crafts unless the nonauthentic Indian arts and crafts are clearly labeled." Indian "products" are defined as those arts and crafts made by enrolled members of a federal- or state-recognized tribe, and the definition also covers those products made by certified "Indian Artisans" who may not be actual enrolled members in a tribe. Various means have been used to circumvent this law; for example, importers may use stickers that can be removed. See "Hopis Ask Arizona Leaders for Protection Against Navajo Carvers," *Indian Trader* 27, no. 3 (1996): 23; Joseph 1996a; McBride 1996; Norrell 1996.

31. See "Brochure Educates Buyers about Fake Hopi Arts and Crafts," *Tutuveni* (September 1996): 10; "Hopis Issue Brochure to Warn Consumers about Fakes," *Indian Trader* 27, no. 4 (1996): 20.

32. Letters from Leigh J. Kuwanwisiwma protesting the sale of Navajo carvings as "Katsinam" were also sent to the president of the Fingerhut Corporation (August 3, 1994) and to the Taylors at New Mexico Catalog (October 24, 1994); see the Hopi Cultural Preservation Office files. He asked both companies to cease advertising and selling these items. In the case of the Taylors at New Mexico Catalog, he called particular attention to the "Removable Mask Kachinas" and described them as "simply profane."

33. *Indian Trader* 29, no. 9 (1998): 20.

34. "Controversy Hits '95 Gallup Ceremonial," *Indian Trader* 26, no. 9 (1995): 5–6.

35. "Controversy Hits '95 Gallup Ceremonial," *Indian Trader* 26, no. 9 (1995): 6.

36. Hopi Cultural Preservation Office Files. There is also a copy of a letter sent May 15, 1995, to the president of *The Native Experience*, a magazine that advertised the Dover Publications, Inc., *Kachina Punch-Out Masks*. Kuwanwisiwma writes: "Every Hopi individual is initiated into the Kachina society around the age of 13 years where he is taught to respect the integrity of that newly acquired knowledge. Both initiated and especially uninitiated Hopi individuals never refer to these beings as masks and the liberal use of that word as well as the reproduction of them is seen as highly sacrilegious. Considering the young audience for which this material is directed, there is also a Hopi cultural standard that is being violated."

37. It should be noted that these mass-produced Christian items do have critics, and that there are Christian factions that protest any kind of imagery.

38. Of note, the marketing of items with Christian imagery is moving in the direction of that of Hopis. Christian companies are being gobbled up by larger firms that do "not care about biblical principles, however they are interpreted" (McDannell 1995, 265).

39. Unidentified copy (magazine or newspaper) in the files of the Hopi Cultural Preservation Office.

40. *Arizona Republic*, October 24 1971, October 27, 1971, and November 14, 1971.

41. Whiteley (1993, 140 n.) points out that "[t]he issue appeared on reservation newsstands right at the time of Powamuy initiation,

when Hopi children are supposed to be learning some of the secrets of the kachina society in a more orthodox way."

42. Meeting minutes are in the files of the Hopi Cultural Preservation Office.

43. A letter of apology dated February 21, 1992, from Marvel Entertainment Group, Inc., signed by Michael Z. Hobson, Group Vice President, and Pamela Rutt, Vice President, Public Relations, is on file at the Hopi Cultural Preservation Office.

44. The "Smoki" Snake Dance was founded in 1921 by a group of Prescott, Arizona, businessmen to imitate Indian ceremonies, in particular the Hopi Snake Dance. As they grew, a fraternal order was formed. Although one of the aims of the organization was anonymity, it is known that influential Euro-American Arizonans, including Barry Goldwater, were members and performed in the ceremonies (Parker and Nelson 1964, 37). The organization was finally forced into bankruptcy in 1991 after Pueblo protests and a Hopi demonstration (Kuwanwisiwma, personal communication, 1994; Clemmer 1995, 329 n. 93).

45. "Club Drops Use of Hopi Ritual After Tribal Protest," *Indian Trader* (February 1996): 8.

46. *Southwest Art* (July 1992): 25.

47. Italian-made figurines were advertised in the following catalogs: *Gift Book* (1994): 8; (spring 1995): 14; (midsummer 1995): 12.

48. Phillips and Steiner (1999) note that since the nineteenth century art historians and anthropologists have rejected commodified objects on the grounds that they exhibit impure styles and that they are produced for an outside market. Steiner (1994) likewise notes westerners' criteria for authentic African art as age, not made for economic gain, made from traditional materials, and used in a "traditional" manner. It is of interest that no art historians, anthropologists, or buyers have rejected Western-style, commodified Katsina carvings on these grounds, but the Hopi themselves use these criteria to distance commodified carvings from traditional ones suitable for ceremonies. For discussions of art and "authenticity," see Duffek 1983; Kasfir 1992; *African Arts* 25, no. 3 (1992): 14–32; *African Arts* 25, no. 4 (1992): 18–103. For definitions of authenticity and tradition in legal trials concerning Native American material, see Evans-Pritchard (1990).

49. See Phillips and Steiner (1999) for a discussion of other issues inherent in the shift from anthropology to art.

50. Whiteley (1993, 129) feels that in some instances Hopi meaning is entirely bypassed. In May 1991 Sotheby's auctioned two Hopi "masks," among the most sacred of Hopi items. One, Ahöla, sold for $24,200. "[T]he object's newfound commodity status, not its Hopi meaning, was the sole criterion of value."

51. A great deal has been written on tourism and the lure of the Southwest. Some of the recent literature includes: Babcock and Wilder 1990; Deitch 1989; Dilworth 1996a; Francaviglia and Narrett 1994; Greenwood 1989; Hinsley 1992; Howard and Pardue 1996; Norris 1994; Rodriguez 1994; Wade 1985; Weigle 1989, 1990, 1994; Weigle and Babcock 1996.

52. Residents responded to a questionnaire, and Halle and his co-workers visited their homes. All visual material—critically acclaimed, mass-produced, photographs, and other—that was

deemed "primitive" was included. As would be expected from the geographical area, the majority of the material (67 percent) was African and African American. Only 10 percent was Native American. Halle, however, is certain from his results that in a survey of any area where native people live, the art collected is "likely to resonate with symbolic meanings that express residents' feelings toward these 'native' peoples" (Halle 1993, 162). It is Halle's method rather than his results that are important here. His results are not directly comparable to the material at hand because he, first, included all objects that fall under the "primitive" rubric, not only those bought as souvenirs or mementos, and, second, surveyed only areas in and around New York City.

Chapter 4 (Bol)

1. Breunig and Lomatuway'ma confirm this: *tihu* "are traditionally fashioned as gifts from the kachinas to uninitiated girls. Originally the gifts served a purpose similar to the paaho (prayer stick) out of which they may have evolved. When a little girl received one, it was, in effect, a prayer wish that she would grow, be healthy and fertile, and in turn have healthy children of her own" (1992, 8).

2. In the case of the boy, the gift of the miniature gourd rattle is probably a prayer for his participation in the ceremonies as he matures, and the miniature bow and arrow refer to a prayer for ability in providing food.

3. Fewkes confirms: "They have a conventionalized human form which is adhered to throughout, but the special or individual character intended to be represented is indicated by appropriate symbolism in the accompanying markings" (1894, 46).

4. See Howard and Pardue for the details of the Dorsey-Voth relationship (1996, 26–32). The catalogs that Dorsey wrote for the twelve collections that the Carnegie Museum of Natural History purchased from the Fred Harvey Company in 1903–1904 demonstrate his flamboyant tendency to embellish the facts.

5. The Sa'lakwmana appears as a pair of marionettes that grind corn in a night kiva performance, described in Stephen (1936, 335–36); Titiev (1972, 324–25); and Fewkes (1903, 114–16).

6. J. J. Brody recognized that some of the *tithu* purchased from Volz are in the collection that the Carnegie Museum of Natural History purchased from the Fred Harvey Company in 1904 (Brody, correspondence, January 4, 1993). Another large group is in the Fred Harvey Collection at the Heard Museum.

Chapter 5 (Wright)

1. For pottery, see: Woodbury and Smith 1966, fig. 77c; E. C. Adams 1991, fig. 3.12; Hays 1992, figs. 1, 2. For wooden images, see: McGregor 1965, fig. 75; Haury 1945, 199. Stone images are included in the collections of the Southwest Museum (Highland Park, California), Museum of New Mexico (Santa Fe), and the Brooklyn Museum. For petroglyphs see: Grant 1979, CDN-7, CDC-121. For cliff drawings, see: P. Schaafsma 1980, fig. 272. For presence of images in homes and *kivas*, see Espejo 1929, 78.

2. Smithsonian Museum of Natural History, SNM.9567.

3. Personal communication with staff of the Smithsonian Museum of Natural History, 1967.

4. Smithsonian Museum of Natural History specimen numbers: 16486, 22933, 22934, 22936, 22937, 22141, 23143, 31141, 35404.

5. Expeditions to the Pueblo Indians of Arizona and New Mexico, 1879–1881. National Museum. Bureau of Ethnology. Catalog of acquisitions. Cushing was an ethnologist on this expedition.

6. Thomas Varker Keam, an Englishman, established a post in what is now known as Keams Canyon. As a trader he undoubtedly took in Katsina dolls along with pottery and basketry and sold them. The beginning date of collecting is unknown, but there is no evidence that he ever commissioned dolls to be made. Frederick Volz was a trader at Canyon Diablo and Orayvi. In the manner of all traders he took in numbers of Katsina dolls. He did not commission these dolls. Reverend H. R. Voth ran a Mennonite Mission at Orayvi. During his stay he amassed a large collection of Hopi artifacts. I have no evidence that he commissioned any dolls (but see Bol, this volume—ed.).

7. As chief of Old Orayvi and in charge of all Katsina ceremonies but not of their ownership, Tawakwaptiwa would have been committing a great breech of authority by making genuine dolls. To avoid this he made doll "combinations" that are not any particular Katsina.

Chapter 7 (Spencer)

1. From the preface to *Intellectual Property Rights for Indigenous Peoples: A Sourcebook* (Greaves 1994, vi).

2. Zena Pearlstone, this volume, provides a voluminous and richly detailed account of contemporary commodification and exploitation of Katsina imagery.

3. See Greaves 1994, and Ziff and Rao 1997.

4. United Nations Department of Public Information, *Indigenous People* (New York: United Nations Department of Public Information, 1992).

5. See the Hopi Cultural Preservation Office Web site: www.nau.edu/~hcop-p/current/hopi_nis.htm.

6. See, for example, H. R. Voth, *The Oraibi Summer Snake Ceremony* (1901), *The Traditions of the Hopi* (1905), and *Brief Miscellaneous Hopi Papers* (1912b), all published by the Chicago Field Columbian Museum as Papers of the Stanley McCormick Hopi Expedition.

7. See the *Hopi Journal of Alexander M. Stephen*, edited and annotated by Elsie Clews Parsons (Stephen 1936). This two-volume set provides a detailed chronicle of Hopi life during Stephen's residency on First Mesa, 1891–1894.

8. "Cultural Preservation Office: Signs Are a Hopi Request for Respect," *Hopi Tutuveni* (July 21, 1995): 8.

9. Eric Volante, "Book by Anglo on Hopi Prophecy Offends Tribal Members," *Arizona Daily Star* (September 16, 1996): B1–2.

10. "Cultural Preservation Office Update, Kachina Klub: A Corporate Taking of the Hopi Culture," *Hopi Tutuveni* (December 15, 1995): 13.

11. "Cultural Preservation Office Update, Kachina Klub: A Corporate Taking of the Hopi Culture," *Hopi Tutuveni* (December 15, 1995): 13.

12. *Indian Trader* (1996): 8.

13. *Hopi Tutuveni* (March 20, 1998).

14. *Hopi Tutuveni* (March 20, 1998).

15. "Tidwell Trial Assaults Hopi Religion," *Navajo-Hopi Observer* (March 11, 1998): 1.

16. "Tidwell Trial Assaults Hopi Religion," *Navajo-Hopi Observer* (March 11, 1998): 1.

17. "Hopis Charged with Selling Artifacts Illegally," *Navajo-Hopi Observer* (May 27, 1998): 1.

18. "Hopi Tribe Charges Nine with Artifact Trafficking," *Navajo-Hopi Observer* (May 24, 1998): 2.

References Cited

Acker, Annie
1993 "Hopi Kachina Doll Carving: Reflections of Cultural Change." Master's thesis, California Institute of Integral Studies.

Adair, John
1944 *The Navajo and Pueblo Silversmiths.* Norman: University of Oklahoma Press.

Adams, E. Charles
1991 *The Origin and Development of the Pueblo Katsina Cult.* Tucson: University of Arizona Press.
1994 "The Katsina Cult: A Western Pueblo Perspective." In *Kachinas in the Pueblo World,* edited by Polly Schaafsma. Albuquerque: University of New Mexico Press.

Adams, Jenny L.
1980 *Perishable Artifacts from Walpi.* Walpi Archaeological Project, Phase II, vol. 5, part I. Flagstaff: Museum of Northern Arizona.

Anderson, Benedict
1991 *Imagined Communities: Reflections on the Origin and Spread of Nationalism.* Rev. ed. London: Verso.

Appadurai, Arjun
1986 "Introduction: Commodities and the Politics of Value." In *The Social Life of Things: Commodities in Cultural Perspective,* edited by Arjun Appadurai, 3–63. Cambridge: Cambridge University Press.

A:shiwi A:wan
1994 *A:shiwi A:wan: Belonging to the Zuni.* Albuquerque: University of New Mexico Art Museum.

Babcock, Barbara A.
1990a "By Way of Introduction." *Journal of the Southwest* 32, no. 4: 383–99.
1990b "A New Mexican Rebecca: Imaging Pueblo Women." *Journal of the Southwest* 32, no. 4: 400–437.
1993 "Bearers of Value, Vessels of Desire: The Reproduction of the Reproduction of Pueblo Culture." *Museum Anthropology* 17, no. 3: 43–57. Special issue, "Museums and Tourism," edited by Edward M. Bruner.
1996 'First Families': Gender, Reproduction, and the Mythic Southwest." In *The Great Southwest of the Fred Harvey Company and the Santa Fe Railway,* edited by Marta Weigle and Barbara A. Babcock, 201–17. Phoenix: The Heard Museum.

Babcock, Barbara A., and Nancy J. Parezo
1988 *Daughters of the Desert: Women Anthropologists and the Native American Southwest.* Albuquerque: University of New Mexico Press.

Babcock, Barbara A., and Joseph C. Wilder, eds.
1990 "Inventing the Southwest: Region as Commodity." *Journal of the Southwest* 32, no. 4. Special issue.

Bassman, Theda
1991 *Hopi Kachina Dolls and Their Carvers.* West Chester, Penn.: Schiffer Publishing Ltd.
1994 *The Kachina Dolls of Cecil Calnimptewa.* Tucson: Treasure Chest Publications, Inc.
1996 *Treasures of the Zuni.* Flagstaff: Northland Publishing.
1997 *Treasures of the Hopi.* Flagstaff: Northland Publishing.

Bassman, Theda, and Michael Bassman
1992 *Zuni Jewelry.* West Chester, Penn.: Schiffer Publishing Ltd.

Bendheim, Anne
1982 "Hopi Magic Blends with Mozart for Fantastic 'Flute.'" *Phoenix Gazette,* 15 April.

Benedict, Ruth
1934 *Patterns of Culture.* Boston: Houghton Mifflin.

Benjamin, Walter
1969 "The Work of Art in the Age of Mechanical Reproduction." In *Illuminations,* edited by Hannah Arendt, 217–51. New York: Schocken.

Beyal, Duane
1998 "Hopis 'Start from Scratch' in Attracting Tourists." *The Indian Trader* 29, no. 2: 21–22.

Bhabha, Homi.
1994 *The Location of Culture.* New York: Routledge.

Bourdieu, Pierre
1984 *Distinction: A Social Critique of the Judgement of Taste.* Cambridge, Mass.: Harvard University Press.

Bourke, Lt. John G.
1884 *The Snake Dance of the Moquis of Arizona.* London: Sampson, Low, Marston, Searle, & Livingston.

Breunig, Robert, and Michael Lomatuway'ma
1992 "Form and Function in Hopi Tithu." *Plateau* 63, no. 4: 3–13.

Brew, Joseph O.
1949 "The History of Awatovi." In *Franciscan Awatovi: The Excavation and Conjectural Reconstruction of a Seventeenth-Century Spanish Mission Establishment at a Hopi Indian Town in Northeastern Arizona,* edited by Ross Gordon Montgomery, Gordon Smith, and John Otis Brew. Cambridge, Mass.: Peabody Museum.

Broder, Patricia Janis
1978 *Hopi Painting: The World of the Hopi.* New York: E. P. Dutton, A Brandywine Press Book.

Brody, J. J.
1971 *Indian Painters and White Patrons.* Albuquerque: University of New Mexico Press.
1979 "Pueblo Fine Arts." In *Handbook of North American Indians,* vol. 9, edited by Alfonso Ortiz, 603–8. Washington, D.C.: Smithsonian Institution.

1980 "Modern Hopi Painting." In *Hopi Kachina: Spirit of Life.* San Francisco: California Academy of Sciences.

1991 *Anasazi and Pueblo Painting.* Albuquerque: University of New Mexico Press.

1994 "Kachina Images in American Art: The Way of the Doll." In *Kachinas in the Pueblo World,* edited by Polly Schaafsma, 147–60. Albuquerque: University of New Mexico Press.

1997 *Pueblo Indian Painting: Tradition and Modernism in New Mexico, 1900–1930.* Santa Fe: School of American Research Press.

Bromberg, Erik
1986 *The Hopi Approach to the Art of Kachina Doll Carving.* West Chester Penn.: Schiffer Publishing.

Byrkit, James W.
1992 "Land, Sky, and People: The Southwest Defined." *Journal of the Southwest* 34, no. 3: 257–387.

Cart, Julie
1998 "Kachina-Doll Feud Divides Two Tribes." *Los Angeles Times,* 25 August: A5.

Chavez, Cynthia
1997 "Felice Lucero and Her Art: Working in and around Cultural Boundaries." Master's thesis, University of California, Los Angeles.

Cirillo, Dexter
1992 *Southwestern Indian Jewelry.* New York: Abbeville Press.

Clay, Rebecca
1988 "Blazing Colors: Painter Dan Namingha Skyrockets to Success." *New Mexico Magazine* (May): 47–53.

Clemmer, Richard O.
1995 *Roads in the Sky: The Hopi Indians in a Century of Change.* Boulder: Westview Press.

Clifford, James
1988 *The Predicament of Culture: Twentieth-Century Ethnography, Literature, and Art.* Cambridge, Mass.: Harvard University Press.

Colton, Harold S.
1949 *Hopi Kachina Dolls with a Key to Their Identification.* Albuquerque: University of New Mexico Press.

Coze, Paul
1957 "Kachinas: Masked Dancers of the Southwest." *National Geographic* 112, no. 2: 218–36.

Culin, Stewart
1905 "Thomas Varker Keam." *American Anthropologist* 7: 171–72.

Curtis, Natalie
1907 *The Indians' Book.* New York: Harper & Brothers.

Danson, Edward B.
1966 "Six Startling Statuettes Added to Museum Here." *The Sun,* 26 August: 11.

Davenport, Natalie
1996 "An Ethnographic Case Study of Anthropologists and Hopis Concerning Intellectual Property Rights." Master's thesis, Northern Arizona University.

David, Neil, Sr.
1993 *Kachinas: Spirit Beings of the Hopi.* Albuquerque: Avanyu Publishing Inc.

Davis, Carolyn O'Bagy
1997 *Hopi Quilting: Stitched Traditions from an Ancient Community.* Tucson: Sanpete Publications.

Day, Jonathan S.
2000 *Traditional Hopi Kachinas: A New Generation of Carvers.* Flagstaff: Northland Publishing.

Deats, Suzanne
1998 "Dan Namingha." *Indian Artist* 4, no. 3: 30–35.

Deitch, Lewis I.
1989 "The Impact of Tourism on the Arts and Crafts of the Indians of the Southwestern United States." In *Hosts and Guests: The Anthropology of Tourism,* edited by V. L. Smith, 223–35. 2d ed. Philadelphia: University of Pennsylvania Press.

D'Emilio, Sandra, and Suzan Campbell.
1991 *Visions and Visionaries: The Art and Artists of the Santa Fe Railway.* Salt Lake City: Peregrine Smith Books.

Dilworth, Leah
1996a *Imagining Indians in the Southwest: Persistent Visions of a Primitive Past.* Washington: Smithsonian Institution Press.

1996b "Discovering Indians in Fred Harvey's Southwest." In *The Great Southwest of the Fred Harvey Company and the Santa Fe Railway,* edited by Marta Weigle and Barbara Babcock, 159–67. Phoenix: The Heard Museum.

Dockstader, Frederick J.
1954 *The Kachina and the White Man: A Study of the Influences of White Culture on the Hopi Kachina Cult.* Bloomfield Hills, Mich.: Cranbrook Institute of Science.

1985 *The Kachina and the White Man: The Influences of White Culture on the Hopi Kachina Cult.* 2d ed. Albuquerque: University of New Mexico Press

Donaldson, Thomas
1893 *Moqui Pueblo Indians of Arizona and Pueblo Indians of New Mexico: Extra Census Bulletin.* Washington, D.C.: U.S. Census Office.

Donovan, Bill
1987 "The Controversy Surrounding Navajo Carvings." *The Indian Trader* 18, no. 7: 4.

1998 "The Controversy Heats Up over Navajo Dolls." *The Indian Trader* 29, no. 9: 5–6.

Dorsey, George Ames
1899 "The Voth Collection." *American Anthropologist* 1: 394–95.

1903 *Indians of the Southwest.* N.p.: Passenger Department, Atchinson, Topeka & Santa Fe Railway System.

Dorsey, George Ames, and Henry R. Voth
1901   *The Oraibi Soyal Ceremony.* Field Columbian Museum
        Publications, Anthropological Series 3. Chicago: Field
        Columbian Museum.

Douglas, Mary, and Baron Isherwood
1996   *The World of Goods: Towards an Anthropology of Consumption.*
        London: Routledge.

Duarte, Carmen
1998   "Artist's Kachina Creations Are Treat for Eyes."
        The Arizona Daily Star (January) 14: 4.

Duffek, Karen
1983   "'Authenticity' and the Contemporary Northwest Coast
        Indian Art Market." *BC Studies* 57: 99–111.

Dunn, Dorothy
1968   *American Indian Painting of the Southwest and Plains Areas.*
        Albuquerque: University of New Mexico Press.

Earle, Edwin, and Edward Kennard
[1938] 1971   *Hopi Kachinas.* Reprint. New York: Museum of the
        American Indian, Heye Foundation.

Eggan, Dorothy
1943   "The General Problem of Hopi Adjustment." *American
        Anthropologist* 45: 357–73.

Eggan, Frederick R.
1950   *Social Organization of the Western Pueblos.* Chicago:
        University of Chicago Press.
1979   "Pueblos: Introduction." In *Handbook of North American
        Indians,* vol. 9, edited by A. Ortiz, 224–35. Washington,
        D.C.: Smithsonian Institution.

Ehn, Jack
1981   "Mural to be Destroyed: Zuni Artwork Offends Other
        Pueblos." *Albuquerque Tribune,* 24 November: A1, A6.

Ehrlich, Gretel
1985   *The Solace of Open Spaces.* New York: Viking.

Erickson, Jon T.
1977   *Kachinas: An Evolving Hopi Art Form?* Phoenix: The Heard
        Museum.

Espejo, Antonio de
1929   *Expedition into New Mexico Made by Antonio de Espejo.*
        Los Angeles: Quivera Society.

Evans-Pritchard, Deirdre
1989   "How 'They' See 'Us': Native American Images of
        Tourists." *Annals of Tourism Research* 16: 89–105.
1990   "Tradition on Trial: How the American Legal System
        Handles the Concept of Tradition." Ph.D. Diss.,
        University of California, Los Angeles.

Farago, Claire
1998   "New Mexican Santos in Theory and in History:
        Managing the Interstices with a Measure of Creativity."
        Unpublished manuscript.

Ferguson, T. J., Kurt Dongoske, Leigh Jenkins, Mike Yeatts,
    and Eric Polingyuomo
1993   "Working Together: The Roles of Archaeology and
        Ethnohistory in Hopi Cultural Preservation." *Cultural
        Resource Management* 16: 27–37. Special issue.

Fewkes, J. Walter
1892   "A Few Summer Ceremonials at the Tusayan Pueblos."
        Journal of American Ethnology and Archaeology 2.
1894   "Dolls of the Tusayan Indians." *Internacionales Archiv für
        Ethnographie* 7: 45–74.
1897   "A Group of Tusayan Ceremonials Called Katcinas."
        Bureau of American Ethnology Annual Report for 1893–94 15:
        245–313.
1901   "An interpretation of Katcina worship." *Journal of
        American Folklore* 14: 81–94.
[1903] 1969   "Hopi Katcinas Drawn by Native Artists." *Bureau
        of American Ethnology Annual Report for 1899–1900* 21:
        3-126. Washington, D.C.: Bureau of American Ethnology.
        Reprint. Glorieta, N.Mex.: The Rio Grande Press, Inc.

Francaviglia, Richard, and David Narrett
1994   *Essays on Changing Images of the Southwest.* College
        Station: Texas A & M University Press.

Frigout, Arlette
1979   "Hopi Ceremonial Organization." In *Handbook of North
        American Indians,* vol. 9, edited by Alfonso Ortiz, 564–76.
        Washington, D.C.: Smithsonian Institution.

Frost, Richard H.
1980   "The Romantic Inflation of Pueblo Culture." *The
        American West* 17, no. 1: 4–9, 56–60.

Gill, Sam D.
1976   "The Shadow of a Vision Yonder." In *Seeing with a Native
        Eye,* edited by W. H. Capps, 44–57. New York: Harper & Row.
1977   "Hopi Kachina Cult Initiation: The Shocking Beginning to
        the Hopis' Religious Life." *Journal of the American
        Academy of Religion* 45: 447–64. Supplement.

Goldwater, Barry
1969   *The Goldwater Kachina Doll Collection.* Tempe: Arizona
        Historical Foundation.

Gonzales, Paul D.
1996   "Borrowing Cultural Images." *Indian Artist* 11, no. 4: 30–31.

Gottlieb, Alma
1982   "Americans' Vacations." *Annals of Tourism Research* 9: 165–87.

Graburn, Nelson H. H.
1976   "Introduction: The Arts of the Fourth World." In *Ethnic
        and Tourist Arts: Cultural Expressions from the Fourth World,*
        edited by Nelson H. H. Graburn, 1–32. Berkeley:
        University of California Press.
1989   "Tourism: The Sacred Journey." In *Hosts and Guests: The
        Anthropology of Tourism,* edited by V. L. Smith, 21–36. 2d
        ed. Philadelphia: University of Pennsylvania Press.

Grant, Campbell
1979   *Canyon de Chelly: Its People and Rock Art.* Tucson:
        University of Arizona Press.

Greaves, Tom, ed.
1994 *Intellectual Property Rights for Indigenous Peoples: A Sourcebook.* Oklahoma City: Society for Applied Anthropology.

Green, Rayna
1995 *From Ritual to Retail.* Phoenix: Heard Museum. Video produced for the *Inventing the Southwest* exhibition.

Greenblatt, Stephan
1991 *Marvelous Possessions: The Wonder of the New World.* Chicago: University of Chicago Press.

Greenwood, Davydd J.
1989 "Culture by the Pound: An Anthropological Perspective on Tourism as Cultural Commoditization." In *Hosts and Guests: The Anthropology of Tourism,* edited by V. L. Smith, 171–85. 2d ed. Philadelphia: University of Pennsylvania Press.

Greer, Sandy
1995 "Internal Interpretations of Intellectual Property Rights." *Winds of Change* (winter).

Grilli, Peter
1997 "Eastern Roots, Western Ties: A Collaboration in Japan." *New York Times,* 17 August: H35–36.

Guthrie, Patricia
1987 "Kachina Dolls: Hopi Makers Rap Imitations, Would Mark Their Work." *Gallup Independent.*

Hait, Pam
1986 "Reaching Out, Reaching In." *Air and Space* (June/July 1986): 96–101.

Hall, Tom
1996 "Imitation Katsina Dolls Sell 'Like Hotcakes' Just off the Reservation." *Hopi Tutuveni,* 8 November: 9, 12.

Halle, David
1993 *Inside Culture: Art and Class in the American Home.* Chicago: University of Chicago Press.

Handler, Richard
1986 "Authenticity." *Anthropology Today* 2, no. 1: 2–4.

Harvey, Byron III
1963a "The Fred Harvey Collection, 1899–1963." *Plateau* 36: 33–53.
1963b "New Mexican Kachina Dolls." *The Masterkey* 37, no. 1: 4–8.
1976 *The Fred Harvey Fine Arts Collection.* Phoenix: The Heard Museum.

Haury, Emil W.
1945 *The Excavations of Los Muertos and Neighboring Ruins in the Salt River Valley, Southern Arizona.* Papers of the Peabody Museum of Archaeology and Ethnology, vol. 24, no. 1. Cambridge, Mass.: Harvard University Press.

Hayden, Ferdinand Vandever
1870 *The Geological and Geographical Survey of the Territories.* Washington: Department of the Interior.

Hays, Kelley Ann
1992 "Shalako Depictions on Prehistoric Hopi Pottery." *The Archaeological Society of New Mexico* 18.

1994 "Kachina Depictions on Prehistoric Pueblo Pottery." In *Kachinas in the Pueblo World,* edited by Polly Schaafsma, 47–62. Albuquerque: University of New Mexico Press.

Hieb, Louis A.
1979 "Hopi World View." In *Handbook of North American Indians,* vol. 9, edited by Alfonso Ortiz, 577–80. Washington, D.C.: Smithsonian Institution.
1994 "The Meaning of Katsina: Toward a Cultural Definition of 'Person' in Hopi Religion." In *Kachinas in the Pueblo World,* edited by Polly Schaafsma, 22–23. Albuquerque: University of New Mexico Press.

Hightower, Marvin
1994 "Ancient Symbols in Modern Art." *Harvard Gazette* (September 8): 5.

Hiller, Susan, ed.
1991 *The Myth of Primitivism: Perspectives on Art.* London and New York: Routledge.

Hinsley, Curtis M.
1992 "Collecting Cultures and Cultures of Collecting: The Lure of the American Southwest, 1880–1915." *Museum Anthropology* 16, no. 1: 12–20.

Hopi Dictionary Project
1998 *The Hopi Dictionary/Hopìikwa Lavàytutuveni: A Hopi-English Dictionary of the Third Mesa Dialect.* The Hopi Dictionary Project, Bureau of Applied Research in Anthropology, University of Arizona. Tucson: University of Arizona Press.

Howard, Kathleen L., and Diana F. Pardue, eds.
1996 *Inventing the Southwest: The Fred Harvey Company and Native American Art.* Flagstaff: Northland Publishing and the Heard Museum.

Hughte, Phil
1994 *A Zuni Artist Looks at Frank Hamilton Cushing.* Zuni, N.Mex.: Pueblo of Zuni Arts and Crafts.

Indyke, Dottie
1997 "Meeting Carver/Painter Gregory Lomayesva." *Indian Artist* 3, no. 4: 46–49.

James, Harry C.
1990 *Pages from Hopi History.* Tucson: University of Arizona Press.

Joseph, Jennifer
1995 "Award Winning Kachina Painting by Navajo Artist Raises Ethical Questions." *Hopi Tutuveni* 5, no. 17: 1–2, 6.
1996a "Arts and Crafts Bill Killed in State Legislature: Efforts Continue." *Hopi Tutuveni,* 12 April, 6, no. 6: 1, 3.
1996b "Tourist Trap Trinkets Masquerade as Authentic Hopi Art and Crafts." *Hopi Tutuveni,* 11 October: 1–2.

Jules-Rosette, Bennetta
1984 *The Messages of Tourist Art: An African Semiotic System in Comparative Perspective.* New York: Plenum Press.

Kabotie, Fred
1977 *Fred Kabotie, Hopi Indian Artist: An Autobiography, Told with Bill Belknap.* Flagstaff: Museum of Northern Arizona with Northland Press.

Kabotie, Fred, with Bill Belknap
1977   *Fred Kabotie, Hopi Indian Artist: An Autobiography.* Flagstaff: Museum of Northern Arizona with Northland Press.

Kasfir, Sydney
1992   "African Art and Authenticity: A Text with A Shadow." *African Arts* 25, no. 2: 40–96.

Kenagy, Suzanne G.
1986   "The A. C. Vroman Collection of Southwest Artifacts at the Southwest Museum." *Masterkey* 63, no. 1: 12–23.

LaFarge, Oliver
1940   *As Long As the Grass Shall Grow.* New York: Alliance Book Corp.

Laird, W. David
1977   *Hopi Bibliography: Comprehensive and Annotated.* Tucson: University of Arizona Press.

Lekson, Stephen H., and Catherine M. Cameron
1995   "The Abandonment of Chaco Canyon, the Mesa Verde Migrations, and the Reorganization of the Pueblo World." *Journal of Anthropological Archaeology* 14: 184–202.

Link, Martin
1994   "Hopis Continue to Complain about Navajo Dolls." *Indian Trader* 25, no. 1: 5.

Loftin, John D.
1991   *Religion and Hopi Life in the Twentieth Century.* Bloomington: Indiana University Press.

Lomatewama, Ramson
1992   "I Sing When I Carve." *Native Peoples* 6, no. 1: 20–24.

Lomawaima, Hartman
1986   "Introductory Notes on Hopi." In *Hopi: Songs of the Fourth World, A Resource Handbook,* 4–5. San Francisco: Ferrero Films.
1996   "Hopi." In *The Encyclopedia of American Indians,* edited by Frederick E. Hoxie, 253–55. Boston: Houghton Mifflin.

Lummis, Charles F.
1893   *The Land of Poco Tiempo.* Albuquerque: University of New Mexico Press.

MacCannell, Dean
1989   *The Tourist: A New Theory of the Leisure Class.* New York: Schocken.
1992   *Empty Meeting Grounds: The Tourist Papers.* London: Routledge.

Mails, Thomas E.
1988   *Secret Native American Pathways: A Guide to Inner Peace.* Tulsa: Council.
1997   *The Hopi Survival Kit.* Arcana: The Penguin Group.

Mails, Thomas E., and Dan Evehema
1995   *Hotevilla: Hopi Shrine of the Covenant—Microcosm of the World.* New York: Marlowe and Company.

Marcus, George E., and Fred R. Myers
1995   "The Traffic in Art and Culture: An Introduction." In *The Traffic in Culture: Refiguring Art and Anthropology,* edited by George E. Marcus and Fred R. Myers, 1–51. Berkeley: University of California Press.

Marcy, Randolph B.
1866   *Thirty Years of Army Life on the Border.* New York: Harper & Brothers.

Masayesva, Marilyn
1996   "Protection Paramount for Hopi Arts, Crafts and Culture." *Hopi Tutuveni,* 11 October, 6, no. 1: 3, 8.

McBride, Ann
1996   "Hopis Lose Indian Art Fraud Legislation in Arizona." *Indian Trader* 27, no. 5: 23.

McCune, Patrick
1993   "'Bahana' Carves 'Hopi Inspired' Kachinas." *Yuma Daily Sun,* 28 March.

McDannell, Colleen
1995   *Material Christianity: Religion and Popular Culture in America.* New Haven: Yale University Press.

McGregor, John C.
1965   *Southwestern Archaeology.* Urbana: University of Illinois Press.

McLuhan, T. C.
1985   *Dream Tracks: The Railroad and the American Indian, 1890–1930.* New York: Harry N. Abrams, Inc.

McNitt, Frank
1962   *The Indian Traders.* Norman: University of Oklahoma Press.

Meinig, D. W.
1971   *Southwest: Three Peoples in Geographical Change, 1600–1970.* New York: Oxford University Press.

Messinger, Phyllis
1989   *The Ethics of Collecting Cultural Property: Whose Culture? Whose Property?* Albuquerque: University of New Mexico Press.

Moore, R. Laurence
1994   *Selling God: American Religion in the Marketplace of Culture.* New York: Oxford University Press.

Mullin, Molly H.
1995   "The Patronage of Difference: Making Indian Art 'Art, Not Ethnology.'" In *The Traffic in Culture: Refiguring Art and Anthropology,* edited by George E. Marcus and Fred R. Myers, 166–98. Berkeley: University of California Press.

Myers, Fred R.
1995   "Representing Culture: The Production of Discourse(s) for Aboriginal Acrylic Paintings." In *The Traffic in Culture: Refiguring Art and Anthropology,* edited by George E. Marcus and Fred R. Myers, 55–95. Berkeley: University of California Press.

Naranjo-Morse, Nora
1992   *Mud Woman: Poems from the Clay.* Tucson: University of Arizona Press.

Nequatewa, Edmund
1948   "Chaveyo: The First Katsina." *Plateau* 20, no. 4: 60–62.

Niebuhr, Gustav
1995   "Zunis Mix Tribe Spirit with Icons of Church." *New York Times,* 29 January, national report.

Norrell, Brenda
1994a   "Navajo Healers Call for Removal of Ceremonial Figures on Public Art." *The Indian Trader* (November): 17–18.
1994b   "Navajo Healing Society Calls for Removal of Ceremonial Art." *Indian Country Today* 14, no. 11: B1–2.
1995a   "Gallup: Where the Rich Get Richer." *Indian Country Today* (week of February 23): B1–2.
1995b   "Navajo Artist Defends Tipis." *Indian Country Today* (week of March 2): B1–2.
1996   "Hopi Support Protective Bill." *Indian Country Today* (week of February 8): C1.

Norris, Scott, ed.
1994   *Discovered Country: Tourism and Survival in the American West.* Albuquerque: Stone Ladder Press.

Ortiz, Alfonso
1972   "Ritual Drama and the Pueblo World View." In *New Perspectives on the Pueblos,* edited by Alfonso Ortiz, 135–61. Albuquerque: University of New Mexico Press.

Ostler, James, Marian Rodee, and Milford Nahohai
1996   *Zuni: A Village of Silversmiths.* Zuni: A:shiwi Publishing.

Owens, Craig
1992   *Beyond Recognition: Representation, Power, and Culture.* Edited by Scott Bryson, Barbara Kruger, Lynne Tillman, and Jane Weinstock. Berkeley: University of California Press.

Padget, Martin
1995   "Travel, Exoticism and the Writing of Region: Charles Fletcher Lummis and the 'Creation' of the Southwest." *Journal of the Southwest* 37, no. 3: 421–49.

Page, Susanne, and Jake Page
1994   *Hopi.* New York: Harry N. Abrams.

Papastergiadis, Nikos, and Laura Turney
1996   *On Becoming Authentic: Interview with Jimmie Durham.* Cambridge: Prickly Pear Press.

Parezo, Nancy J.
1983   *Navaho Sandpainting: From Religious Act to Commercial Art.* Albuquerque: University of New Mexico Press.

Parker, Charles Franklin, and Kitty Joe Parker Nelson
1964   *Arizona Highways* 40: 36–41.

Parsons, Elsie Clews
1930   "Spanish Elements in the Kachina Cult of the Pueblos." *Proceedings of the Twenty-Third International Congress of Americanists:* 582–603.
1933   *Hopi and Zuni Ceremonialism.* Memoirs of the American Anthropological Association, no. 39.
1939   *Pueblo Indian Religion.* 2 vols. Chicago: University of Chicago Press.

Pearlstone, Zena
1995a   "Native American Stereotypes in Advertising." *American Indian Art Magazine* 20, no. 3: 36–43.
1995b   Review of "Kachinas: Spirit Beings of the Hopi." *American Indian Culture and Research Journal* 19, no. 2: 198–201.
Forthcoming   "Mail-Order 'Katsinam' and the Issue of Authencity." *Journal of the Southwest.*

Pearson, Julie
1989   "Charlie Pratt." *Southwest Art* (May): 96–100, 180.

Phillips, Ruth B., and Christopher B. Steiner
1999   "Art, Authenticity and the Baggage of Colonial Encounter." In *Unpacking Culture: Art and Commodity in Colonial and Postcolonial Worlds,* edited by Ruth B. Phillips and Christopher B. Steiner, 3–19. Berkeley: University of California Press.

Pinel, Sandra Lee, and Michael J. Evans,
1994   "Tribal Sovereignty and the Control of Knowledge." In *Intellectual Property Rights for Indigenous Peoples: A Sourcebook,* edited by T. Greaves, 41–55. Oklahoma City: Society for Applied Anthropology.

Posey, Darrell A.
1994   "International Agreements and Intellectual Property Right Protection for Indigenous Peoples." In *Intellectual Property Rights for Indigenous Peoples: A Sourcebook,* edited by T. Greaves, 223–51. Oklahoma City: Society for Applied Anthropology.

Price, Sally
1989   *Primitive Art in Civilized Places.* Chicago: University of Chicago Press.

Rhodes, Colin
1994   *Primitivism and Modern Art.* New York: Thames and Hudson.

Riley, Michael J.
1994   "Constituting the Southwest. Contesting the Southwest. Re-Inventing the Southwest." *Journal of the Southwest* 36, no. 3: 221–41.

Rivera, Eladia Valentina
1990   Unwelcome Guests: Hopi Resistance to Tourism. Masters thesis, University of Denver.

Rodriguez, Sylvia
1989   "Art, Tourism, and Race Relations in Taos: Toward a Sociology of the Art Colony." *Journal of Anthropological Research* 45: 77–99.
1994   "The Tourist Gaze, Gentrification, and the Commodification of Subjectivity in Taos." In *Essays on the Changing Images of the Southwest,* edited by Richard Francaviglia and David Narrett, 105–26. College Station: Texas A & M University Press.

Root, Deborah
1996   *Cannibal Culture: Art, Appropriation, and the Commodification of Difference.* Boulder: Westview Press.

Rothman, Hal K.
1998   *Reopening the American West.* Tucson: University of Arizona Press.

Rubin, Arnold
1989   *Art as Technology: The Arts of Africa, Oceania, Native America, and Southern California,* edited by Zena Pearlstone. Beverly Hills: Hillcrest Press.

Rubin, William, ed.
1984   *"Primitivism." In Twentieth Century Art: Affinity of the Tribal and the Modern.* New York: The Museum of Modern Art.

Rushford, Scott, and Steadman Upham
1992   *A Hopi Social History: Anthropological Perspectives on Sociocultural Persistence and Change.* Austin: University of Texas Press.

Rushing, W. Jackson
1995   *Native American Art and the New York Avant Garde.* Austin: University of Texas Press.

Schaafsma, Polly
1980   *Indian Rock Art of the Southwest.* Santa Fe: School of American Research.
1994   "The Prehistoric Kachina Cult and Its Origins as Suggested by Southwestern Rock Art." In *Kachinas in the Pueblo World,* edited by Polly Schaafsma, 63–79. Albuquerque: University of New Mexico Press.

Schaafsma, Polly, ed.
1994   *Kachinas in the Pueblo World.* Albuquerque: University of New Mexico Press.

Schaafsma, Curtis F.
1994   In *Kachinas in the Pueblo World,* edited by Polly Schaafsma, 121–37. Albuquerque: University of New Mexico Press.

Scholes, France [*sic*] V.
1937   "Troublous Times in New Mexico, 1659–1670." *New Mexico Historical Review* 4, no. 1: 45–58; 4, no. 2: 195–201.

Schwartz, Hillel
1996   *The Culture of the Copy: Striking Likenesses, Unreasonable Facsimiles.* New York: Zone Books.

Scott, Jay
1989   *Changing Woman: The Life and Art of Helen Hardin.* Flagstaff: Northland Publishing.

Seaman, P. David, ed.
1993   *Born a Chief: The Nineteenth Century Hopi Boyhood of Edmund Nequatewa (as told to Alfred F. Whiting).* Tucson: University of Arizona Press.

Secakuku, Alph H.
1995   *Following the Sun and Moon: Hopi Kachina Tradition.* Flagstaff: Northland Publishing and the Heard Museum.

Secakuku, Ferrell
1996   "Secakuku Comments on the Defeat of Senate Bill 1169." *Hopi Tutuveni,* 12 April, vol. 6, no. 6: 3.

Sekaquaptewa, Emory
1976   "Hopi Indian Ceremonies." In *Seeing with a Native Eye,* edited by W. H. Capps, 35–43. New York: Harper & Row.

Sekaquaptewa, Helen
1969   *Me and Mine: The Life Story of Helen Sekaquaptewa (as told to Louis Udall).* Tucson: University of Arizona Press.

Seowtewa, Ken
1992   "Adding a Breath to Zuni Life." *Native Peoples* 5, no. 2: 10–16.

Seymour, Tryntje Van Ness
1988   *When the Rainbow Touches Down.* Phoenix: The Heard Museum.

Shaffer, Mark
1992   "Hopis Outraged over Portrayal in Comic Book." *Arizona Republic,* 15 February.

Shaffer, Mark, and Bill Donovan
1994   "Fake Kachinas Offend Hopis." *Albuquerque Journal,* 30 January: A1, 11.

Sikorsky, Kathryn
1958   "Zuni Jewelry." *Arizona Highways* 6, no. 8: 5–12.

Simmons, Leo W., ed.
1942   *Sun Chief: The Autobiography of a Hopi Indian.* New Haven: Yale University Press.

Smith, Watson
1952   *Kiva Mural Decoration at Awotovi and Kawaika'a, with a Survey of Other Wall Paintings in the Pueblo Southwest.* Papers of the Peabody Museum of American Archaeology and Ethnology, no. 37. Cambridge Mass.: Harvard University.
1980   "Mural Decoration from Ancient Hopi Kivas." In *Hopi Kachina: Spirit of Life,* edited by D. K. Washburn, 29–38. San Francisco: California Academy of Sciences

Snodgrass, Jeanne O., comp.
1968   *American Indian Painters: A Biographical Directory.* New York: Museum of the American Indian, Heye Foundation.

Spooner, Brian
1986   "Weavers and Dealers: The Authenticity of an Oriental Carpet." In *The Social Life of Things: Commodities in Cultural Perspective,* edited by Arjun Appadurai, 195–235. Cambridge: Cambridge University Press.

Spurr, David.
1993   *The Rhetoric of Empire: Colonial Discourse in Journalism, Travel Writing, and Imperial Administration.* Durham: Duke University Press.

Steiner, Christopher B.
1994   *African Art in Transit.* Cambridge: Cambridge University Press.
1999   "Authenticity, Repetition and the Aesthetics of Seriality: The Work of Tourist Art in the Age of Mechanical Reproduction." In *Unpacking Culture: Art and Commodity in Colonial and Postcolonial Worlds,* edited by Ruth B. Phillips and Christopher B. Steiner, 87–103. Berkeley: University of California Press.

Steinway, Frederick
1994   "Kachina Spirit Acupuncture." *Santa Fe Sun* 6, no. 10: 5.

Stephen, Alexander M.
1893 "Description of a Hopi Ti-Hu." *Folklorist* 1: 83–88.
1929 "Hopi Tales." *Journal of American Folklore* 42: 1–72.
1936 *Hopi Journal of Alexander M. Stephen.* Edited by Elsie Clews Parsons. 2 vols. New York: Columbia University Press.

Stevenson, James
1879–81 *Expeditions to the Pueblo Indians of New Mexico and Arizona.* Washington, D.C.: Bureau of Ethnology, National Museum.
1881 *Illustrated Catalogue of the Collections Obtained from the Indians of New Mexico and Arizona in 1879.* Bureau of American Ethnology Annual Report for 1880–81, vol. 2: 307–422.
1882 *Illustrated Catalogue of the Collections Obtained from the Pueblos of Zuni, New Mexico, and Wolpi, Arizona, in 1881.* Bureau of American Ethnology Annual Report for 1881–82, vol. 3: 511–94.

Stewart, Susan
1984 *On Longing: Narratives of the Miniature, the Gigantic, the Souvenir, the Collection.* Baltimore: The Johns Hopkins Press.

Suina, Joseph H.
1992 "Pueblo Secrecy Result of Intrusions." *New Mexico Magazine* 70, no. 1: 60–63.

Taussig, Michael
1993 *Mimesis and Alterity: A Particular History of the Senses.* New York: Routledge.

Tedlock, Barbara
1995 "Aesthetics and Politics: Zuni War God Repatriation and Kachina Representation." In *Looking High and Low: Art and Cultural Identity,* edited by B. J. Bright and L. Bakewell. Tucson: University of Arizona Press.

Tedlock, Dennis
1994 "Stories of Kachinas and the Dance of Life and Death." In *Kachinas in the Pueblo World,* edited by Polly Schaafsma, 161–74. Albuquerque: University of New Mexico Press.

Teiwes, Helga
1991 *Kachina Dolls: The Art of Hopi Carvers.* Tucson: University of Arizona Press.
1996 *Hopi Basket Weaving: Artistry in Natural Fibres.* Tucson: University of Arizona Press.

Ten Kate, Dr. Herman Fredrik Carel, Jr.
1885 *Reizen en Onderzoakingen in Noord-Amerika.* Leiden: E. J. Brill.

Thomas, Alfred B.
1941 *Teodoro de Croix and the Northern Frontier of New Spain, 1776–1783.* Norman: University of Oklahoma Press.

Thomas, Nicholas
1991 *Entangled Objects: Exchange, Material Culture and Colonialism in the Pacific.* Cambridge, Mass.: Harvard University Press.
1994 *Colonialism's Culture: Anthropology, Travel and Government.* Cambridge: Polity Press.

Titiev, Mischa
1944 *Old Oraibi: A Study of the Hopi Indians of Third Mesa.* Peabody Museum of American Archaeology and Ethnology, Papers, vol. 22, no. 1. Cambridge, Mass.: Peabody Museum of American Archaeology and Ethnology.
1972 *The Hopi Indians of Old Oraibi: Change and Continuity.* Ann Arbor: University of Michigan Press.

Uzzell, David
1984 "An Alternative Structuralist Approach to the Psychology of Tourism Marketing." *Annals of Tourism Research* 11: 79–99.

Voth, H. R.
1901 *The Oraibi Powamu Ceremony.* Field Museum Publication 61, Anthropological Series 3, no. 2. Chicago: Field Columbian Museum.
[1912a] 1967 *The Henry R. Voth Hopi Indian Collection at Grand Canyon, Arizona; A Catalogue Prepared for the Fred Harvey Company in 1912.* Edited by Byron Harvey III. Reprint. Phoenix: Arequipa Press.
1912b "Notes on the Eagle Cult of the Hopi." *Brief Miscellaneous Hopi Papers: Field Museum of Natural History Anthropological Series* 11: 105–10.

Wade, Edwin L.
1976 "The History of the Southwest Indian Ethnic Art Market." Ph.D. Diss., University of Washington.
1985 "The Ethnic Art Market in the American Southwest 1880–1890." In *Objects and Others: Essays on Museums and Material Culture,* edited by George W. Stocking, 167–91. Madison: University of Wisconsin Press.
1995 "The Day the Katsinas Came Home," with Vernon Masayesva and Leigh Jenkins. *Canyon Journal* 1, no. 1:16–31.

Wallis, Tom
1992 "A Bridge across the Centuries." *Native Peoples* 5, no. 3: 46–49.

Walsh, Barry
1993 "The Emerging Trend of Old Style Hopi Kachina Dolls." *The Indian Trader* (September) 24, no. 9: 7–8.
1994 "The Navajo Doll and the Dispute with the Hopis." *The Indian Trader* (March): 5–9.

Warburg, Aby M.
1995 *Images from the Region of the Pueblo Indians of North America.* Translated with an interpretive essay by Michael P. Steinberg. Ithaca: Cornell University Press.

Webb, William, and Robert A. Weinstein
1973 *Dwellers at the Source: Southwestern Indian Photographs of A. C. Vroman, 1895–1904.* New York: Grossman Publishers.

Weigle, Marta
1989 "From Desert to Disney World: The Santa Fe Railway and the Fred Harvey Company Display the Indian Southwest." *Journal of Anthropological Research* 45: 115–37.
1990 "Southwest Lures: Innocents Detoured, Incensed, Determined." *Journal of the Southwest* (Inventing the Southwest) 32, no. 4: 499–540.
1992 "Exposition and Mediation: Mary Colter, Erna Fergusson, and the Santa Fe/Harvey Popularization of the Native Southwest, 1902–1940." *Frontiers* 13, no. 3: 117–50.

1994   "Selling the Southwest: Santa Fe InSites." In *Discovered Country: Tourism and Survival in the American West,* edited by Scott Norris, 210–24. Albuquerque: Stone Ladder Press.

1996   "'Insisted on Authenticity': Harveycar Indian Detours, 1925–1931." In *The Great Southwest of the Fred Harvey Company and the Santa Fe Railway,* edited by Marta Weigle and Barbara A. Babcock, 47–59. Phoenix: The Heard Museum.

Weigle, Marta, and Barbara A. Babcock, eds.
1996   *The Great Southwest of the Fred Harvey Company and the Santa Fe Railway.* Phoenix: The Heard Museum.

Wheeler, Lt. George M.
1871   *Geographical Surveys West of the 100th Meridian.* War Department.

Whiteley, Peter M.
1988   *Deliberate Acts: Changing Hopi Culture through the Oraibi Split.* Tucson: University of Arizona Press.

1993   "The End of Anthropology (at Hopi)?" *Journal of the Southwest* 35, no. 2: 125–57.

Whiting, Alfred F.
1964   "Hopi Kachinas." *Plateau* 37, no. 1: 1–7.

Wilks, Flo
1978   "A Spiritual Escape from the World of Reality." *Southwest Art* (August): 66–69.

Wilson, Jane
1994   "Namingha." *The Aspen Times* (February 26–27): 1B, 16B.

Wilson, Maggie
1982   "Magic Flute Gets Hopi Facelift." *Arizona Republic,* 27 March.

Wood, Paul
1996   "Commodity." In *Critical Terms for Art History,* edited by R. S. Nelson and R. Schiff, 257–80. Chicago: University of Chicago Press,

Woodbury, Richard, and Watson Smith
1966   "Specimen." *Museum of the American Indian* 20.

Wright, Barton
1973   *Kachinas: A Hopi Artist's Documentary,* Illustrated by Cliff Bahnimptewa. Flagstaff: Northland Press.

1975   *Kachinas: The Barry Goldwater Collection at the Heard Museum.* Phoenix: The Heard Museum.

1977   *Hopi Kachinas: The Complete Guide to Collecting Kachina Dolls.* Flagstaff: Northland Press.

1979   *Hopi Material Culture: Artifacts Gathered by H. R. Voth in the Fred Harvey Collection.* Flagstaff: Northland Press.

1985   *Kachinas of the Zuni.* Original Paintings by Duane Dishta. Flagstaff: Northland Press.

1988   *Patterns and Sources of Zuni Kachinas.* Harmsen Publishing Company.

1989   "Change and the Hopi Kachina Doll." In *Seasons of the Kachina: Proceedings of the California State University Hayward Conferences on the Western Pueblos, 1987–1988,* edited by Lowell John Bean, 65–72. Novato: Ballena Press.

1994   *Clowns of the Hopi: Tradition Keepers and Delight Makers.* Flagstaff: Northland Publishing.

Wright, Margaret Nickelson
1989   *Hopi Silver: The History and Hallmarks of Hopi Silversmithing.* Flagstaff: Northland Publishing.

Yava, Albert
1978   *Big Falling Snow: A Tewa-Hopi Indian's Life and Times and the History and Traditions of his People.* Edited by H. Courlander. Albuquerque: University of New Mexico Press.

Ziff, Bruce, and Pratima V. Rao, eds.
1997   *Borrowed Power: Essays on Cultural Appropriation.* New Brunswick NJ: Rutgers University Press.

Zwinger, Ann.
1987   "Writers of the Purple Figwort." In *Old Southwest, New Southwest,* edited by Judy Nolte Lensink, 143–54. Tucson: The Tucson Public Library.